Susette M Taylor, H. R Millar

The Humour of Spain

Susette M Taylor, H. R Millar

The Humour of Spain

ISBN/EAN: 9783337245535

Printed in Europe, USA, Canada, Australia, Japan

Cover: Foto ©ninafisch / pixelio.de

More available books at **www.hansebooks.com**

HUMOUR SERIES
Edited by W. H. DIRCKS

THE HUMOUR OF SPAIN

ALREADY ISSUED

FRENCH HUMOUR
GERMAN HUMOUR
ITALIAN HUMOUR
AMERICAN HUMOUR
DUTCH HUMOUR
IRISH HUMOUR
SPANISH HUMOUR

"WHILE YOUR DAUGHTER WALKS OUT WITH HER BLACK EYES." P. 318.

THE
HUMOUR OF SPAIN

SELECTED, WITH AN IN-
TRODUCTION AND NOTES,
BY SUSETTE M. TAYLOR;
ILLUSTRATIONS BY H. R.
MILLAR

LONDON
1894

WALTER SCOTT
LTD

CONTENTS.

	PAGE
INTRODUCTION	xi
MY CID PLEDGES TWO COFFRES FULL OF SAND TO THE JEWS RACHEL AND VIDAS—*Twelfth Century* .	1
THE COWARDICE OF THE INFANTES OF CARRION WHEN THE LION BREAKS LOOSE—*Thirteenth Century* . .	4
THE CAT TURNED NUN—*Fourteenth Century* . . .	8
THE MADMAN IN THE BATH—*Don Juan Manuel* .	10
THE NAKED KING—*Don Juan Manuel* . . .	10
"NOT EVEN THE DAY OF THE MUD?"—*Don Juan Manuel* .	16
THE TAMING OF THE SHREW—*Don Juan Manuel* . .	18
A LONG TALE—*Fifteenth Century*	22
ELECTIO NULLA DEBET ESSE IN MALIS—*Fifteenth Century* .	23
THE BITER BIT—*Fifteenth Century* . . .	23
CALISTO IS SMITTEN WITH MELIBEA'S CHARMS—*Rodrigo Cota*	26
LOVE AND DEATH	31
THE EATEN PANCAKE—*Lope de Rueda* .	33
THE FAIR CELIBATE—*Gil Vicente* . . .	36

CONTENTS.

	PAGE
"THE TABLE-BOOK AND TRAVELLERS' JOY"—	
THE RUSTIC AND THE LACKEYS	38
THE CONTRARY WIFE	40
AN AFFECTIONATE WIFE	42
CHASTISE WITH GOOD WORDS	42
THE ACCOMMODATING FARMER	44
THE ACCOMMODATING LORD	44
DIAMOND CUT DIAMOND	44
THE BEST HOUR TO DINE	45
THE BEST WIFE IN THE WORLD	45
A PIOUS WISH	45
"THE BOOK OF JOKES"—TRAVELLERS' TALES	54
TALES OF ROGUES—	
LAZARO DECLARETH WHOSE SON HE WAS—*Hurtado de Mendoza*	57
HOW LAZARO SERVES A BLIND MAN—*Hurtado de Mendoza*	58
LAZARO IS SERVANT TO A PRIEST—*Hurtado de Mendoza*	60
A TAILOR WOULD FAIN LEARN OF GUZMAN TO WRITE HIS NAME, OR TO MAKE FIRMA, OR MARK, AND THE REASON WHY—*Mateo Aleman*	70
EPISODE OF THE OFFICIOUS PHYSICIAN—*Mateo Aleman*	71
OF THE PLEASANT LIFE GUZMAN LED AMONG HIS BRETHREN, AND AN ACCOUNT OF HIS VISIT TO GATEA—*Mateo Aleman*	72
OF THE WICKED OLD HOUSEKEEPER, AND THE FIRST KNAVISH PRANKS PAUL PLAYED AT ALCALA—*Quevedo*	79
ESTEBANILLO ACTS ON THE CARDINAL'S BIRTHDAY!—*Estebanillo Gonzalez*	86

CONTENTS

	PAGE
THE INGENIOUS GENTLEMAN, DON QUIXOTE OF LA MANCHA —*Miguel Cervantes*	90
THE LOVERS' RUSE—*Lope de Vega*	128
AUNTS—*Jacinto Polo*	131
THE MISER CHASTISED—*Doña Maria de Zayas*	132
THE MARKET OF ANCESTORS—*Velez de Guevara*	139
VISION OF THE LAST JUDGMENT—*Gomez de Quevedo*	141
THE REVENGE OF DON LUCAS—*Francesco Rojas de Zorrilla*	155
THE MAYOR OF ZALAMEA—*Calderon de la Barca*	160
THE SIMPLE GROOMS—*Santos*	178
PORTUGUESE EPITAPHS AND SAYINGS—*Seventeenth Century*	180
LA TARASCA AND THE CARRIERS—*Santos*	181
PEDIGREE OF FOOLS—*Seventeenth Century*	183
THE FAMOUS PREACHER, FRIAR BLAS	184
THE MUSICAL ASS—*Yriarte*	187
THE BASHFUL SHEPHERDESS—*Iglesias*	189
THE BEAR, THE APE, AND THE PIG—*Yriarte*	189
THE FROG AND THE HEN—*Yriarte*	190
MARIQUITA THE BALD—*Juan Eugenio Hartzenbusch*	191
PULPETE AND BALBEJA; OR, AN ANDALUSIAN DUEL—*Estébanez Calderón*	207
SEVILLE—*José Zorrilla*	213
AFTER THE BULL-FIGHT—*Mesonero Romanos*	213
DELIGHTS OF A MADRID WINTER—*Wenceslao Ayguals de Izco*	216
IN THE EARLIER DAYS OF PHOTOGRAPHY—*M. Ossorio y Bernard*	218
THE OLD CASTILIAN—*Mariano José de Larra*	221
A DEMAGOGIC JOURNALIST—*Antonio Maria Segovia*	233

CONTENTS.

	PAGE
A Cat Chase during the Siege of Gerona—*Perez Galdos*	238
A Well-won Dish of Cherries—*Perez Galdos*	242
First Love—*Emilia Pardo Bazan*	246
The Account Book—*Pedro Antonio de Alarcon*	254
Sister Saint Sulpice—*A. Palacio Valdés*	261
Pepita—*Juan Valera*	275
If She could only Write—*Campoamor*	288
Doctor Pertinax—*Leopoldo Alas*	291
A Few Thoughts on Light—*José Selgas*	300
Epigrams	302
Folk-Tales	305
Miracles of St. Isidro, Patron-Saint of Madrid	309
The Wedding-Night	313
Father Cobos' Hint—*Juan Martinez Villergas*	316
Popular Songs	318
Proverbs	321
Anecdotes	325
Eccentricities of Englishmen—*A. Ribot y Fontseré*	329
Newspaper Humour	332
Humorous Advertisements	338
At the Theatre	341
Notes—Critical and Biographical	345

INTRODUCTION.

A CERTAIN mysterious charm clings to the Spanish people, by reason of the long domain of more than seven hundred years of the Moors over the Peninsula, and consequent intermingling, to some degree, of race, and considerable Oriental influence on the national life and characteristics. The chief sport of the Spaniards, the bull-fight, is of Moorish origin; their popular dances and songs raise recollections of Indian Nautch-girls and the choruses in Moroccan coffee-houses; their predominant sentiment, the jealousy over their women, points back to the strict seclusion of the harem. To divert to another paramount influence, Spain, to this day the most Catholic country in the world, is in history of awful interest as the country in which the dread Inquisition took root most firmly: here alone 32,000 persons were condemned to the *auto-da-fe!* Gloominess, pride, and reserve have for centuries been the reputed qualities of the Spaniards. Oriental races are not mirthful; it is difficult to make the dignified Moor smile, much less laugh: the influence of the Moor, therefore, and the absolute power of the Church as little, could scarcely be conducive to merriment. And yet Spanish literature is illumined throughout with bright flashes of humour, like the silver lining to the dark cloud of the history of the people—a humour which shows itself in almost every phase of the national literature, from the twelfth to the nineteenth century: from incidents in the "Poema del Cid" which tickled the rough sense of humour of the warriors of the Middle Ages, to the delicate and subtle irony of Valera in "Pepita Jimenez"— quaint and naïve in the ballads and collections of tales, sprightly in the drama, boisterous in the "Novela Picaresca," inimitable in "Don Quixote." A humour, moreover, not laboured, not purely literary (though the latter kind is not lacking), but spontaneous, and embodying the salient features of the national life and characteristics.

It is both unnecessary and invidious to descant upon "Don Quixote," *par excellence* the work of Spanish Humour. The death-blow to the chivalrous literature throughout civilised Europe (in Spain more rankly luxuriant than elsewhere, and where it perhaps reached its climax of absurdity), this marvellous work spread rapidly from land to land, and was first put into English in the year 1612. It is here given from the latest and most scholarly translation, the labour of love for eighteen years of Mr. H. E. Watts. It may be as well, however, to draw attention to the special phase of Spanish life round which Spanish humour collected in the sixteenth and seventeenth centuries—namely, the life of rogues in the "Novela Picaresca"—to which a section of this volume has been devoted, and the influence of which is traceable in other authors (such as Guevara and Santos) not included in that section. This peculiar taste, called El Gusto Picaresco (*picaro* = rogue) owes its origin, according to Ticknor, to the condition of certain portions of society in the reigns of Charles V. and Philip II., and it has ever been in popular favour. Le Sage boldly imitated it in his famous "Gil Blas";[1] and Fielding, Smollet, and other English authors show its influence upon English literature. This typical rogue, who generally starts in life as a servant, has his counterpart on the stage in the Gracioso (the valet), prototype of the Barbier de Seville of Beaumarchais, and Molière's Scapin.

As this collection is not intended to be comprehensive, no apology need be made for omissions obvious perhaps to Spanish scholars. Among other works, such as those of the Archpriest of Hita, of Castillejo, Forner, Pitillas, and Moratin, the "Gatomaquia" (*see* Notes) and "Mosquea," burlesque epics after the pattern of the "Batrachomyomachia," are not represented; nor yet the famous "Murciliego Alevoso" (in which is displayed a humour not unlike Pope's) of Gonzalez, and the celebrated periodical *El Padre Cobos*.[2] That the drama, however, the richest in Europe, and original and characteristic as only either the Greek or the English drama, should be so little represented is due to the fact that the fun of a Spanish comedy generally lies in the plot and in comic situations.

With regard to the tales and anecdotes (both ancient and modern), the difficulty is any certainty

---

[1] See note on *Ib.*   [2] See note on *Newspaper Humour*.

of their origin, though this applies to the literature of all countries. The story of the cook and the crane is a common chestnut (with us the crane is a goose), the travellers' tale of the huge cauldron and the cabbage is perhaps too familiar to please; but they are here of interest as from Spanish Tablebooks of so long ago as the sixteenth century.

To come to the nineteenth century, our English periodical essayists of the eighteenth — Addison, Steele, and Johnson—will be recognised as prototypes of Figaro, El Curioso Parlante, El Solitario, &c. These Spanish *Tatlers* and *Spectators* are, however, on the whole, no servile imitators, and are justly held in high esteem by the Spaniards, though little known outside the Peninsula.[1] The nineteenthcentury novel, in which critics see the continuity of the Spanish genius, is here well represented by Valera's "Pepita Jiménez," and "Sister Saint Sulpice" of Valdés; other novelists, the rightly popular Alarcon, and the distinguished authoress, Emilia Pardo Bazan, have contributed short tales.

The chronological order, which on the whole is adhered to down to the eighteenth century, is somewhat neglected in the nineteenth for the sake of variety and harmony in the arrangement of the selections. It is also to be feared that a few names of minor importance have crept in among the authors of the present century.

[1] Blanco Garcia, the latest authority upon modern Spanish literature, ignores the English periodical essayists, and ascribes the introduction of this style of literature into Spain to the amusing and humorous work, "Ermite de la Chaussée d' Antin," of M. de Jouy (d. 1846), which work, however, was, according to Gustave Masson, written in imitation of the *Spectator*.

This compilation is based upon Ticknor's great work upon Spanish literature [1] and Padre Blanco Garcia's "History of the Literature of the Nineteenth Century" (published 1891), besides some valuable advice, generously given under great stress of work and worry, by Señor Don Rubió y Lluch, professor of Spanish Literature to the University of Barcelona. Other authorities consulted, biographies, &c., are too numerous to detail.

Existing translations have been used, and the translators' names appended. Among these many famous ones from Elizabethan to modern times will be noticed. Many of the selections have been considerably adapted for various reasons, principally to suit the requirements of a work intended to be popular. Others are almost literal. In many cases it has been no little difficulty to select passages comprehensive enough to dispense with explanations or a long introductory notice.

On the whole liveliness and attractiveness (whether with success or no) is aimed at rather than scholarly exactness, though it is to be hoped the collection will also be of interest to the student, and give a faithful reflection of Spanish humour so far as possible in a foreign garb.

With regard to the insertion of extracts from translations or Spanish originals published within the last ten years, I have to thank the Cassell Publishing Co., New York, for "The Account

---

[1] This last edition of 1863, enlarged and corrected by reference to a German annotated translation and to the Spanish translation (with ample notes) of his first edition by Don Pascual de Gayangos and Enrique de Vedia.

Book," translated by Mary J. Serrano; Messrs. Thomas J. Crowell & Co., New York, for the extracts from "Sister Saint Sulpice," translated by N. H. Dole; Mr. Heinemann, for his kind permission to insert the given extract from the translation of "Pepita Jiménez"; Messrs. Kegan Paul, Trench, Trübner, and Co. for permission to insert the ballad from Mr. Gibson's Spanish Romances; Señora Doña Emilia Pardo Bazan for her gracious permission to select from her tales; Mr. H. E. Watts for permission to insert extracts from his translation of "Don Quixote."

Finally, my best thanks are due to kind friends in Catalonia (possessors in the Catalan of a distinct tongue and valuable literature, if less important than the Castilian) for their great help during my residence at Barcelona by the furthering of my Spanish studies, privately, and at the University. While I owe much, to cultured Spaniards, from Santander to Seville, for valuable information on their national life and customs, and to my Mother, a patient and enthusiastic traveller, and the origin, in more than one way, of my sojourn and travels in Spain.

SUSETTE M. TAYLOR.

THE HUMOUR OF SPAIN.

MY CID PLEDGES TWO COFFRES FULL OF SAND TO THE JEWS RACHEL AND VIDAS.

MARTIN ANTOLINEZ, a dowghtye lance art thow
And be my troth thy hire shall ne stinted be, I vow
My gold, alack, is all yespent and eke the silver toe,
And richesse here I none with me as God on hye is trewe.
With an ill wille I do itte, for my brave companye's sake,
Togither with thy gude reade tweye strong chests we will make,
The leather schal be cramasie, the nails schal be of gold,
And we'll fill them ful of gravele, as much as thei can hold
Toe Rachel and to Vidas, now hie thee speedilee :
An outlawe I from Burgos towne, the Kyng is wrath with me,
I needs must leave my tresor because of its sore weyt,
And I wil plege it to them at an anantageus rate."
Martin Antolinez spedde to towne without delai,
And saw the tweye Jewes upon that verye day.
"O Rachel and thow Vidas, dere frendes are ye in trothe,
A message I have privyly to telle onto youe bothe."
They did not keep him waiting, they went asyde all thre.
"Here Rachel, and thow Vidas, praye giv your handes to me,
Betray me not to Xtian nor yet to any More,
And I will make you ryche, you schal never more be poor.
The Campeador alate gathered in the landes dutie,
And keped from the Kyng grete and mickle bootie ;

Tweye coffres he has gotten brimful of shin and gold
And he cannot bere hem with him, unless he had them sold;
But he'll give them in your keepyng, and borrow what is just,
Soe take the coffres in your care, with hem we youe entrust,
And laye your handes within mine and tel me one and bothe,
That you wil not look insyde them al this yere upon your oathe'—
"And what will my Cid paye toe us for keepyng safe his treasure?"—
Quoth Martin Antolinez, "He will paye you in due measure
But now he needes a hundred markes, and you can paye them here."—
"We never paye," the Jewes sayde," afore we have the ware."
Soe they mounted ther swift corsiares and rade richt speedilee,
Wen my Cid saw them comynge, he lought most lustilee.
The Jewes bent loe and kissed his hande, Martin wrote down the deed,
Thei sholde have care of the coffers but of lookyng in tayk heed.
The myrth youe sholde have witnest wen the chests were borne away,
They coulde not bere them by themselves all gyf no striplings they.
Sayd Rachel to the Campeador, "O Cid, I kisse thy hand,
Myght I a fyn red moorish skynne on thi returne demande?"
"Richt willyngley," sayde my Cid, "sych gifts I gladly offer,
Shoulde I perchaunce forget itte, youe must count it on the coffer."

THE CID PLEDGES TWO COFFERS OF SAND TO THE JEWS.

In the middle of the hall they stretch'd a carpet fringed and
    rare,
And a shete of fyn bleached linen was also laid out ther.
In a single lot of silver thre hundrith markes they payed ;
Brave Antolinez counted them but did not have hem weyed.
Thre hundrith more he toke in gold, and then bespake the
    two :
" O Rachel and thow Vidas, mickle gain I've brought to
    you,
And in soth I've earned your thanks gif not a pair of
    breeches toe."
Vidas and Rachel youde asyde and speedilye agreed
That Antolinez verile had earned of them ryche meede.
"Thritte odde markes, wich is but just, Martin, we'll giv
    to youe,
And you can buye some fur, a cloake, and paire of breeches
    toe."
Soe Antolinez took the markes and thanked them hertelye,
And tayking curteous leave of them spedde backe richt
    merrylye.

" Poema del Cid" (Twelfth Century).

THE COWARDICE OF THE INFANTES OF CARRION WHEN THE LION BREAKS LOOSE.

TWO years after their marriage did the Infantes of Carrion sojourn in Valencia in peace and pleasure, to their own great contentment, and their uncle Suero Gonzalez with them ; and at the end of those two years there came to pass a great misadventure, by reason of which they fell out with the Cid, in whom there was no fault. There was a lion in the house of the Cid who had grown a large one, and a strong, and was full nimble ; three

BRAVERY OF THE CID WHEN THE LION BREAKS LOOSE.

men had the keeping of this lion, and they kept him in a den which was in a courtyard, high up in the palace; and when they cleansed the court they were wont to shut him up in his den, and afterward to open the door that he might come out and eat: the Cid kept him for his pastime, that he might take pleasure with him when he was minded so to do. Now it was the custom of the Cid to dine every day with his company, and after he had dined he was wont to sleep awhile upon his seat. And one day when he had dined there came a man and told him that a great fleet was arrived in the port of Valencia, wherein there was a great power of the Moors, whom King Bucar had brought over, the son of the Miramamolin of Morocco. And when the Cid heard this his heart rejoiced and he was glad, for it was nigh three years since he had had a battle with the Moors. Incontinently he ordered a signal to be made that all the honourable men who were in the city should assemble together. And when they were all assembled in the Alcazar, and his sons-in-law with them, the Cid told them the news, and took counsel with them in what manner they should go out against this great power of the Moors. And when they had taken counsel the Cid went to sleep upon his seat, and the Infantes and the others sat playing at tables and chess. Now at this time the men who were keepers of the lion were cleaning the court, and when they heard the cry that the Moors were coming, they opened the den, and came down into the palace where the Cid was, and left the door of the court open. And when the lion had ate his meat and saw that the door was open he went out of the court and came down into the palace, even into the hall where they all were; and when they who were there saw him, there was a great stir among them; but the Infantes of Carrion showed greater cowardice than all the rest. Ferrando Gonzalez having no shame, neither for the Cid nor for the others who were present, crept under the seat whereon the Cid was sleeping, and in his haste he burst his mantle and his doublet also at the shoulders. And Diego Gonzalez, the other, ran to a postern door, crying, "I shall never see Carrion again!" This door opened upon a courtyard where there was a wine-press, and he jumped out, and by reason of the great height could not keep on his feet, but fell among the lees and defiled himself therewith. And all the others who were in the hall wrapped their cloaks around their arms, and stood round about the seat whereon the Cid was sleeping, that they might defend him. The noise which they made awakened the Cid, and he saw the lion coming towards him, and he lifted up his hand and said, "What is this?" . . . And the lion, hearing his voice, stood still; and he rose up and took him by the mane as if he had been a gentle mastiff, and led him back to the court where he was before, and ordered his keepers to look better to him for the time to come. And when he had done this he returned to the hall and took his seat again; and all they who beheld it were greatly astonished.

After some time, Ferrando Gonzalez crept from under the seat where he had hidden himself, and he came out with a pale face, not having yet lost his fear, and his brother Diego got from among the lees: and when they who were present saw them in this plight you never saw such sport as they made; but my Cid forbade their laughter. And Diego went out to wash himself and change his garments, and he sent to call his brother forth, and they took counsel together in secret.

"*Chronicle of the Cid*" (*Thirteenth Century*).
Trans. Southey.

THE CAT TURNED NUN.

IN a certain convent there was a cat which had killed all the mice in the convent but one, which was very big, which she could not catch. The cat mused in her heart in what manner she might deceive the mouse that she might kill him; and thought so long till she agreed she must take the veil, and clothe herself in nun's garb, and sit amongst the nuns at table, and then she might get at the mouse; and she did as she had thought. The mouse, when he saw the cat eating with the nuns, rejoiced greatly, and thought, since the cat had become religious, that she would henceforth do him no harm, insomuch that Don Mouse came near to where the nuns were eating, and began to leap about here and there. Then the cat rolled her eyes as one who has no longer eyes for any vanity or folly, and she kept a peaceful and humble countenance; and the mouse, seeing that, drew near little by little; and when the cat saw him nigh her she sprang upon him with her claws and began to throttle him. And the mouse said, "How is it that thou, a nun, art so cruel as to wish to kill me?" Whereupon the cat replied, "Think not thy cries will cause me to free thee; for know, brother, that when it pleases me I am a nun, and when it pleases me a canoness."[1]

"*The Book of Cats*" (*Fourteenth Century*).
Author unknown.

---

[1] That a canoness is a woman who enjoys a prebend, without being obliged to make any vows, or renounce the world, may be unknown to some readers.

"THE MOUSE, WHEN HE SAW THE CAT EATING WITH THE NUNS, REJOICED GREATLY."

THE MADMAN IN THE BATH.

NOW it chanced that a good man kept some baths, and a neighbour, a madman, was the first to come daily to this bath; afterwards awaiting the arrival of the people to bathe, he commenced, as soon as he saw them, to beat them with sticks or throw stones at them, so that the proprietor of the baths soon lost all his customers. The good man, seeing this, determined to rise very early one day, undressed himself, and went into the bath before the madman arrived, having at hand a pail full of very hot water and a wooden club. When the madman came to the bath, determined, as usual, to attack all who came in his way, the good man, seeing him enter, allowed him to approach, when he suddenly upset the pail of hot water over his head, attacking him at the same time with the club. The madman now gave himself up for dead; nevertheless, he managed to escape, and, running away, he told every one he met to be careful, for there was a madman in the bath.

Don Juan Manuel (d. 1347). Trans. James York.

THE NAKED KING.

THREE impostors came to a king and told him they were cloth-weavers, and could fabricate a cloth of so peculiar a nature that a legitimate son of his father could see the cloth; but if he were illegitimate, though believed to be legitimate, he could not see it.

Now the King was much pleased at this, thinking that by this means he would be able to distinguish the men in his kingdom who were legitimate sons of their supposed

"SUDDENLY UPSET THE PAIL OF HOT WATER."

fathers from those who were not, and so be enabled to increase his treasures, for among the Moors only legitimate children inherit their father's property; and for this end he ordered a palace to be appropriated to the manufacture of this cloth. And these men, in order to convince him that they had no intention of deceiving him, agreed to be shut up in this palace until the cloth was manufactured, which satisfied the King.

When they were supplied with a large quantity of gold, silver, silk, and many other things, they entered the palace, and, putting their looms in order, gave it to be understood that they were working all day at the cloth.

After some days, one of them came to the King and told him the cloth was commenced, that it was the most curious thing in the world, describing the design and construction; he then prayed the King to favour them with a visit, but begged he would come alone. The King was much pleased, but wishing to have the opinion of some one first, sent the Lord Chamberlain to see it, in order to know if they were deceiving him. When the Lord Chamberlain saw the workmen, and heard all they had to say, he dared not admit he could not see the cloth, and when he returned to the King he stated that he had seen it; the King sent yet another, who gave the same report. When they whom he had sent declared that they had seen the cloth, he determined to go himself.

On entering the palace and seeing the men at work, who began to describe the texture and relate the origin of the invention, as also the design and colour, in which they all appeared to agree, although in reality they were not working; when the King saw how they appeared to work, and heard the character of the cloth so minutely described, and yet could not see it, although those he had sent had seen it, he began to feel very uneasy, fearing he might not be the son of the King who was supposed to be his father,

"HE MOUNTED ON HORSEBACK AND RODE INTO THE CITY."

and that if he acknowledged he could not see the cloth he might lose his kingdom; under this impression he commenced praising the fabric, describing its peculiarities after the manner of the workmen.

On the return to his palace he related to his people how good and marvellous was the cloth, yet at the same time suspected something wrong.

At the end of two or three days the King requested his "Alguacil" (or officer of justice) to go and see the cloth. When the Alguacil entered and saw the workmen, who, as before, described the figures and pattern of the cloth, knowing that the King had been to see it, and yet could not see it himself, he thought he certainly could not be the legitimate son of his father, and therefore could not see it. He, however, feared if he was to declare that he could not see it he would lose his honourable position; to avoid this mischance he commenced praising the cloth even more vehemently than the others.

When the Alguacil returned to the King and told him that he had seen the cloth, and that it was the most extraordinary production in the world, the King was much disconcerted; for he thought that if the Alguacil had seen the cloth, which he was unable to see, there could no longer be a doubt that he was not the legitimate son of the King, as was generally supposed; he therefore did not hesitate to praise the excellency of the cloth and the skill of the workmen who were able to make it.

On another day he sent one of his Councillors, and it happened to him as to the King and the others of whom I have spoken; and in this manner, and for this reason, they deceived the King and many others, for no one dared to say he could not see the cloth.

Things went on thus until there came a great feast, when all requested the King to be dressed in some of the cloth; so the workmen, being ordered, brought some rolled up in a very fine linen, and inquired of the King how much of it he wished them to cut off; so the King gave orders how much and how to make it up.

Now when the clothes were made, and the feast day had arrived, the weavers brought them to the King, informing his Majesty that his dress was made of the cloth as he had directed, the King all this time not daring to say he could not see it.

When the King had professed to dress himself in this suit, he mounted on horseback and rode into the city; but fortunately for him it was summer time. The people seeing his Majesty come in this manner were much surprised: but knowing that those who could not see this cloth would be considered illegitimate sons of their fathers, kept their surprise to themselves, fearing the dishonour consequent upon such a declaration. Not so, however, with a negro, who happened to notice the King thus equipped; for he, having nothing to lose, came to him and said, "Sire, to me it matters not whose son I am, therefore I tell you that you are riding without any clothes." On this the King commenced beating him, saying that he was not the legitimate son of his supposed father, and therefore it was that he could not see the cloth. But no sooner had the negro said this, than others were convinced of its truth, and said the same; until, at last, the King and all with him lost their fear of declaring the truth, and saw through the trick of which these impostors had made them the victims. When the weavers were sought for they were found to have fled, taking with them all they had received from the King by their imposition.

Don Juan Manuel. Trans. James York.

"NOT EVEN THE DAY OF THE MUD?"

THE King Abit, of Seville, was married to Romaquia, and he loved her better than anything in the world. She was a very virtuous woman, and the Moors recount many of her good acts. But in one thing she did not display much wisdom; this was that she generally had some caprice or other which the King was always willing to gratify.

One day, being in Cordova during the month of February, there happened to be (which was very unusual) a very heavy fall of snow. When Romaquia saw this she began to weep. The King, seeing her so afflicted, desired to know the cause of her grief.

"I weep," said she, "because I am not permitted to live in a country where we sometimes see snow."

The King, anxious to gratify her, ordered almond-trees to be planted on all the mountains surrounding Cordova, for, it being a very warm climate, snow is seldom or never seen there. But now, once a year, and that in the month of February, the almond-trees came forth in full blossom, which, from their whiteness, made it appear as if there had been a fall of snow on the mountains, and was a source of great delight to the Queen for a time.

On another occasion Romaquia, being in her apartment, which overlooked the river, saw a woman without shoes or stockings kneading mud on the banks of the river for the purpose of making bricks. When Romaquia saw this she began to cry, which the King observing, begged to know the cause of her grief.

She replied, "It is because I am not free to do as I please; I cannot do as yonder woman is doing."

Then the King, in order to gratify her, ordered a lake at Cordova to be filled with rose-water in place of ordinary

"THE KING ORDERED A LAKE AT CORDOVA TO BE FILLED WITH ROSE-WATER."

water, and to produce mud he had this filled with sugar, powdered cinnamon and ginger, beautiful stones, amber, musk, and as many other fragrant spices and perfumes as could be procured, and in place of straws he ordered to be placed ready small sugar-canes. Now when this lake was full of such mud, as you may imagine, the King informed Romaquia that now she might take off her shoes and stockings and enjoy herself by making as many bricks as she pleased.

Another day, taking a fancy for something not immediately procurable, she began weeping as before. The King again entreated to know the cause of her grief.

"How can I refrain from tears," said she, "when you never do anything to please me?"

The King, seeing that so much had been done to please and gratify her caprices, and feeling now at his wits' end, exclaimed, in Arabic, "*Eha alenahac aten*," which means, "Not even the day of the mud." That is to say, that, although all the rest had been forgotten, she might at least have remembered the mud he had prepared to humour her.

Don Juan Manuel (d. 1347). *Trans. James York.*

THE TAMING OF THE SHREW.

THERE lived in a city a Moor who was much respected, and who had a son, the most promising youth in the world, but not being rich enough to accomplish the great deeds which he felt in his heart equal to, he was greatly troubled, having the will and not the power. Now in the same town there lived another Moor who held a higher position, and was very much richer than his father, and who had an only daughter, the very reverse in character and appearance of the young man, she being of so very violent a temper that no one could be found willing to marry such a virago. One day the young man came to his father and said, "You know that your means will not allow you to put me in a position to live honourably," adding that, as he desired to live an easy and quiet life, he thought it better to seek to enrich himself by an advantageous marriage, or to leave that part of the country. The father told him that he would be very happy if he could succeed in such a union. On this the son proposed, if it were agreeable to his father, to seek the daughter of their neighbour in marriage. Hearing this, the father was much astonished, and asked how he could think of such a thing when he knew that no man, however poor, could be induced to marry her.

Nevertheless the son insisted, and although the father thought it a strange whim, in the end he gave his consent. The good man then visited his neighbour telling him the wish of his son.

When the good man heard what his friend said, he answered, "By heaven, my friend, were I to do such a thing I should prove myself a very false friend, for you have a worthy son, and it would be base in me to consent to his injury or death, and I know for certain that, were he to live with my daughter, he would soon die, or death, at least, would be preferable to life. Do not think I say this from any objection to your alliance, for I should only be too grateful to any man who would take her out of my house."

The young man's father was much pleased at this, as his son was so intent on the marriage. All being ultimately arranged, they were in the end married, and the bride taken home, according to the Moorish fashion, to the house of her husband, and left to supper, the friends and relations returning to their respective homes, waiting anxiously for the following day, when they feared to find the bridegroom either dead or seriously injured.

Now, being left alone, the young couple sat down to supper, when the bridegroom, looking behind him, saw his mastiff, and said to him, "Bring me water wherewith to wash my hands." The dog naturally taking no notice of this command, the young man became irritated, and ordered the animal more angrily to bring him water for his hands, which the latter not heeding, the young man arose in a great rage, and, drawing his sword, commenced a savage attack on the dog, who to avoid him ran away, but finding no retreat jumped on the table, then to the fireplace, his master still pursuing him, who, having caught him, first cut off his head, then his paws, hewing him to pieces, covering everything with blood. Thus furious and blood-stained he returned to the table, and looking round saw a cat. "Bring me water for my hands," said he to him. The animal not noticing the command, the master cried out, "How, false traitor, did you not see how I treated the mastiff for disobeying me? If you do not do as I tell you this instant you shall share his fate." The poor little harmless cat continuing motionless, the master seized him by the paws and dashed him to pieces against the wall. His fury increasing, he again placed himself at the table, looking about on all sides as if for something to attack next. His wife, seeing this, and supposing he had lost his senses, held her peace. At length he espied his horse, the only one he had, and called to him fiercely to bring him water to wash his hands. The animal not obeying he cried out in a rage, "How is this? Think you that because you are the only horse I have, you may dare thus to disobey my orders? Know, then, that your fate shall be the same as the others, and that any one living who dares to disobey me shall not escape my vengeance." Saying this he seized the horse, cut off his head, and hacked him to pieces.

And when the wife saw this, and knowing he had no other horse, felt that he was really in earnest, she became dreadfully alarmed.

He again sat down to table, raging and all bloody as he was, swearing he would kill a thousand horses, or even men or women, if they dared to disobey him. Holding at the same time his bloody sword in his hand, he looked around with glaring eyes until, fixing them on his wife, he ordered her to bring him water to wash his hands.

The wife, expecting no other fate than to be cut to pieces if she demurred, immediately arose and brought him the water.

"Ha! thank God you have done so!" said he, "otherwise, I am so irritated by these senseless brutes, that I should have done by you as by them." He afterwards commanded her to help him to meat. She complied; but he told her, in a fearful tone of voice, to beware, as he felt as if he was going mad. Thus passed the night, she not daring to speak, but strictly obeying all his orders. After letting her sleep for a short time he said to her, "Get up; I have been so annoyed that I cannot sleep, take care that nothing disturbs me, and in the meanwhile prepare me a good and substantial meal."

While it was yet early the following morning the fathers, mothers, and other relatives came stealthily to the door of the young people, and, hearing no movement, feared the bridegroom was either dead or wounded, and seeing the bride approach the door alone were still more alarmed.

She, seeing them, went cautiously and tremblingly towards them, and exclaimed: "Traitors, what are you doing? How dare you approach this gate? Speak not—be silent, or all of us, you as well as I, are dead."

When they heard this they were much astonished, and on learning what had taken place the night previous they esteemed the young man very much who had made so good a commencement in the management of his household; and from that day forward his wife became tractable and complaisant, so that they led a very happy life. A few days later his father-in-law, wishing to follow the example of his son, likewise killed a horse in order to intimidate his wife, but she said to him, "My friend, it is too late to begin now; it would not avail you to kill a hundred horses: we know each other too well."

> "Who would not for life be a henpecked fool,
> Must show, from the first, that he means to rule."

Don Juan Manuel. Trans. James York.

A LONG TALE.

A KING kept a man to tell him fables and tales at night before going to sleep. And one night the King, troubled with anxious thoughts, could not sleep, and the man told him three tales more than on other nights. And the King bade him tell still more, but he was unwilling, having told many. And the King said, "Thou hast told many, but they were short; tell me a long one, and then thou canst hie thee to bed." The man, agreeing, began thus: "A countryman had a thousand shillings, and went to the fair and bought two thousand sheep at sixpence each, and on his way back he found the water had risen in the river, and that he could not cross by either bridge or ford; but he found a little boat, and putting in two sheep, rowed across. And now, the river is wide, the boat very small, and the sheep many; when the rustic has ferried his flock across, I will go on with the tale." And he got up and hied him to bed.

"Libro de los Exemplos" (Fifteenth Century).

ELECTIO NULLA DEBET ESSE IN MALIS.

A KNAVISH fool condemned to death, asked the judge if he might choose the tree whereon he should be hanged; and this wish granted him, he was taken to the mountains, but could see no tree to please him. And they took him before the King, who asked why he was not yet hanged, to which the fool replied, the fact was he could not find a tree on which he felt he would like to be hanged.
"*Libro de los Exemplos*" (*Fifteenth Century*).

THE BITER BIT.

" Who thinks to take another in
Is oft in his turn taken in."

TWO townsmen and a countryman, on a pilgrimage to Mecca, agreed to share provisions till they should reach Mecca. But the victuals ran short, so that they had nothing left but a little flour—enough to make a loaf. And the townsmen, seeing that, said one to the other: "We have but little food, and our companion eats much, how shall we bring about that he shall eat none of the bread, and that we alone eat it?" And they took this counsel—they would make the loaf, and whilst it was baking should all go to sleep, and whoever dreamed the most marvellous thing in that time, he should alone eat the bread. This they did, thinking to betray the simple rustic, and they made the loaf and put it to bake, and then lay down to sleep. But the rustic saw through their treachery, and when the companions were sleeping took the half-baked bread, eat it, and turned to sleep. Then one of the townsmen awoke as one dreaming and afraid, and called to his companion; and the other said, "What hast thou?"

"I saw a marvellous vision: methought two angels opened the gates of heaven, and bore me before the face of God."

And his companion said, "Marvellous is that vision. But I dreamed that two angels seized me, and, cleaving the earth, bore me to hell."

The rustic heard all this and pretended to sleep, but the others called out to him to awake, and he discreetly, as one amazed, replied, "Who are ye that are calling me?"

They replied, "We are thy companions."

And he said, "Have ye returned?"

And they said, "Whence wouldst thou have us return?"

And the rustic said, "But now methought I saw two angels take the one of you to heaven, and then two other angels take the other to hell; and seeing this, and thinking you would neither return, I got up and ate the loaf."

"*Libro de los Exemplos*" (*Fifteenth Century*).

"WHO ARE YE THAT ARE CALLING ME?"

CALISTO IS SMITTEN WITH MELIBEA'S CHARMS.

ARGUMENT.—CALISTO, *entering into a garden after his usuall manner, met there with* MELIBEA, *with whose love being caught, he began to court her; by whom being sharply checkt and dismist, he gets him home.*

Calisto. Sempronio, Sempronio, why Sempronio, I say, Where is this accursed Varlet?

Sempronio. I am heere, Sir, about your horses.

Calisto. My horses (you knave), how haps it then that thou comst out of the hall?

Sempronio. The Gyrfalcon bated, and I came in to set him on the Pearch.

Calisto. Is't e'en so? Now the divell take thee; misfortune waite on thy heeles to thy destruction; mischiefe light upon thee; let some perpetuall intolerable torment seyze upon thee in so high a degree that it may be beyond all comparison, till it bring thee (which shortly I hope to see) to a most painfull, miserable, and disastrous death. Goe, thou unlucky rogue, goe I say, and open the chamber doore, and make ready my bed.

Sempronio. Presently, Sir, the bed is ready for you.

Calisto. Shut the windowes, and leave darknesse to accompany him, whose sad thoughts deserve no light. Oh death! how welcome art thou, to those who out-live their happinesse! how welcome, wouldst thou but come when thou art call'd! O that Hypocrates and Galen, those learned Physicians, were now living, and both heere, and felt my paine! O heavens! if yee have any pitty in you, inspire that Pleberian heart therewith, lest that my soule, helplesse of hope, should fall into the like misfortune with Pyrramus and Thisbe.

Sempronio. What a thing is this? What's the matter with you?

Calisto. Away, get thee gone, doe not speake to me, unlesse thou wilt, that these my hands, before thy time be come, cut off thy daies by speedy death.

Sempronio. Since you will lament all alone, and have none to share with you in your sorrowes, I will be gone, Sir.

Calisto. Now the divell goe with thee.

Sempronio. With me Sir? There is no reason that he should goe with me, who stayes with you. O unfortunate, O sudden and unexpected ill: what contrarious accident, what squint-ey'd starre is it that hath robbed this Gentleman of his wonted mirth? and not of that alone, but of it (which is worse) his wits. Shall I leave him all alone? or shall I goe in to him? If I leave him alone, he will kill himselfe. If I goe in, he will kill me. Let him bide alone, and bite upon the bit, come what will come, I care not. Better it is that hee dye, whose life is hatefull unto him, than that I dye, when life is pleasing unto mee, and say that I should not desire to live, save only to see my Elicia, that alone is motive inoughe to make mee louke to my selfe, and guard my person from dangers. . . . Well, I will let him alone awhile, and give his humour leave to work out it selfe; . . . againe, if he see me in sight, I shall see him more incensed against me: For there the sun scorcheth most where he reflecteth most. . . . And therefore I think it my best play, to play least in sight, and to stay a little longer; but if in the meanewhile he should kill him selfe, then farewell he. Perhaps I may get more by it than every man is aware of, and cast my skinne, changing rags for robes, and penury for plenty. But it is an old saying, He that lookes after dead-men's shoes, may chance to goe barefoote: Perhaps also the divell hath deceived me. And so his death may be my death, and then all the fat is in the fire: The rope will go after the Bucket: and one losse follows another;— on the other side, your wise men say, That it is a great ease to a grieved soule to have a companion, to whom he may communicate his sorrow. Besides, it is generally received, that the wound which bleedes inward, is ever the more dangerous. Why then in these two extremes hang I in suspense. What I were best to doe? Sure the safest is to enter. . . .

Calisto. Sempronio!
Sempronio. Sir.
Calisto. Reach me that Lute.
Sempronio. Sir, heere it is.
Calisto. "Tell me what griefe so great can be
    As to equall my misery."

Sempronio. This Lute, Sir, is out of tune.

Calisto. How shall he tune it, who himselfe is out of tune? . . . Or how can he do anything well, whose will is not obedient to reason? who harbors in his brest needles, peace, warre, truce, love, hate, injuries and suspicions; and all these at once, and from one and the same cause. Doe thou therefore take this Lute unto thee, and sing me the most dolefull ditty thou canst devise.

Sempronio.
"Nero from Tarpey, doth behold
How Rome doth burne all on a flame;
He heares the cries of young and old,
Yet is not grieved at the same."

Calisto. My fire is farre greater, and lesse her pity whom now I speake of——

Sempronio. I was not deceived when I sayd, my Master had lost his wits.

Calisto. Whats that (Sempronio) thou muttrest to thy selfe?

Sempronio. Nothing Sir, not I.

Calisto. Tell me what thou saidst: Be not afraid.

Sempronio. Marry I said, How can that fire be greater which but tormenteth one living man, than that which burnt such a Citty as that was, and such a multitude of men?

Calisto. How? I shall tell thee. Greater is that flame which lasteth fourscore yeeres than that which endureth but one day. And greater that fire which burneth one soule, than that which burneth an hundred thousand bodies: See what difference there is betwixt apparencies and existencies; betwixt painted shadowes, and lively substances. . . . So great a difference is there betwixt that fire which thou speakest of and that which burneth mee.

Sempronio. I see, I did not mistake my byas; which runnes worse and worse. Is it not enough to shew thy selfe a fool, but thou must also speake prophanely?

Calisto. Did I not tell thee, when thou speakest, that thou shouldest speake aloud? Tell me what's that thou mumblest to thy selfe.

Sempronio. Onely I doubted of what religion your Worship was.

Calisto. I am a Melibean, I adore Melibea, I believe in Melibea, and I love Melibea.

Sempronio. My Master is all Melibea: whose heart not able to containe her, like a boyling vessell, goes bubbling her name in his mouth. Well, I have now as much as I desire: I know on which foot you halt. I shall heale you.

Calisto. Thou speakest of matters beyond the Moone. It is impossible.

Sempronio. O Sir, exceeding easie: for the first recovery of sicknesse, is the discovery of the disease. . . . Ha, ha, ha, Calisto's fire; these, his intolerable paines: as if love shot all his arrowes only against him. O Cupid, how high and unsearchable are thy mysteries! What reward has thou ordained for love, since that so necessary a tribulation attends on lovers? That hast set his bounds, as markes for men to wonder at: Lovers ever deeming that they only are cast behinde; that all men breake thorow but themselves, like your light-footed bulls, which being let loose in the Place, and galled with darts, take over the bars as soone as they feele themselves prickt.

Calisto. Sempronio.

Sempronio. Sir.

Calisto. Doe not you goe away.

Sempronio. This pipe sounds in another tune.

Calisto. What dost thou think of my malady?

Sempronio. Why, that you love Melibea.

"*Celestina, or the Tragicomedy of Calisto and Melibœa.*"
   The first Act is attributed to Rodrigo Cota, 1480.
   Trans. Puede-Ser, or Mabbe.

LOVE AND DEATH.

TAPAROUSE EN UNA VENTA.

DEATH and Cupid chanced to meet,
On a day when they were roaming,
At a wayside country inn,
After sunset in the gloaming.
Cupid he was bound for Seville,
Death was marching to Madrid,
Both with knapsacks on their shoulders,
Where their wicked wares were hid.

Seemed to me that they were fleeing
From the clutches of the law,
For the couple gained a living
Dealing death on all they saw.
Cupid slily glanced at Death,
As they sat around the board,
Marvelled at her ugly visage,
Shook his merry sides and roared.

"Madam," quoth he, "'tis so rude
To behave in such a way;
But, in sooth, so fair a fright
I've not seen for many a day."
Death, whose cheeks grew red and fiery,
Put an arrow in her bow;
Cupid put in his another,
And to combat they would go.

Quick the landlord slipped between them,
As they scowled on one another,
Made them swear eternal friendship,
Bade them sit and sup together.

In the kitchen, by the ingle,
They were fain to lay them down,
For no bed was in the tavern,
And the landlord he had none.

They their arrows, bows and quivers,
Gave into Marina's care,
She, a buxom wench who waited
On the guests that harboured there;
On the morrow at the dawning,
Cupid started from the floor,
Bade the landlord fetch his arms,
Broke his fast and paid his score.

"Twas the arms of Death the landlord
In his haste to Cupid brought,
Cupid flung them on his shoulder,
Took the road and gave no thought.
Death rose up a little after,
Sour, and limp, and woe-begone,
Took at once the arms of Cupid,
Shouldered them, and wandered on.

From that very day to this,
Cupid's shafts no more revive;
Youths who feel his fatal arrows
Pass not over twenty-five.
And, 'tis stranger still, the old ones,
Whom Death's arrows used to slay,
When they feel the shafts of Cupid,
Gain a new life and a gay.

What a world, so topsy-turvey!
What a change in people's lives!
Cupid giving life destroys,
Death destroying life revives!

Trans. J. Y. Gibson.

THE EATEN PANCAKE.

Leno. Ah, Troico, are you there?
Troico. Yes, my good fellow, don't you see I am?
Leno. It would be better if I did not see it.
Troico. Why so, Leno?
Leno. Why, then you would not know a piece of ill-luck that has just happened.
Troico. What ill-luck?
Leno. What day is it to-day?
Troico. Thursday.
Leno. Thursday? How soon will Friday come, then?
Troico. Friday will come to-morrow.
Leno. Well, that's something;—but tell me, are there not other days of ill-luck as well as Fridays?
Troico. Why do you ask?
Leno. Because there may be unlucky pancakes, if there are unlucky Thursdays.
Troico. I suppose so.
Leno. Now, stop there;—suppose one of yours had been eaten of a Thursday, on whom would the ill-luck have fallen—on the pancake, or on you?
Troico. On me, of course.
Leno. Then, my good Troico, comfort yourself, and begin to suffer and be patient; for men, as the saying is, are born to misfortunes, and these are matters, in fine, that come from God; and in the order of time you must die yourself, and, as the saying is, your last hour will then be come and arrived. Take it, then, patiently, and remember that we are here to-morrow and gone to-day.
Troico. For heaven's sake, Leno, is anybody in the family dead? Or else why do you console me so?
Leno. Would to heaven that were all, Troico!
Troico. Then what is it? Can't you tell me without

so many circumlocutions? What is all this preamble about?

Leno. When my poor mother died, he that brought me the news, before he told me of it, dragged me round through more turn-abouts than there are windings in the rivers Pisuerga and Zapardiel.

Troico. But I have got no mother, and never knew one. I don't know what you mean.

Leno. Then smell this napkin.

Troico. Very well, I have smelt it.

Leno. What does it smell of?

Troico. Something like butter.

Leno. Then you may surely say, "Here Troy was.'

Troico. What do you mean, Leno?

Leno. For you it was given to me; for you Donna Timbria sent it, all stuck over with nuts;—but, as I have (and Heaven and everybody else knows it) a sort of natural relationship for whatever is good, my eyes watched and followed her just as a hawk follows chickens.

Troico. Followed whom, villain? Timbria?

Leno. Heaven forbid! But how nicely she sent it, all made up with butter and sugar!

Troico. And what was that?

Leno. The pancake, to be sure,—don't you understand?

Troico. And who sent a pancake to me?

Leno. Why, Donna Timbria.

Troico. Then what became of it?

Leno. It was consumed.

Troico. How?

Leno. By looking at it?

Troico. Who looked at it?

Leno. I, by ill-luck.

Troico. In what fashion?

Leno. Why, I sat down by the way-side.

Troico. Well, what next?

Leno. I took it in my hand.

Troico. And then?

Leno. Then I tried how it tasted; and what between taking and leaving all around the edges of it, when I tried to think what had become of it, I found I had no sort of recollection.

Troico. The upshot is that you ate it?

Leno. It is not impossible.

Troico. I' faith you are a trusty fellow!

Leno. Indeed! do you think so? Hereafter, if I bring two, I will eat them both, and so be better yet.

Troico. The business goes on well, truly!

Leno. And well advised, and at small cost, and to my content. But now, go to; suppose we have a little jest with Timbria.

Troico. Of what sort?

Leno. Suppose you make her believe you ate the pancake yourself, and, when she thinks it is true, you and I can laugh at the trick till you split your sides. Can you ask for anything funnier?

Troico. You counsel well, indeed.

Leno. Well, Heaven bless the men that listen to reason! But tell me, Troico, do you think you can carry out the jest with a grave face?

Troico. I? What have I to laugh about?

Leno. Why, don't you think it is a laughing matter to make her believe you ate it, when all the time it was your own good Leno that did it?

Troico. Wisely said! But now hold your tongue, and go about your business!

Lope de Rueda. "*Timbria*" (*fl.* 1565). *Trans. Ticknor.*

THE FAIR CELIBATE.

THEY say, "'Tis time, go, marry! go!"
But I'll no husband! not I! no!

For I would live all carelessly,
Amidst these hills, a maiden free,
And never ask, nor anxious be,
Of wedded weal or woe.
Yet still they say, "Go, marry! go!"
But I'll no husband! not I! no!

So, mother, think not I shall wed,
And through a tiresome life be led,
Or use, in folly's ways instead,
What grace the heaven's bestow—
Yet still they say, "Go, marry! go!"
But I'll no husband! not I! no!

The man has not been born, I ween,
Who as my husband shall be seen;
And since what frequent tricks have been
Undoubtingly I know,—
In vain they say, "Go, marry! go!"
For I'll no husband! not I! no!

Gil Vicente (d. 1557). Trans. Ticknor.

THE FAIR CELIBATE.

"THE TABLE-BOOK AND TRAVELLERS' JOY."

THE RUSTIC AND THE LACKEYS.

A RUSTIC desirous to see the King, thinking he was more than man, put his wages in his pocket and took leave of his master. But the pennies soon melted away on the long journey to the capital. Having arrived and seen the King, whom he found to be a man like himself, he was so disgusted at having spent upon this all his money excepting half a real, that a tooth began to ache, and what with hunger tormenting him too he did not know what to do, for he said to himself, "If I have the tooth drawn, and give my half real for that, I shall die of hunger; while, if I eat the half real, my tooth will go on aching." As he was thus debating he approached a pastrycook's stall, and gazed with longing eyes at the tarts displayed. By chance two lackeys were passing by, who, seeing him so taken up with the pastry, cried out, to make sport—

"Hola, rustic, how many tarts would you venture to make a meal of?"

"By heavens! I could swallow fifty."

"Go to the devil!" said they.

"Gentlemen," he replied, "you are easily frightened."

Upon which they offered to lay a wager.

"Done," said the rustic; "if I don't eat fifty, you can draw this tooth," and he pointed to the one that ached.

"THE OTHERS, MAKING VERY MERRY, BADE A BARBER DRAW THE TOOTH."

All parties pleased, the countryman, very much to his taste, began whetting his teeth upon the tarts. When his hunger was satisfied he stopped, saying, "Gentlemen, I have lost." The others, making very merry, indulged in much laughter, bade a barber draw the tooth—though at this our friend feigned great grief—and the more to jeer at him cried out to the bystanders—

"Did you ever see such a fool of a clown as to lose an ivory to satiate himself with tarts?"

"Yours is the greater folly," retorted he; "you have satisfied my hunger and drawn a grinder which has been aching all the morning."

The crowd burst out laughing at the trick the rustic had played upon the lackeys, who, paying the pastrycook and barber, turned their backs and went away.

THE CONTRARY WIFE.

A TAMBOURINIST had so contrary a wife, he never could get her to do anything he asked. One day, on their way to a wedding, at which he was to play, she was riding an ass and carrying his tambourine, and he cried out, as they were fording a river, "Woman, don't play the tambourine, for you'll frighten the ass." No sooner said than she began thrumming; the ass, shying, lost its footing, and threw our dame into the river; while the husband, however much he wished to help her, could do no good. Seeing she was drowned, he went up-stream in search of her body.

"My good fellow," said a looker-on, "what are you seeking?"

"My wife," replied he, "who is drowned."

"And you are looking for her up-stream, friend?"

"Oh, yes, sir, she was always contrary."

"THE ASS, SHYING, LOST HIS FOOTING, AND THREW OUR DAME INTO THE RIVER."

AN AFFECTIONATE WIFE.

MATTERS came to such a pass between a husband and wife—who, having married against their will, lived a cat and dog life—that the husband one day gave his spouse a box on the ears, whereupon she, knowing he had a few days before killed a neighbour, began, without the least caring about the issue, to raise her voice, crying, "Seize the villain; he wants to kill me as he did So-and-so." Somebody heard her, and the man was accused, and, in accordance with his own confession, condemned to be hanged. On his way to the gallows he begged to be allowed to speak with his wife. She came, and he stopped on the road; but the good woman, eager to see the last of his days, cried, "Husband, why stop still? Let us walk while we talk, and lose no time."

CHASTISE WITH GOOD WORDS.

AN honest husband, so ill-starred as to have married a troublesome widow, beat her with a light stick, whereupon she went and complained to her kinsfolk. The latter reprehended her husband, bidding him not treat his wife thus, but chastise her with good words. This he said he would do, whereupon the skittish widow conducted herself much worse. The good fellow, not to break his promise, took a cudgel, into which he cut the *Pater Noster* on one side, and the *Ave Maria* on the other, and when she misbehaved herself beat her with that. The wife renewing her complaints, her relations came to tell him he had ill kept his word. "Not so, friends," replied the young man; "I have done what you bade me, and only chastised her with good words; read what is written on the cudgel."

CHASTISE WITH GOOD WORDS. 43

"READ WHAT IS WRITTEN ON THE CUDGEL."

THE ACCOMMODATING FARMER.

A FARMER who had on his land a fig-tree, on which several poor wretches had from time to time done away with themselves, determined to fell it as a thing of evil omen; but before so doing sent a cryer through the town: Should any one wish to hang himself on that fig-tree, he was to make up his mind within three days, for it was going to be cut down.

THE ACCOMMODATING LORD.

AS a great lord was dining, his servants at the sideboard turning their backs, there entered a thief, who took one of the best dishes on the table, and, seeing the master of the house looking at him, signed to him to keep quiet, and made off. When the dish was found missing, the lord said, "A thief took it, I saw him do so."

"Then why didn't your lordship cry out?"

"Oh, he bade me be quiet."

DIAMOND CUT DIAMOND.

A CHAPLAIN devouring a fine roast pigeon at an inn was asked by a fresh arrival to let him eat with him and he would pay his share. This was refused, and the pedestrian sat down and ate his dry bread, saying afterwards, "Know, reverend sir, you by tasting, and I by smelling, have both eaten the pigeon, although against your wish."

"If that is so, you must pay your part of the pigeon," replied the chaplain.

The chaplain insisting, the other refusing, they finally made the village sacristan judge between them. The sacristan, asking what the bird cost, was told half a real, and then made the pedestrian disburse a farthing, which he took and rang on the table, saying, "Reverend sir, inasmuch as he ate by the smell of the pigeon, consider yourself paid by the sound of the money."

THE BEST HOUR TO DINE.

A GREAT nobleman asked certain physicians what was the best time of the day to dine. One replied, at ten; another, at eleven; another, at noon. The oldest said, "My lord, the perfect hour for dining is for the rich man when he feels inclined, for the poor man when he has something to eat."

THE BEST WIFE IN THE WORLD.

A CERTAIN Valencian dame, a very good wife, had one fault: at times she wagged her tongue more than was needful. One evening at a ball she was seized with faintness, and they ran for her husband, telling him his wife had lost her speech. "Let her alone! Let her alone!" said he. "If this lasts, she'll be the best wife in the world!"

A PIOUS WISH.

A CAPTAIN, when in Flanders, being robbed of some half-boots made to measure for his feet, which were maimed and crooked, exclaimed, upon discovering his loss, "Please God, they may fit the rogue who stole them!"

A country squire, who had killed a crane, bade his cook roast it. As his master was late to dinner, the cook ate one leg, and when the bird was sent up to table and the other leg asked for, he replied cranes only had one leg. Out shooting cranes another day with his master, he said, "See, sir, they only have one" (for the bird raises one when standing). "S-s-s-s-t!" cried the Squire, and the cranes flew up, each showing two legs. "Oh!" exclaimed the cook, "if you had said 'S-s-s-s-t!' to the one on the dish, he would also have brought out his other leg."

An old man, jealous of his pretty young wife and a certain friend of his, a merchant and widower, fell ill of a mortal disease. Knowing his case was hopeless, he said to his wife, "You know, my dear, that I cannot escape this deadly sickness; what I beg of you is, if you care to please me, that you will not marry that friend of mine, who often comes to the house, and of whom I have been somewhat jealous." "Dear husband," replied she, "even if I wished, I could not, for I am already engaged to somebody else."

An old bachelor, having married at seventy, was reproached by his friends for having committed a folly, and replied they said true: Man with years loses his prudence; when he was a young man, and had any, he never could be induced to marry.

An astrologer, whose wife was with child, cast the horoscope of the unborn infant and discovered two sons would be born to him, and that the first would be a cutpurse, the second a murderer. This so grieved him that he was unable to conceal his sorrow, which being

"'s-s-s-t!' CRIED THE SQUIRE, AND THE CRANES FLEW UP."

perceived by his wife, was unburdened to her. "There is a cure for this case," said she. "We will make the first a purse-maker, and he will cut purses; the second a butcher, and he can slay oxen."

———

A village maiden, driving before her an ass, which, as it was returning to its foal, went quicker than the girl, met a courtier. "Where do you live, my pretty maiden?" "At Getafe," replied she. "Tell me, do you know the daughter of the innkeeper in that village?" "Very well," replied she. "Then be so kind as to take her a kiss from me!" "Give it to my donkey, sir; she'll get there first."

———

A father sending his son to study at Salamanca, bade him eat the cheapest food. The youth on his arrival asked the price of an ox, and was told ten ducats; then of a partridge, and was told a real. "Oh!" said he, "then I am bidden to eat partridges!"

———

Two friends, a weaver and a tailor, became in time enemies, so much so that the tailor spoke much evil of the weaver behind his back, though the weaver always spoke well of the tailor. Upon a lady asking the weaver why he always spoke so well of the tailor, who spoke so ill of him, he replied: "Madam, we are both liars."

———

Two thieves were breaking into a door when the master of the house, hearing them, looked out of the window and said: "Friends, come a little later, we are not yet in bed."

"THEN HE ASKED ME TO TAKE HER A KISS FROM ME."

A man of evil life and fame having built a beautiful house, had inscribed on the lintel: "Let no evil cross this threshold." A wit reading it, said, "Then wherever does the master of the house enter?"

A knight having received a dish of cherries early in the season, had them placed before him above the dais. His children, a bastard and a legitimate son, were seated at another table apart, and seeing they got no cherries, the bastard up with his hand and soundly boxed his brother's ears. "How now, you villain," said the father, "why did you do that?" "Because, sir, he kept on saying, 'You won't get any cherries, you won't.'" Upon which the father, much amused, gave some to both.

A prince had a jester who kept a book of fools, in which he put everybody deserving that title. One day at table the prince asked the jester to bring him the book, and opening it saw his own name, and below, "His Highness, on such a day, gave fifty ducats to an alchemist with which to go to Italy and bring back materials for making gold and silver." "And what if he returns?" said the Prince. "Oh, then she will scratch out your Highness and put him in."

A collegian of the Archbishop of Seville's college was one day at table overlooked by the prebendary who doles out everybody's rations. Somewhat embarrassed as to how he should ask for his food, he suddenly observed a cat mewing in front of him, which he addressed in a loud voice so that the prebendary might hear, "Why the deuce are you mewing and licking your chops at me? I have not

"YOU WON'T GET ANY CHERRIES, YOU WON'T!"

yet got my rations, and you must needs already begin bothering me for the bones."

A Biscayan, just finished working on the belfry in a small town, where there chanced to be a man condemned to death, was told by the authorities that, as they had no executioner, they would give him a ducat and the condemned man's clothes to do the job, with which our Biscayan was well content. A few months after, finding himself penniless, and remembering how much he had gained by so light a task, he climbed the belfry, and when the townsfolk hurried by upon the pealing of the bells, he looked down at them, saying: "Gentlemen, it is I have called your worships. You must know I have not a blessed farthing, and you remember you gave me a ducat the other day to hang a man. Now I have been thinking that, from the smallest to the biggest of your worships, I should like to hang the whole town at half a ducat each."

A blind man hid some money at the foot of a tree in a field belonging to a rich farmer. Visiting it one day he found it gone, and suspecting the farmer, went to him and said, "Sir, as you seem an honest man, I have come to ask your advice. I have a sum of money in a very safe place, and now I have just as much more, and do not know if I should hide it where the other is, or somewhere else." The farmer replied, "Truly, if I were you, I would not change the place, it being as safe as you say." "That's just what I thought," said the blind man, and took his leave. The farmer hurriedly put back the money, hoping to get it doubled, and the blind man in his turn dug it up, greatly rejoicing at recovering what he had lost.

Juan de Timoneda (*fl.* 1590).

"I SHOULD LIKE TO HANG THE WHOLE TOWN AT HALF A DUCAT EACH."

"THE BOOK OF JOKES."

TRAVELLERS' TALES.

IN Monzon de Campos a nobleman returned from India, as he was one day relating wonders of those regions to some neighbours, told them how he had seen a cabbage so immense that three hundred mounted men could rest under its shade. "I don't think much of that," cried a servant of the Marquess of Poza. "In Biscay I saw a cauldron so vast that two hundred men were hammering at it, and yet stood so far from each other that no man heard the noise of his neighbour's hammer." The Indian, much surprised, inquired the use of this cauldron. "Sir, to cook the cabbage you have just told us about."

Don Rodrigo Pimentel, Count of Benavente, was a master much feared by his servants. One day at Benavente, as he was writing some important despatches, certain of his pages stood round about discussing their fear of him, and one said, "What will you give me if I go up, just as he is now, and give him a hard smack on the back of his neck?" The others eagerly laid a wager with him. Hereupon goes my good page as if to see if his lord wanted anything, and gives him a sound slap, crying "St. George!" "What's that?" said the Count. "Sir, a large spider was crawling

"HEREUPON GOES MY GOOD PAGE AND GIVES HIM A SOUND SMACK."

down your Excellency's neck." The Count sprang up much disturbed, saying, "What became of it? Did you kill it?" "I knocked it down, sir, and it's gone away." And his delighted comrades willingly paid the wager he had so cleverly and boldly won.

Luis de Pinedo (*Sixteenth Century*).

A great favourite of Cardinal Loaysa came one day to speak with him on a certain matter, arriving so early that the Cardinal was asleep. The nobleman's importunity was so great that the servants awoke his Eminence, telling him who was there. The Cardinal finally ordered him to be shown in, and learning his business, said, "My friend, I knew long ago that you wasted your time ; but that you got up so early to do so, that I did not know."

A pupil at the grammar school of Alcalá once said to the vice-rector, who, for the sake of economy, always made boys eat very stale bread, "Domine, fac ut lapides isti panes fiant."

Bachelor N., at Salamanca, gave bad wine to some pupils, one of whom, a bold fellow, tasting it, rose, and taking off his hat, said to him, "Domine, si potest fieri, transeat a me calix iste."

In the madhouse of Toledo a madman cried out in a loud voice to some visitors shown round, " I am the angel Gabriel, who came with the tidings to Our Lady," and said, " Ave Maria," &c. Another madman near him upon this exclaimed, " He is lying ; I am God the Father and I sent him on no such errand."

TALES OF ROGUES.

LAZARO DECLARETH WHOSE SON HE WAS.

"YOUR Worship shall understand, before all things, that my name is Lazaro de Tormes, son of Thomas Gonzalez and Antonia Pelez, native of Tejares, a village near Salamanca. I was born within the river called Tormes, whereof I took my surname. My father (whom God pardon) had the charge of a mill standing upon that river, wherein he supplied the room of a miller about fifteen years. It fortuned on a night, my mother being great with child was there brought to bed, and there was I born; therefore now I may truly report the river itself to be the place of my nativity; and after the time I came to the age of eight years, there was laid to my father's charge that he had shamefully cut the seams of men's sacks that came thither to grind; wherefore he was taken and imprisoned, and being tormented, he confessed the whole matter, denying nothing, wherefore he was persecuted. I trust in God he is now in Paradise, seeing the Gospel doth say that blessed are such as confess their faults."

"*Lazarillo de Tormes*," *Hurtado de Mendoza*, 1503-1575.
Trans. David Rowland.

HOW LAZARO SERVES A BLIND MAN.

I AM sorry to say that I never met with so avaricious and so wicked an old curmudgeon; he allowed me almost to die daily of hunger, without troubling himself about my necessities; and, to say the truth, if I had not helped myself by means of a ready wit and nimble fingers, I should have closed my account from sheer starvation.

Notwithstanding all my master's astuteness and cunning, I contrived so to outwit him that generally the best half came to my share. But to accomplish this I was obliged to tax my powers of invention to the uttermost. The old man was accustomed to carry his bread, meat, and other things, in a sort of linen knapsack, which was closed at the mouth with an iron ring, and secured also by a padlock; but in adding to his store, or taking from it, he used such vigilance that it was almost an impossibility to cheat him of a single morsel. However, when he had given me my pittance, which I found no difficulty in dispatching at about two mouthfuls, and closed his budget, thinking himself perfectly secure from depredation, I began my tactics, and by means of a small rent, which I slyly effected in one of the seams of the bag, I used to help myself to the choicest pieces of meat, bacon, and sausage, taking care to close the seam according as opportunity occurred. But in addition to this, all that I could collect together, either by fraud or otherwise, I carried about me in half farthings; so that when the old man was sent for to pray, and they gave him farthings (all which passed through my hands, he being blind), I contrived to slip them into my mouth, by which process so quick an alteration was effected that when they reached his hands they were invariably reduced to half the original value.

"I PROCURED A LARGE STRAW."

The cunning old fellow, however, suspected me, for he used to say, "How the deuce is this? ever since you have been with me they give me nothing but half-farthings, whereas before it was not an unusual thing to be paid with halfpence, but never less than farthings. I must be sharp with *you*, I find." Whenever we ate, the old man took care to keep a small jar of wine near him, which was reserved for his own especial service, but I very soon adopted the practice of bestowing on this favourite jar sundry loving though stolen embraces. Such pleasures were but short-lived, for the fervency of my attachment was soon discovered in the deficiency of the wine; and the old man afterwards, to secure his draught, never let the jar go without tying it to him by the handle. But I was a match for him even there; for I procured a long straw, and, dipping it into the mouth of the jar, renewed my intimacy with such effect that but a small share was his who came after me. The old traitor was not long in finding me out; I think he must have heard me drink, for he quickly changed his plan, and placed the jar between his knees, keeping the mouth closed with his hand, and in this manner considered himself secure from my depredations.

Hurtado de Mendoza. Trans. Roscoe.

LAZARO IS SERVANT TO A PRIEST.

IT was during this trying and afflicting time, when, seeing things going from bad to worse, without any one to advise with, I was praying with all Christian humility that I might be released from such misery, that one day, when my wretched, miserable, covetous thief of a master had gone out, an angel, in the likeness of a tinker, knocked at the door—for I verily believe he was directed by Providence to assume that habit and employment—and inquired whether

"THE ANGELIC TINKER DREW FORTH A LARGE BUNCH OF KEYS AND
BEGAN TO TRY THEM."

I had anything to mend? Suddenly a light flashed upon me, as though imparted by an invisible and unknown power. "Uncle," said I, " I have unfortunately lost the key of this great chest, and I'm sadly afraid my master will beat me; for God's sake, try if you can fit it, and I will reward you." The angelic tinker drew forth a large bunch of keys, and began to try them, while I assisted his endeavours with my feeble prayers; when lo, and behold! when least I thought it, the lid of the chest arose, and I almost fancied I beheld the divine essence therein in the shape of loaves of bread. "I have no money," said I to my preserver, "but give me the key and help yourself." He took some of the whitest and best bread he could find, and went away well pleased, though not half so well as myself. I refrained from taking any for the present, lest the deficiency might be noticed, and contented myself with the hope that, on seeing so much in my power, hunger would hardly dare to approach me.

My wretched master returned, and it pleased God that the offering my angel had been pleased to accept remained undiscovered by him. The next day, when he went out, I went to my farinaceous paradise, and, taking a loaf between my hands and teeth, in a twinkling it became invisible; then, not forgetting to lock the treasure, I capered about the house for joy to think that my miserable life was about to change, and for some days following I was as happy as a king. But it was not predestined for me that such good luck should continue long; on the third day symptoms of my old complaint began to show themselves, for I beheld my murderer in the act of examining our chest, turning and counting the loaves over and over again. Of course I dissimulated my terror, but it was not for want of my prayers and invocations that he was not struck stone-blind like my old master, but he retained his eyesight.

After he had been some time considering and counting, he said, " If I were not well assured of the security of this chest, I should say that somebody had stolen my bread; but, however, to remove all suspicion, from this day I shall count the loaves; there remain now exactly nine and a piece."

"May nine curses light upon you, you miserable beggar," said I to myself, for his words went like an arrow to my heart, and hunger already began to attack me, seeing a return to my former scanty fare now inevitable.

No sooner did the priest go out than I opened the chest to console myself even with the sight of food, and as I gazed on the nice white loaves a sort of adoration arose within me, which the sight of such tempting morsels could alone inspire. I counted them carefully to see if, perchance, the curmudgeon had mistaken the number; but, alas! I found he was a much better reckoner than I could have desired. The utmost I dared do was to bestow on these objects of my affection a thousand kisses, and, in the most delicate manner possible, to nibble here and there a morsel of the crust. With this I passed the day, and not quite so jovially as the former, you may suppose.

But as hunger increased, and more so in proportion as I had fared better the few days previously, I was reduced to the last extremity. Yet all I could do was to open and shut the chest and contemplate the divine image within. Providence, however, who does not neglect mortals in such an extreme crisis, suggested to me a slight palliation of my present distress. After some consideration, I said within myself, "This chest is very large and old, and in some parts, though very slightly, is broken. It is not impossible to suppose that rats may have made an entrance and gnawed the bread. To take a whole loaf would not be wise, seeing that it would be missed by my most liberal master, but the other plan he shall certainly have the benefit of." Then I began to pick the loaves on some tablecloths which were there, not of the most costly sort, taking one loaf and leaving another, so that in the end I made up a tolerable supply of crumbs, which I ate like so many sugar-plums; and with that I in some measure consoled myself and contrived to live.

The priest, when he came home to dinner and opened the chest, beheld with dismay the havoc made in his store; but he immediately supposed it to have been occasioned by rats, so well had I imitated the style of those depredators. He examined the chest narrowly, and discovered the little holes through which the rats might have entered, and calling me, he said, "Lazaro, look what havoc has been made in our bread during the night." I seemed very much astonished, and asked "what it could possibly be?" "What has done it?" quoth he; "why, rats; confound 'em, there is no keeping anything from them." I fared well at dinner, and had no reason to repent of the trick I played, for he pared off all the places which he supposed the rats had nibbled at, and, giving them to me, he said, "There, eat that; rats are very clean animals." In this manner, adding what I thus gained to that acquired by the labour of my hands, or rather my nails, I managed tolerably well, though I little expected it. I was destined to receive another shock when I beheld my miserable tormentor carefully stopping up all the holes in the chest with small pieces of wood, which he nailed over them, and which bade defiance to further depredations. "Oh, Lord!" I cried involuntarily, "to what distress and misfortunes are we unhappy mortals reduced, and how short-lived are the pleasures of this our transitory existence. No sooner did I draw some little relief from the measure which kind fortune suggested, than it is snatched away; and this last act is like closing the door of consolation against me, and opening that of my misfortunes."

It was thus I gave vent to my distress, while the careful workman, with abundance of wood and nails, was finishing his cruel job, saying with great glee. "Now, you rascals of rats, we will change sides, if you please, for your future reception in this house will be right little welcome."

The moment he left the house I went to examine his work, and found he had not left a single hole unstopped by which even a mosquito could enter. I opened the chest, though without deriving the smallest benefit from its contents; my key was now utterly useless; but as I gazed with longing eyes on the two or three loaves which my master believed to be bitten by the rats, I could not resist the temptation of nibbling a morsel more, though touching them in the lightest possible manner, like an experienced swordsman in a friendly assault.

Necessity is a great master, and being in this strait, I passed night and day in devising means to get out of it. All the rascally plans that could enter the mind of man did hunger suggest to me, for it is a saying, and a true one, as I can testify, that hunger makes rogues, and abundance fools. One night, when my master slept, of which disposition he always gave sonorous testimony, as I was revolving in my mind the best mode of renewing my intimacy with the contents of the chest, a thought struck me, which I forthwith put in execution. I arose very quietly, and, taking an old knife which, having some little glimmering of the same idea the day previous, I had left for an occasion of this nature, I repaired to the chest, and at the part which I considered least guarded I began to bore a hole. The antiquity of the chest seconded my endeavours, for the wood had become rotten from age, and easily yielded to the knife, so that in a short time I managed to display a hole of very respectable dimensions. I then opened the chest very gently, and, taking out the bread, I treated it much in the same manner as heretofore, and then returned safe to my mattress.

The next day my worthy master soon spied my handiwork, as well as the deficiency in his bread, and began by wishing the rats at the devil. "What can it mean?" said he; "during all the time I have been here there have never been rats in the house before." And he might say so with truth; if ever a house in the kingdom deserved to be free from rats, it was his, as they are seldom known to visit where there is nothing to eat. He began again with nails and wood, but when night came, and he slept, I resumed my operations, and rendered nugatory all his ingenuity.

In this manner we went on; the moment he shut one door, I opened another; like the web of Penelope, what he spun by day I unravelled by night, and in the course of a few nights the old chest was so maltreated that little remained of the original that was not covered with pieces and nailing. When the unhappy priest found his mechanical ability of no avail, he said, "Really, this chest is in such a state, and the wood is so old and rotten, that the rats make nothing of it. The best plan I can think of, since what we have done is of no use, is to arm ourselves within against these cursed rats." He then borrowed a rat-trap, and baiting it with bits of cheese which he begged from the neighbours, set it under the chest. This was a piece of singular good fortune for me, for although my hunger needed no sauce, yet I did not nibble the bread at night with less relish because I added thereto the bait from the rat-trap. When in the morning he found not only the bread gone as usual, but the bait likewise vanished, and the trap without a tenant, he grew almost beside himself. He ran to the neighbours and asked of them what animal it could possibly be that could positively eat the very cheese out of the trap, and yet escape untouched. The neighbours agreed that it could be no rat that could thus eat the bait, and not remain within the trap, and one more cunning than the rest observed, "I remember once seeing a snake about your premises, and depend on it that is the animal which has done you this mischief, for it could easily pick the bait from the trap without entering entirely, and thus too it might easily escape." The rest all agreed that such must be the fact, which alarmed my master a good deal.

He now slept not near so soundly as before, and at every little noise, thinking it was the snake biting the chest, he would get up, and taking a cudgel which he kept at his bed's head for the purpose, began to belabour the poor chest with all his might, so that the noise might frighten the reptile from his unthrifty proceedings. He even awoke the neighbours with such prodigious clamour, and I could not get a single minute's rest. He turned me out of bed, and looked amongst the straw, and about the blanket, to see if the creature was concealed anywhere; for, as he observed, at night they seek warm places, and not unfrequently injure people by biting them in bed. When he came I always pretended to be very heavy with sleep, and he would say to me in the morning, "Did you hear nothing last night, boy? The snake was about, and I think I heard him at your bed, for they are very cold creatures, and love warmth." " I hope to God he will not bite me," returned I, " for I am very much afraid." He was so watchful at night that, by my faith, the snake could not continue his operations as usual, but in the morning, when the priest was at church, he resumed them pretty steadily as usual.

Looking with dismay at the damage done to his store, and the little redress he was likely to have for it, the poor priest became quite uneasy from fretting, and wandered about all night like a hobgoblin. I began very much to fear that, during one of these fits of watchfulness, he might discover my key, which I placed for security under the straw of my bed. I therefore, with a caution peculiar to my nature, determined in future to keep this treasure by night safe in my mouth; and this was an ancient custom of mine, for during the time I lived with the blind man my mouth was my purse, in which I could retain ten or twelve maravedies in farthings, without the slightest inconvenience in any way. Indeed, had I not possessed this faculty, I should never have had a single farthing of my own, for I had neither pocket nor bag that the old man did not continually search. Every night I slept with the key in my mouth without fear of discovery; but, alas! when misfortune is our lot, ingenuity can be of little avail.

It was decreed, by my evil destiny, or rather, I ought to say, as a punishment for my evil doings, that one night, when I was fast asleep, my mouth being somewhat open, the key became placed in such a position therein that my breath came in contact with the hollow of the key, and caused—the worst luck for me!—a loud whistling noise. On this my watchful master pricked up his ears, and thought it must be the hissing of the snake which had done him all the damage, and certainly he was not altogether wrong in his conjectures. He arose very quietly, with his club in his hand, and stealing towards the place whence the hissing sound proceeded, thinking at once to put an end to his enemy, he lifted his club, and with all his force discharged such a blow on my unfortunate head that it needed not another to deprive me of all sense and motion. The moment the blow was delivered he felt it was no snake that had received it, and, guessing what he had done, called out to me in a loud voice, endeavouring to recall me to my senses. Then, touching me with his hands, he felt the blood, which was by this time in great profusion about my face, and ran quickly to procure a light. On his return he found me moaning, yet still holding the key in my mouth, and partly visible, being in the same situation which caused the whistling noise he had mistaken for the snake. Without thinking much of me, the attention of the slayer of snakes was attracted by the appearance of the key, and drawing it from my mouth, he soon discovered what it was, for of course the wards were precisely similar to his own. He ran to prove it, and with that at once found out the extent of my ingenuity.

"Thank God," exclaimed this cruel snake hunter, "that the rats and the snakes which have so long made war upon me, and devoured my substance, are both at last discovered."

Of what passed for three days afterwards I can give no account, but that which I have related I heard my master recount to those who came there to see me. At the end, however, of the third day I began to have some consciousness of what was passing around me, and found myself extended on my straw, my head bound up and covered with ointment and plaisters.

"What is the meaning of all this?" I cried in extreme alarm. The heartless priest replied, "I have only been hunting the rats and the snakes, which have almost ruined me." Seeing the condition in which I was, I then guessed what had happened to me. At this time an old nurse entered, with some of the neighbours, who dressed the wounds on my head, which had assumed a favourable appearance; and as they found my senses were restored to me, they anticipated but little danger, and began to amuse themselves with my exploits, while I, unhappy sinner, could only deplore their effects.

With all this, however, they gave me something to eat, for I was almost dying with hunger, and at the end of fourteen or fifteen days I was able to rise from my bed without danger, though not even then without hunger, and only half cured. The day after I got up my worthy and truly respectable master took my hand, and, opening the door, put me into the street, saying, "Lazaro, from this day look out for yourself; seek another master, and fare you well. No one will ever doubt that you have served a blind man, but for me, I do not require so diligent nor so clever a servant." Then shaking me off, as though I was in league with the Evil One, he went back into his house and shut the door.

Hurtado de Mendoza. Trans. Roscoe.

A TAILOR WOULD FAIN LEARN OF GUZMAN TO WRITE HIS NAME, OR TO MAKE FIRMA, OR MARK, AND THE REASON WHY.

IT was my hap one day to bear in my basket, which I brought from the Shambles, a quarter of Mutton, for a certain Hosier, or Gentleman Tailor. I had by chance at that time about me, certain old Coplas, or Ballads, which in a kind of broken tune still, as I read this or t'other line, I fell a-singing, as I went along. My good Master having (as it should seem) listened unto me, looked back on the sudden, and smiling, said—

"How now, my tattered Rascal, a pox take you for a ragga-muffin. Can you read, you Rogue?"

"Yes, marry, can I, Sir," quoth I. "I thank God I can read reasonable well, but my writing is better than my reading."

"Sayst thou so, Boy?"

And with that he entreated me, that I would teach him to write his name, or to make some mark that might serve for a subscription, or undersigning. He cared not which, for either would serve his turn.

"I pray, Sir," said I. "what good can this do you? What can you benefit yourself, by having learnt to make a bare mark and no more? Methinks you should have no great use for that alone, unless you could write too."

"Yes, marry, have I, Sir," quoth he, "for I have much work goes through these hands, of such and such great men, I make all the clothes their children wear" (and there, by the way, he reckons me up a beadroll of these and these Lords) "and therefore I would very fain, if I knew how, learn to write my Name, or to make my Mark, that if occasion were offered I might not be taken for an Ass, and say like a fool as I am when I am called to subscribe, 'Indeed, Sir, you must pardon me, I cannot write.'"

And so this business broke off as abruptly, as it began. And I making a large soliloquium, and meditation to myself, went on.

"*Guzman d'Alfarache*," *Mateo Aleman* (*fl.* 1609).
Trans. Mabbe.

EPISODE OF THE OFFICIOUS PHYSICIAN.

(In Spain your physician's fee is ordinarily two shillings; the better sort give four shillings; and the best seldom above a crown.)

NOW methought I saw Heaven opened, and my honest Carrier appearing unto me in the shape of an Angel. His face was as joyful unto me, as that of the desired Physician is to him that is afflicted with sickness. I say, desired; because (as perhaps you may have heard) a Physician hath three faces: Of a man, when we see him, and have no need of him: of an angel when we are sick, and cannot be without him: and of a Devil, when at one and the self-same time our sickness, and our purse ends together, and yet for his private interest and to gain a fee, he follows us with daily visits. As it happened to a Gentleman in Madrid, who having sent for a physician, for a certain infirmity, wherewithal he was troubled, every visit that he made, gave him a crown. The humour ceased; but his physician was not in the humour to cease from coming unto him.

Now the Gentleman, when he saw that he was thorough

well, and that his Physician did still continue his visits, he got him up one morning very early and went to Church.

Now, when the Physician came to visit him, and found him not at home, he asked his servant whither he was gone. He (like a fool as he was), for there are Servants still enow for their masters' hurt, but few for their profit, told him, that he was gone forth to Mass to such a Church. My nimble Doctor, putting spurs to his Mule for to make the more haste, went with all speed to the said Church, and, searching for him, at last he found him; and then said unto him—

"What in God's name, Sir, do you mean to commit so great an excess, as to go abroad without my leave?"

The Gentleman, who knew well enough what he came for, and seeing that now he had no more need of him, put his hand in his pocket, took out his purse, drew forth a crown, and putting it in his hand, told him, "Here, take it, master Doctor; for by the faith of a Gentleman, I now perceive even this sacred place cannot privilege me from you."

Mateo Aleman. Trans. Mabbe.

OF THE PLEASANT LIFE GUZMAN LED AMONG HIS BRETHREN, AND AN ACCOUNT OF HIS VISIT TO GAETA.

IN the evenings we used to assemble, some ten or twelve of us, and amused ourselves with discussing the different kind of new exclamations we had hit upon, to rouse public sympathy in our behalf. Such was the skill of a few, that they had invented forms of benediction from which they derived considerable profit by the sale of them to other less ingenious heads than their own; so great was their novelty and efficacy with all classes.

On every festival we went early in the morning to church, where plenary indulgence was always granted us. We placed ourselves in the most convenient stations; we continued there the whole morning; and towards evening we issued forth into the neighbouring villages, calling at the country seats and farmhouses on our road. From these we usually brought away some slices of bacon, bread and cheese, eggs, and sometimes old clothes and other articles; so successfully did we work upon the charity of the good people. Did a person above the common rank happen to make his appearance, we instantly united in setting up a loud lamentation, even at a distance, giving him time to put his hand into his pocket, and vociferating louder and louder the nearer he came, so as to compel him in a manner to be charitable.

If we met a number of good citizens together, and had leisure to prepare to accost them in due form, each played his own part—one the *blind*, another the *halt*, a third the *dumb*, a fourth the *paralytic*, a fifth the *idiotic*, and some with crutches, making altogether a complication of human misery and distortion, which, with the most able at our head, was sure to penetrate into the pockets even of the callous. Could you but have heard the concord of sweet sounds we made at the crisis that decided the balance in our favour! We beseeched the Lord to bless them with lovely children—to return their bounty a hundred fold—and long to preserve their precious health. Not a party of pleasure could be got up, not a single festival pass, but we had some share in it; so that however much others expended we gained by them; and so acute was our scent that we could smell the preparation for them at an enormous distance.

In the same way the mansions of the cardinals, the bishops, and ambassadors, with all kind of open houses, were successfully besieged and occupied by us. Thus we might truly be said to possess all, levying as we did a tax upon all, though really having nothing. I know not how my comrades felt inclined on receiving charity from the hands of a pretty lady; but for my part, miserable sinner, when I accosted a young creature, enchanting both in face and figure, I looked her steadily in the face while I asked with my eyes fixed upon hers. If she gave me anything, I caught her hand, pressed it affectionately, and imprinted upon it a kiss in the fervour of my gratitude, before she had time to withdraw it. Yet so respectfully, or rather, hypocritically, was this done, that the lady, not being previously alarmed, took the whole in good part, as a transport of grateful joy.

What are called the pleasures of life—erroneously supposed to be monopolised by the great and the wealthy of this best of worlds—are, in fact, the chief property of us mendicants, who feel no drawback, but taste their flavour with a double relish, without a tithe of their anxiety and trouble to obtain them. Had the happy fellows no other privilege than that of asking freely, and receiving without the least touch of shame or pain, it is such a one as the rest of mankind cannot boast; if we only except monarchs and their royal families, who, without a blush, can demand what they please from their good people, while the sole difference between them and other beggars is, that they always wring out silver and gold even from the poorest people, while we require nothing but a mere trifle from the most proud and wealthy. There is no condition, therefore, more happy and respectable than that of the mendicant, but all do not know their own happiness—"beati si sua bona norint."

The most part of us—wholly sunk in the enjoyment of mere animal life; insensible of the true pleasure of living independently, free from strife, from all speculative losses, all intrigues of State, eternal business; in short, from the infernal embarrassment in which the great are involved—to the day of their death have the folly to envy what they ought to avoid. The first man who embraced our kind of life must, from his very nature, have been much better than the great—I mean a great philosopher.

I had been led to think that this noble fraternity was safe from the usual shocks of fortune, but the malicious goddess made them occasionally feel the effects of her ire—throwing little stumbling-blocks in their way, much like the one I broke my shins over, when on a visit at Gaeta, whither I had gone out of curiosity, and in the idea that a man already able in the profession would only need to enter the town to feel a revivifying shower of alms poured upon him from all sides. No sooner was I there than, having assumed a new complexion, I placed myself at the entrance into a church. As luck would have it, the governor of the place was then passing, and, after looking at me very earnestly for a few moments, he gave me alms. A number of the natives immediately followed his example, and it acted as a continued benediction for me during more than a week; but there is a medium in all things, and I did not observe the golden rule. On the next festival, my complexion appearing no longer ingenious enough, I changed it for a huge ulcer on my leg, and for this purpose I put in practice one of the choicest secrets of my craft.

After having put my leg into an elegant case, I took an advantageous station at the entrance to a well-frequented church. There, setting up a sorrowful howl, caused by the new pain I felt from the ulcer, I caught the eye of almost every one that passed. I thought I excited the compassion of all who looked on me, but unluckily my rubicund complexion, which I had neglected to sicken over with white, seemed to give the lie to my lamentations, and might well excite suspicion; but good people are not over suspicious, and I heard the golden shower dropping sweetly and plentifully as they went into the house of prayer. In short, I got more than all the rest of my brethren put together, and they wished me at the devil, with my ulcer, that brought the capital into one bank.

As the stars at last would have it, there came the governor to hear mass at this very church—surely for my sins—and he recognised my voice in a moment, surveying me intently from head to foot. Yes, it was my voice, for elsewhere I was impenetrable; my whole person being disguised in the most effectual manner, with a huge napkin round my head, reaching down to my nose. Alas! he was a man of strong natural penetration, and suspicious as the devil; for, as he fixed me with his eyes, he seemed to be saying within himself, "For these several days past I have heard, I have seen, this odd-looking fish; is it possible he has got so dreadful an ulcer—all at once? Let us examine a little farther." "Friend," he observed, "you seem in a sad plight; your case truly deserves compassion; come, follow me, I will at least give you a shirt to your back."

I had the indiscretion to obey, for I suspected nothing. Had I so done, spite of all the people at his heels, I vow I would have given him the slip, and saved my unfortunate carcase. He had no sooner got me safely housed than he assumed a cold and severe aspect, from which I augured nothing pleasant. He then asked me sharply if I were not the person he had seen at the door of a church, with a complexion as pale as death. I grew pale enough indeed at this, and lost all presence of mind; I could not deny it: and when he asked me how I had got so speedily cured of my scalded head and other infirmities I was still more puzzled than before. "Besides," he continued, "I cannot comprehend how, with that ruddy complexion of thine, thou hast got such a terrible ulcer in the leg." "My lord," replied I, quite disconcerted, and trembling in every

"COME, FOLLOW ME, I WILL AT LEAST GIVE YOU A SHIRT TO YOUR BACK."

limb, " I know not how it is, except that it is the will of God."

But what was my anxiety when I heard the governor direct one of his messengers to go and call in a surgeon. I saw what was coming, and would have made an attempt to save myself had not the doors been already closed upon me. Not a chance was left me; the dreaded surgeon came, he examined my leg; but, with all his ability and experience, he would perhaps have been deceived had not the cruel governor privately communicated the reasons he had to believe me an impostor. Of course, he had little merit after that of probing the thing to the bottom; he unbundled it all anew, and putting on a knowing face: " I verily believe," he said, "the rogue has nothing amiss with his leg, any more than I have with my eyes; I see through it; bring me some warm water;" which being done, he proceeded to restore it to its natural form and colour. I had not a word to say in my defence, and held my tongue.

The governor then ordered me to be presented with a shirt, as he had promised, and this was nothing but a most severe flagellation, administered by a stout fellow, who laid on, at the governor's special order, with right good will on my bare carcase. After thirty lashes he stopped; I was dressed by the same surgeon, and told to take myself off, spite of my smarting, at double quick time, under a more terrible penalty were I again found in the same territories. This advice was quite superfluous. I hastened from the accursed spot, shrugging up my shoulders, and marched as quickly as possible to reach the milder government of the Pope. I uttered a thousand benedictions at the sight of my well-loved Rome once more; I wept for joy as I entered it, and wished that I had arms long enough to embrace it with the devoted love of some returning prodigal son or happy pilgrim.

I rejoined my comrades, and took care not to say a word

of the new marks of honour I had brought back with me
there would have been no end to their raillery, and I should
never have heard the last of it. I merely said I had been
making a little excursion to the adjacent villages, but, with
the exception of Rome, there was no place on which our
profession could fairly rely, either for profit or safety. I
had indeed been a great ass to leave such a city at all.

Mateo Aleman. Trans. Roscoe.

OF THE WICKED OLD HOUSEKEEPER, AND THE FIRST KNAVISH PRANKS PAUL PLAYED AT ALCALA.

WHEN you are at Rome, do as they do at Rome, says the old proverb; and it is well said. I took it so seriously into consideration, that I fully resolved to play the knave among knaves, and to excel them all if possible. I know not whether I succeeded to my wish, but I am sure I used all my endeavours. In the first place, I made a law that it should be no less than death for any pigs to cross the threshold of our house, or for any of the old housekeeper's chickens to run out of the yard into our room. It happened that one day two of the cleverest porkers that ever my eyes beheld slipped into our dominions; I was then at play with the other servants, and hearing them grunt, said to one of my companions, "Go see who it is that grunts in our house:" he went, and brought word they were actually two swine.

No sooner did I hear, then off I set in a passion, exclaiming— "It was a great deal of impudence in them to grunt in other people's houses." Then slamming to the door, in a sudden heat of blood, I ran my sword into the throats of them both, and we afterwards cut off their heads. To prevent their cries for rescue, we all set up our voices to the highest pitch during the operation, and between us they soon gave up the ghost. We next paunched them, saved the blood, and by the help of our straw bed half roasted them in the yard, so that all was over before our masters came home, except the mere making of the black puddings. Don Diego and our steward were informed of this exploit, and flew into such a passion, that the other lodgers, highly amused, were fain to take my part.

The don asked me what I should say for myself when the affair should be found out. I replied that I would plead hunger, the common sanctuary of all scholars; and if that was not enough, I would urge that, seeing them come into the house without knocking, just as if they had been at home, I really thought that they were ours. They all laughed, and Don Diego said, "By my faith, Paul, you begin to understand the trade." It was well worth observing the difference between my master and me; he so sober and religious, I so arch and roguish, so that the one was a foil to the other, and served to set off either his virtue or his vice. Our old housekeeper was pleased to the very heart, for we both played our parts, and conspired against the larder. I was caterer, and a mere Judas in my employment, ever since retaining an inclination for cribbing and stealing. The meat always wasted in the old woman's keeping, and she never dressed wedder mutton when she could get ewe or goat. Besides, she picked the flesh off the bones before she boiled them, so that the dishes she served up looked as if the cattle had all died of a consumption. The broth was so clear, that had it been as hard as the bones, it might have passed for crystal; but when she wanted to make it seem a little fat, she clapped in a few candles' ends. When I was by, she would say to my master, "In truth, sir, Paul is the best servant in Spain, bating his unluckiness, but that may well enough be borne with, because he is so honest." I gave her the same character, and so we put upon the whole house between us.

When I bought anything at market for the real value, the old body would pretend to fall out and quarrel; and she, seeming to be in a passion, would say, "Do not tell me, Paul, that this is a pennyworth of salad." At this I pretended to cry and make a great noise, beseeching my master that he would please to send the steward, that he might prove the base calumny of the scolding old woman. By such simple means did we both retain our character for honesty; she appearing to look sharp after me, and I always being found out to be trustworthy. Don Diego, highly pleased, would often say, "Would to God, Paul were as virtuous in other ways as he is honest: I see, my good woman, he is even better than you represent him." It was thus we had leisure and opportunity to feast on them like horse-leeches.

If you ask how much we might cheat them of in the year's round, I can only say it amounted to a considerable sum; yet the old woman never missed going to church daily, nor did I perceive any scruple of conscience she made of it, though she was so great a saint. She always wore a pair of beads about her neck, so big, that the wood of them might have served to roast a sirloin of beef. It was all hung with medals, crosses, pictures, and other trinkets, on all which, she said, she prayed every night for her benefactors. She would pray longer than any fanatical preacher, always in dog Latin, the sound of which almost made us split our sides with laughter.

The old woman kept fowls, and had about a dozen fine grown chickens, which made my mouth water, for they were fit for any gentleman's table. It happened one day, going to feed them, she called, as is the custom in Spain, very loud: "Pio, Pio, Pio." She repeated it so often, that I cried out in a pretended rage—

"'Fore God! nurse, I wish I had seen you kill a man, or clip and coin, for then I might have kept your counsel; but now I must be forced to discover you. The Lord have mercy upon us both, I say."

She, seeing me in such disorder, was somewhat alarmed: "Why, Paul," she said, "what have I done? pray do not jest with me."

"Jest with you, forsooth, a curse on your iniquity! I cannot avoid giving information to the Inquisition, or I shall be excommunicated."

"Oh Lord! the Inquisition; have I committed any crime, then?"

"Have you *not?*" I answered: "don't think to trifle with the Inquisitors; own you are in the wrong; eat your own words as fast as you can, and deny not the blasphemy and irreverence."

She replied in great consternation: "But, Paul, will they punish me if I recant?"

"No," I replied, "they will then only absolve you."

"Then I recant," said she; "only tell me what it is I have to recant; for I know nothing of it, as I hope for mercy."

"Bless me," replied I; "is it possible you should be so dull? the irreverence was so great I hardly know how to express it. Wretch as you are, did you not call the chickens, Pio, Pio; and Pius is the name of several Popes, who are Christ's vicars upon earth, and heads of the church. Now do you consider whether that be any trifling sin?"

She stood as if she had been thunderstruck, and after a while cried: "'Tis true, I said so, Paul; but may I be burnt if I did it with any ill design. I recant—I do, indeed; and try to find some way not to inform of me; for I shall die if they get me into the Inquisition."

"Provided you take your oath on the holy altar that you meant it not for blasphemy; but then you must give me the two chickens you called in that unsanctified way, by the names of the Popes, that they may be burnt by the officers of the Inquisition. This you must do now, or I shall otherwise be compelled to lay an information against you as quick as possible."

She was glad to escape so easily, and instantly consented, giving me three instead of two, which I took to a neighbouring cook, had them dressed, and ate with my companions. Don Diego came to hear of the trick, and made excellent sport of it in the family. The old woman had nearly fretted herself to death for mere vexation, and was a thousand times in the mind of taking revenge, and discovering all my schemes. She was, however, too deeply implicated; and having once quarrelled with me, there was no end to the tricks I played her. In short, I became a great authority in all that the scholars called snatching and shop-lifting, at which I had many pleasant adventures.

One evening, about nine o'clock, as I was passing through the great street, I spied a confectioner's shop open, and in it a frail of raisins upon the counter. I whipped in, took hold of it, and set a-running; the confectioner scoured after me, and so did several neighbours and servants. Being loaded, I perceived that, though I had the start, they would overtake me, and so, turning the corner of a street, I clapped the frail upon the ground and sat down upon it, and wrapping my cloak about my leg, began to cry out, "God forgive him, he has trod upon me and crippled me." When they came up I began to cry, "For God's sake, pity the lame; I pray God you may never be lame!"

"'FRIEND,' THEY EXCLAIMED, 'DID YOU SEE A MAN RUN THIS WAY?'"

"Friend!" they exclaimed, "did you see a man run this way?"

"He is before you," was my answer, "for he trod upon me."

I boasted of this exploit, and with some reason: I even invited them to come and see me steal a box of sweetmeats another night. They came, and observing that all the boxes were so far within the shop, that there was no reaching them, they concluded the thing was impracticable. Drawing my sword, however, about a dozen paces from the shop, I ran on, and crying out at the door, "You are a dead man!" I made a strong pass just before the confectioner's breast, who dropped down calling for help; and my sword running clean through a box of sweetmeats, I drew it, box and all, and took to my heels. They were all amazed at the contrivance, and ready to burst with laughing on hearing him bid the people search him, for that he was badly wounded; even when he found out the cheat he continued to bless himself, while I was employed in eating the fruits of my exploit. My comrades used to say that I could easily maintain my family upon nothing; as much as to say, by my wits and sleight-of-hand. This had the effect of encouraging me to commit more. I used to bring home my girdle, hung all round with little pitchers, which I stole from nuns, begging some water to drink of them; and when they turned it out in their wheel, I went off with the mugs, they being shut up and not able to help themselves.

"*Paul, the Spanish Sharper.*" Quevedo (1580-1645).
Trans. Roscoe.

ESTEBANILLO ACTS ON THE CARDINAL'S BIRTHDAY!

WHEN I had been there five weeks, to reward my good service, I was prefer'd to be under-sweeper below stairs. Thus men rise who behave themselves well in their employment, and are careful to please their superiors. I was bare-foot, half-naked, and as black as a collier, when I entered upon my new charge, where I fared not so well as in the kitchen; for places of honour are not often so profitable as those of less reputation, and nothing could stick to me but the dust of the house, whereas before I never wanted a sop in the pan, or other perquisites.

But Fortune so ordered it that the Cardinal's servants undertook to act a play on his Eminency's birthday; and in distributing the parts, they pitched upon me to represent a young King of Leon, either because I was young, or for being descended from the renowned Fernan Gonzales, who, as I said before, was my progenitor, and Earl of Castile, before there were kings of that country. I took care to learn my part, and persuaded him that took the management of it to give me half a pound of raisins and a couple of oranges every day, that I might eat a little collation at night, and rub my temples with the orange-peels in the morning fasting, telling him that would help my memory, which was very weak, else I should never get it by heart, tho' the whole was not above twenty lines; and assuring him I had seen this done by the most celebrated comedians in Spain, when they acted the greatest parts. When the day of the solemnity came, a stately theatre was erected in the largest room in the palace, making a wood of green boughs at the end next the attiring room, where I was to lye asleep, and Moors to come and carry me away captive. My lord, the Cardinal, invited all the men of quality and ladies of

"I CAME TO THE SEASHORE."

the court to this diversion. Our Merry-Andrew actors dressed themselves like so many Jack-Puddings, and all the palace was richly hung and adorned. They put me on a very fine cloth suit, half cover'd with rich silver loops, and laced down the seams, which was as good as giving me wings to take my flight and be gone. Seeing myself in such equipage as I had never known before, I thought not fit to return to my rags again, but resolv'd to shift for myself. The play began at three in the afternoon, the audience consisting of all the flower of the city. The manager of the representation was so active and watchful, because he had hir'd my clothes, and was bound to see them forthcoming, that he never suffered me to go out of his sight. But when they came to that part where I was to appear as if I had been hunting, and then to lye down in the wood, pretending weariness and sleep; I repeated a few verses, and those who came out with me upon the stage having left me, I turn'd into that green copse, where it cannot be said I was taken napping, for going in at one end I follow'd a narrow path that was left among the boughs, to the other end of the theatre, whence I slipped down, and going along under it to the door of that great hall, bid those who stood about it, make way, for I was going to shift my clothes. Upon this they all let me pass, I made but two steps down the stairs, and flew along the streets like an arrow out of a bow, till I came to the sea-shore, whither I had steer'd my course, in hopes of some conveniency to carry me off. I was told afterwards when I returned to Palermo, that at the time when I quitted the stage, there came out half-a-dozen Christian Moors, well stuff'd with gammon of bacon, and encouraged with rich wine; who coming to the wood to seize their prize, thinking I had been there, cry'd out with loud voice: "Young Christian King, appear!" To which I supposing them to be my servants, was to answer, "Is it time to move?" I being then too far on my way, not for fear of being made a slave among infidels, but rather of being stripped of my fine clothes, could not play my part, or answer to the Moors, because I was a mile off, driving a bargain with Christians. The prompter perceiving I did not answer, was very diligent, repeating what I was to say, as believing I had forgot myself, tho' he was much mistaken, for I had all my business fresh in my head. The Moors being tired with expectation, and concluding I had really fallen asleep, when I ought only to counterfeit, went into the imaginary wood, and found no footsteps of a King. They were all amazed, there was no proceeding on the play; some ran about calling upon me, and others went to enquire after my Majesty, whilst he, who had engag'd for my clothes, tore his hair for vexation, and offer'd vows to Heaven in case I were found, and he escaped that shipwreck. They told the Cardinal I was fled, who answered, I was much in the right to make my escape from the enemies of the Christian religion, and not suffer myself to be made prisoner by them. That, without doubt, I was gone back to the city of Leon, where I kept my court, whence it was likely I would take care to return the clothes; but in the meanwhile, he would pay the value, so that they need not take the trouble of sending after me, for he would not disoblige so great a prince, especially on his birthday. He ordered my part should be read, and the rest of the play acted; which was done accordingly, to the great satisfaction of the audience, and no less of the manager, having such good security for his clothes.

"The Life of Estebanillo Gonzalez" (written by himself in 1646). Trans. Captain John Stevens.

THE INGENIOUS GENTLEMAN, DON QUIXOTE OF LA MANCHA.

Which treats of the condition and way of life of the famous gentleman, Don Quixote of La Mancha.

IN a certain village of La Mancha, whose name I will not recall, there lived not long ago a gentleman—one of those who keep a lance in the rack, an ancient target, a lean hackney, and a greyhound for coursing. A mess of somewhat more beef than mutton, a salad on most nights, a hotch-potch on Saturdays, lentils on Fridays, with the addition of a pigeon on Sundays, consumed three parts of his substance. The rest of it was spent in a doublet of fine broad-cloth, a pair of velvet breeches for holidays, with slippers of the same, and his home-spun of the finest, with which he decked himself on week-days. He kept at home a housekeeper, who was past forty, and a niece who had not yet reached twenty, besides a lad for the field and market, who saddled the nag and handled the pruning-hook.

The age of our gentleman bordered upon fifty years. He was of a vigorous constitution, spare of flesh, dry of visage, a great early riser, and a lover of the chase. They affirm that his surname was Quejada, or Quesada (and in this there is some variance among the authors who treat of the matter), although by very probable conjectures we are led to conclude that he was called Quijana. But this is of small import to our story; enough that in the telling of it we swerve not a jot from the truth.

Be it known, then, that this gentleman above mentioned, during the interval that he was idle, which was the greater part of the year, gave himself up to the reading of books of chivalries, with so much fervour and relish, that he almost entirely neglected the exercise of the chase and even the management of his estate. And to such a pitch did his curiosity and infatuation reach, that he sold many acres of arable land in order to buy romances of chivalry to read; and so he brought home as many of them as he could procure. And of all none seemed to him so good as those composed by the famous Feliciano de Silva, for their brilliancy of style and those entangled sentences seemed to him to be very pearls; and especially when he came to read of the passages of love, and cartels of defiance, wherein he often found written things like these: "*The reason of the unreason which is done to my reason in such wise my reason debilitates, that with reason I complain of your beauteousness.*" And also when he read: "*The lofty heavens which of your divinity do divinely fortify you with the constellations, and make you deserver of the deserts which your mightiness deserves.*"

Over these reasons our poor gentleman lost his senses, and he used to keep awake at night in trying to comprehend them, and in plucking out their meaning, which not Aristotle himself could extract or understand, were he to come to life for that special purpose. He did not much fancy the wounds which Don Belianis gave and received; for he thought that, however potent were the masters who had healed him, the Knight could not but have his face and all his body full of scars and marks. Nevertheless, he praised in the author the ending of his book with the promise of that interminable adventure, and ofttimes he was seized with a desire to take up the pen, and put a finish to it in good earnest, as is there purposed. And doubtless he would have done so—aye, and gone through with it—had not other greater and more lasting thoughts diverted his mind.

Many times he held dispute with the Priest of his village (who was a learned man, a graduate of Siguenza) as to who should have been the better knight, Palmerin of England, or Amadis of Gaul; though Master Nicholas, the Barber of the same village, was used to say that none came up to the Knight of the Sun, and that if any one could compare with him it was Don Galaor, brother of Amadis of Gaul, for he had a very accommodating temper for everything; he was no prudish cavalier, nor such a sniveller as his brother, nor in the article of valour any behind him.

In fine, our gentleman was so absorbed in these studies, that he passed his nights reading from eve to dawn, and his days from dark to dusk; and so with little sleep and much study his brain dried up, to the end that he lost his wits. He filled himself with the imagination of all that he read in the books: with enchantments, with quarrels, battles, challenges, wounds, amorous plaints, loves, torments, and follies impossible. And so assured was he of the truth of all that mass of fantastic inventions of which he read, that for him there was no other history in the world so certain. He would say that the Cid Ruy Diaz must have been a good knight, but not to be named with the Knight of the Flaming Sword, who only with one back-stroke had severed two fierce and monstrous giants through the middle. He better liked Bernardo del Carpio, because at Roncesvalles he had slain Orlando the Enchanted, availing himself of Hercules' trick when he throttled Anteus, son of Terra, in his arms. He spoke very well of the giant Morgante; for, though of that gigantesque brood who are all arrogant and uncivil, he alone was affable and well-mannered. But, above all, he esteemed Rinaldo of Montalvan, especially when he saw him sally from his castle and rob all he met, and when in Heathenric he stole that idol of Mahound, which was all of gold, as his history tells. As for the traitor Galalon, for a volley of kicks at him he would have given his housekeeper—aye, and his niece to boot. In short, his wits utterly wrecked, he fell into the strangest delusion ever madman conceived in the world, and this was, that it was fitting and necessary for him, as he thought, both for the augmenting of his honour and the service of the State, to make himself a Knight Errant, and travel through the world with his armour and his horse seeking for adventures, and to exercise himself in all that he had read that the Knight Errant practised, redressing all kinds of wrong, and placing himself in perils and passes by the surmounting of which he might achieve an everlasting name and fame. Already the poor man imagined himself, by the valour of his arm, crowned with, at the least, the Empire of Trebizond. And so, with these imaginations so delightful, rapt in the strange zest with which they inspired him, he made haste to give effect to what he desired. The first thing he did was to furbish up some armour which had belonged to his great-grandfathers, which, eaten with rust and covered with mould, had lain for ages, where it had been put away and forgotten, in a corner. He scoured and dressed it as well as he was able, but he saw that it had one great defect, which was that there was no covered helmet, but only a simple morion or, headpiece. This his ingenuity supplied, for, with pieces of pasteboard, he fashioned a sort of half-beaver, which, fitted to the morion, gave it the appearance of a complete helmet. The fact is that, to prove it to be strong and able to stand the chance of a sword-cut, he drew his sword and gave it a couple of strokes, demolishing with the very first in a moment what had cost him a week to make. The ease with which he had knocked it to pieces not seeming to him good, in order to secure himself against this danger he set to making it anew, fitting some bars of iron within in such a manner as to leave him satisfied with his defence; and without caring to make a fresh trial of it, he constituted and accepted it for a very perfect good helmet. He went then to inspect his nag, a beast which, though it had more quarters than there are in a real, and more blemishes than the horse of Gonela, who, *tantum pellis et ossa fuit*, appeared to him to surpass Alexander's Bucephalus and the Cid's Bavieca. Four days were spent by our gentlemen in meditating on what name to give him; for, as he said to himself, it was not right that the steed of Knight so famous, and in himself so good, should be without a recognised appellation; and therefore he endeavoured to fit him with one which should signify what he had been prior to his belonging to a Knight Errant, and what he was then; since he thought it but right that, the master having changed his condition, the horse should also change his name, and get him one sublime and high-sounding, as befitted the new order and the new office which he professed. And so, after many names which he devised, effaced, and rejected, amended, re-made and unmade in his mind and fancy, finally he decided to call him ROZINANTE—a name, in his opinion, lofty, sonorous, and significative of what his animal had been when he was a common hackney, before he became what he now was, before, and in front of, all the hackneys in the world.

Having given to his horse a name so much to his liking, he then desired to give one to himself, and the thinking of this cost him eight other days. At last he decided to call himself DON QUIXOTE; whereupon the authors of this truthful history, as has been said, have found occasion to affirm that his name was Quijada, and not Quesada, as others would have it. Then recollecting that the valorous Amadis was not contented with calling himself simply Amadis, but added the name of his kingdom and native country, to make it famous, taking the name of Amadis of Gaul, so he desired, like a good knight, to add to his own the name of his native land, and call himself DON QUIXOTE OF LA MANCHA, whereby, to his seeming, he made lively proclamation of his lineage and his country, and honoured it by taking his surname therefrom.

His armour then being cleaned, his morion manufactured into a helmet, a name given to his horse, and himself confirmed with a new one, it struck him that he lacked nothing else than to look for a lady of whom to be enamoured; for the Knight Errant without amours was a tree without leaves and without fruit, and a body without soul. He would say to himself: "Were I, for my sins, or through good luck, to encounter hereabouts some giant, as usually happens to Knights Errant, and to overthrow him at the onset, or cleave him through the middle of his body, or, in fine, vanquish him and make him surrender, would it not be well to have some one to whom to send him as a present, that he might enter and bend the knee before my sweet mistress, and say with humble and subdued voice: 'I, lady, am the giant Caraculiambro, lord of the island of Malindramia, whom the never-to-be-praised-as-he-deserves Knight, Don Quixote of La Mancha, vanquished in single combat—he who hath commanded me to present myself before your grace that your highness may dispose of me at your pleasure.'"

Oh, how our good knight was pleased with himself when he had delivered this speech!—and the more when he found one to whom to give the name of his lady. It happened, as the belief is, that in a village near his own there was a well-looking peasant girl, with whom he had once fallen in love, though it is understood that she never knew it or had proof thereof. Her name was Aldonza Lorenzo, and upon her he judged it fit to bestow the title of mistress of his fancy; and, seeking for her a name which should not much belie her own, and yet incline and approach to that of a princess or great lady, he decided to call her DULCINEA DEL TOBOSO, for she was a native of El Toboso—a name, in his opinion, musical, romantic, and significant, as were all which he had given to himself and his belongings.

Wherein is related the pleasant method by which Don Quixote got himself dubbed Knight.

. . . . Don Quixote promised to perform all that was recommended to him with all exactness; whereupon he was enjoined forthwith to keep watch over his armour in a large yard by the inn-side. Collecting the pieces all together, he placed them on top of a stone trough which stood near a well, and, buckling on his shield, he grasped his lance, and began with a jaunty air to pace in front of the trough, it being now dark when he commenced his exercise.

The landlord told all who were staying in the inn of his guest's craze, the watching of the armour, and the dubbing of Knighthood which he awaited. Wondering at this strange kind of madness, they went to look at him from afar, and saw him sometimes pacing with a tranquil mien, sometimes resting on his lance, with his eyes fixed on his armour, from which he would not take them off for some time. The night had now closed in, with a moon of such brightness that she might have vied with him who lent it to her,[1] so that whatever our novice did could be plainly seen by all. Just then one of the muleteers who were staying in the inn, wanting to give water to his team, found it necessary to remove Don Quixote's armour from where it lay on the trough. The Knight, seeing the man approach, exclaimed with a loud voice: "O thou, whosoever thou art, rash cavalier! who comest to touch the armour of the most valiant Errant that ever girt sword on himself, take heed

[1] Meaning, of course, the sun.

what thou doest, and touch it not, if thou wouldst not lose thy life in forfeit of thy temerity."

The muleteer paid no regard to these words (and better for him it had been had he regarded them, for he would have re-guarded his safety), but, taking hold of the armour by the straps, flung it some way from him. When Don Quixote saw this, he lifted his eyes to heaven, and addressing himself, as it seemed, to his Lady Dulcinea, cried, "Succour me, mistress mine, in this the first affront which is offered to this enthralled bosom: let not your favour and help fail me in this first trial!"

And uttering these and other such words, and loosing his shield, he raised his lance in both hands, and with it dealt such a mighty blow on the muleteer's head that it felled him to the earth in such ill plight that, if it had been followed up with a second, there would have been no need of a leech to cure him. Soon after, another muleteer, without knowing what had passed (for the first still lay stunned), came up with the same purpose of giving water to his mules, and was going to remove the armour so as to clear the trough, when Don Quixote, without speaking a word or asking any one's favour, again loosed his shield and again raised his lance, and without breaking it made more than three of the second muleteer's head, for he broke it into four pieces. At the noise all the people of the inn ran out, and the landlord among them. Seeing this, Don Quixote buckled on his shield, and, setting his hand to his sword, cried, "O lady of beauty! strength and vigour of this debile heart! now is the hour when you should turn the eyes of your grandeur on this your captive Knight, who is awaiting this mighty adventure!"

Thereupon he seemed to himself to acquire so much courage, that if all the muleteers in the world had assailed him he would not have budged a foot backwards. The companions of the wounded, seeing them in that plight,

"DEALT SUCH A MIGHTY BLOW ON THE MULETEER'S HEAD, THAT IT
FELLED HIM TO THE EARTH."

began to shower stones upon Don Quixote from a distance, who sheltered himself as well as he could with his shield, not venturing to leave the horse-trough lest he should seem to abandon his armour. The innkeeper called out to them to leave him alone, for he had told them already that it was a madman, and being mad he would be scot-free even if he killed them all. Don Quixote also cried out yet louder, calling them cowards and traitors, and declaring the Lord of the castle to be a craven and a base-born Knight for consenting to Knights Errant being so treated, and that if he himself had received the order of Knighthood he would have made him sensible of his perfidy: " But of you, base and wild rabble, I make no account. Shoot! come on! advance! assail me as much as ye are able; you shall see the penalty you have to pay for your folly and insolence!"

This he said with so much spirit and intrepidity that he struck all who heard him with a terrible fear; and therefore, and partly by the host's persuasions, they left off pelting him, and he on his part permitted them to carry off their wounded, returning to the vigil of his arms with the same calmness and composure as before.

These pranks of his guest were not to the innkeeper's liking, so he determined to despatch and give him that plaguy order of Knighthood forthwith, before other mischief should happen. Going up to him, therefore, he apologised for the insolence with which those base fellows had behaved without his knowledge, but, he added, they had been well chastised for their hardihood. And seeing there was no chapel in that castle, as he had said before, there was no need, he declared, for the rest of the performance—that the whole point of Knight-making consisted in the slap of the hand and the stroke on the shoulder, according to his knowledge of the ceremonial of the order, and this could be done in the middle of a field; and that Don Quixote had already accomplished all that pertained to the watching of arms, more by token that he had been more than four hours at what might have been finished off with a two hours' watch.

To all this Don Quixote gave credence, and he said to the host that he was there ready to obey him, praying him to conclude the business as soon as possible, for, were he assaulted again when full Knight, he purposed not to leave any one alive in the castle, except those he might spare at the Castellan's bidding, and out of regard for him.

The Castellan, thus forewarned, and apprehensive of what might happen, brought out a book in which he used to enter the straw and barley which he supplied to the muleteers, and, with a candle-end borne by a lad, the two damsels aforesaid with him, went up to where Don Quixote was standing, whom he ordered to go down on his knees. Reading in his manual as though he were reciting some devout prayer, he broke off in the middle, and, lifting up his hand, dealt Don Quixote a sound blow on the head, and after this a brisk thwack on the shoulder with his own sword, still muttering between his teeth as though he were praying. This done, he commanded one of those ladies to gird on Don Quixote's sword, which she did with much sprightliness and discretion, and it needed no little of that last article to avoid bursting with laughter at each point of the ceremonies, though the prowesses they had witnessed of the new Knight kept their mirth within bounds. At the girding on of the sword the good lady said, "God make your worship a fortunate Knight, and give you good luck in battles!" Don Quixote besought her to tell him her name, that thenceforward he might know to whom he was indebted for the favour received, for he designed to bestow on her some portion of the honour which he was to reap by the valour of his arm. She replied, with much humility, that her name was *La Tolosa*, and that she was the daughter of a cobbler, native of Toledo, who lived among the stalls of Sancho Bienaya, and that wheresoever she might be, she was at his service and took him for her master. Don Quixote begged her in reply, for love of him, henceforth to assume the *Don*, and call herself Donna Tolosa, which she promised to do. The other damsel buckled on him his spurs, with whom there passed almost the same colloquy as with her of the sword. He asked her her name, and she answered that she was called *La Molinera*, and was the daughter of a miller of Antequera. Her also Don Quixote besought to take upon her the *Don*, and call herself Donna Molinera, renewing his offers of service and favour.

These never-before-seen ceremonies having been despatched at a gallop and post-haste, Don Quixote could not rest till he saw himself on horseback, sallying forth in quest of adventures. So saddling Rozinante at once he mounted, and embracing the innkeeper, thanked him for the favour done in the knighting in terms so extravagant that it is impossible to give an exact relation of them. The innkeeper, seeing him well outside his inn, responded to his speeches with others no less flowery although more brief, and, without asking him for the cost of his lodging, let him go with a hearty good will.

Of the good success which Don Quixote had in the terrible and never-before imagined adventure of the windmills, with other events worthy of happy remembrance.

While thus conversing, they caught sight of some thirty or forty windmills which are in that plain, and as soon as Don Quixote perceived them, he exclaimed—

"Fortune is guiding our affairs better than we could have desired, for look yonder, friend Sancho, where thirty or more huge giants are revealed, with whom I intend to do battle, and take all their lives. With their spoils we will begin to enrich ourselves, for this is fair war, and it is doing God great service to clear this evil spawn from off the face of the earth.

"What giants?" asked Sancho Panza.

"Those thou seest there," replied his master, "with the long arms, which some of them are wont to have of two leagues' length."

"Take care, sir," cried Sancho, "for those we see yonder are not giants, but windmills, and what in them look like arms are the sails which, being whirled about by the wind, make the mill-stone to go."

"It is manifest," answered Don Quixote, "that thou art not experienced in this matter of adventures. They are giants, and if thou art afraid get thee away home and dispose thyself to prayer, while I go to engage with them in fierce and unequal combat."

So saying, he clapped spurs to Rozinante, his steed, without heeding the cries which Sancho Panza, his squire, uttered, warning him that those he was going to encounter were beyond all doubt windmills and not giants. But he went on so fully persuaded that they were giants, that he neither listened to the cries of his squire Sancho, nor stopped to mark what they were, but shouted to them in a loud voice—

"Fly not, cowards, vile creatures, for it is a single cavalier who assails you!"

A slight breeze having sprung up at this moment, the great sail-arms began to move, on perceiving which Don Quixote cried—

"Although ye should wield more arms than had the giant Briareus, ye shall pay for it!"

Saying this, and commending himself with his whole soul to his lady Dulcinea, beseeching her to succour him in this peril, well covered with his buckler, with his lance in rest, he charged at Rozinante's best gallop, and attacked the first mill before him and thrusting his lance into the sail the

"THE HORSE AND HIS RIDER SENT ROLLING OVER THE PLAIN SORELY DAMAGED."

wind turned it with so much violence that the lance was shivered to pieces, carrying with it the horse and his rider, who was sent rolling over the plain sorely damaged.

Sancho Panza hastened to his master's help as fast as his ass could go, and when he came up he found the Knight unable to stir, such a shock had Rozinante given him in the fall.

"God bless me," cried Sancho, "did I not tell your worship to look to what you were doing, for they were nought but windmills? And nobody could mistake them but one who had other such in his head."

"Peace, friend Sancho," said Don Quixote; "for the things of war are more than other subject to continual mutation. And, moreover, I believe, and that is the truth, that the same sage Friston, who robbed me of my room and my books, hath turned these giants into windmills, in order to deprive me of the glory of their overthrow, so great is the enmity he bears to me; but in the upshot his evil arts shall little avail against the goodness of my sword."

"God send it as He will," answered Sancho; and helping him to rise, the Knight remounted Rozinante, whose shoulders were half dislocated.

Which treats of the lofty adventure and the rich winning of Mambrino's helmet.

. . . Now, the truth of the matter as to the helmet, the horse, and the Knight that Don Quixote saw was this. There were in that neighbourhood two villages, one so small that it possessed neither apothecary's shop nor barber, which the other, close to it, had; and so the barber of the larger village did duty for the smaller, in which was a sick man who required to be blooded, and another who wanted shaving; on which account the barber was coming, bring-

"BEGAN TO RACE ACROSS THE PLAIN FASTER THAN THE WIND."

ing with him a brass basin; and it chanced that, at the time he was travelling, it commenced to rain, and, not to spoil his hat, which was a new one, he clapt upon his head the basin, which, being a clean one, shone half a league off. He rode upon a grey ass, as Sancho said, and this was how to Don Quixote there appeared the dapple-grey steed and the Knight and the helmet of gold, for all things that he saw he made to fall in very easily with his wild chivalries and his vagabond fancies. And, when he perceived that luckless horseman draw near, without stopping to parley with him, he ran at him with his lance couched at Rozinante's full gallop, with intent to pierce him through and through; and as he came up to him, without abating the fury of his career, he cried out—

"Defend thyself, vile caitiff creature, or render me up of thine own will that which by all right is my due."

The barber, who saw that apparition bearing down upon him, without thought or apprehension of any such thing, had no other way to save himself from the thrust of the lance than to let himself fall off his ass, and no sooner had he touched the ground when he rose more nimbly than a deer, and began to race across the plain faster than the wind. The basin he left upon the ground, with which Don Quixote was well content, remarking that the Paynim had done wisely, and that he had imitated the beaver, who, when he finds himself hard pressed by the hunters, tears and cuts off with his teeth that for which he knows by natural instinct he is chased. He bade Sancho pick up the helmet, who, taking it in his hands, said—

"In sooth the basin is a good one, and worth a real of eight, if it is worth a maravedi."

He gave it to his master, who placed it upon his head, turning it about from side to side in search of the vizor, and, not finding it, he said—

"Doubtless the Paynim to whose measure this famous

headpiece was first forged, must have had a very large head, and the worst of it is that half of it is wanting."

When Sancho heard him call the basin a headpiece, he could not contain his laughter, but bethinking him of his master's wrath, he checked himself in the midst of it.

"What dost thou laugh at?" asked Don Quixote.

"I am laughing," replied he, "for thinking of the big head the Paynim owner of this helmet must have had, for it looks for all the world like nothing but a perfect barber's basin."

"Knowest thou what I suspect, Sancho? That this famous piece of the enchanted helmet must by some strange accident have come into the hands of one who did not know or esteem its worth, and who, ignorant of what he did, seeing it to be of pure gold, must have melted down the other half of it to profit by its worth, and of this half he has made what looks to thee like a barber's basin, as thou sayest. But, be that as it may, to me who recognise it, its transmutation makes no matter, for I will have it rectified in the first village where there is a smith, and in such wise that it shall not be surpassed or even approached by that which was made and forged by the god of smithies for the god of battles. And, in the meantime, I will wear it as I can, for something is better than nothing; all the more as it will well suffice to protect me against any blow from a stone."

Wherein is set forth the highest point and extreme to which the never-before-heard-of courage of Don Quixote reached or could reach; with the happily achieved Adventure of the Lions.

The history tells that Sancho, when Don Quixote called for his helmet, was buying some curds of the shepherds, and in his perturbation at his master's hurried call, knew not what to do with them or how to carry them; so in order not to lose what he had now paid for, he bethought him of clapping them into his master's helmet, and having thus made shift, he turned back to see what Don Quixote wanted, who, on his coming up, cried, "Give me that helmet, friend, for I know little of adventure or that which I descry yonder is one which should require, and does require, me to take to arms."

He of the Green Coat, hearing this, turned his eyes every way, but saw nothing but a cart which came towards them with two or three little flags, which made him think that it must be carrying the King's treasure, and so he told Don Quixote. But the Knight would not credit it, always supposing and imagining that all which happened was adventures, and still adventures; and so he replied—

"Forewarned is forearmed; nothing is lost by taking precaution, for I know by experience that I have enemies visible and invisible, nor know I when, nor where, nor in what moment, nor in what shape I have to encounter them."

And turning to Sancho he asked for his helmet, which the squire, not having an opportunity of relieving it of the curds, was compelled to hand to him as it was. Don Quixote took it, and without giving a look to what it contained, clapped it on his head in all haste; and as the curds were squeezed and pressed, the whey began to pour over all Don Quixote's face and beard, from which he got such a fright that he said to Sancho—

"What is this, Sancho? For methinks my skull is softening, or my brains are melting, or I sweat from feet to head. And if it is that I am sweating, truly it is not from fear. Without doubt I believe this is terrible, the adventure that now means to befall me. Give me something, if you can, with which to wipe myself, for this copious sweat doth blind my eyes."

Sancho held his tongue and gave him a cloth, and with it thanks to God that his master had not found out the truth. Don Quixote wiped himself, and took off the helmet to see what it was which seemed to chill his head, and finding the white clots within his headpiece, held them to his nose, and smelling them, cried—

"By the life of my lady Dulcinea del Toboso, but these are curds thou hast put here, thou traitor! villain, brazen-faced squire!"

To which, with much deliberation and command of countenance, Sancho replied, "If they are curds give them to me, your worship, and I will eat them; but let the devil eat them, for it must be he who put them there. I to dare soil your worship's helmet! You must know who it is that's so bold. In faith, sir, as God reads my mind, I, too, must have enchanters who persecute me as a creature and limb of your worship; and they will have put that nastiness there to move your patience to anger, and make you baste my ribs as you are wont to do; but, in truth, this time they have jumped wide of the mark, for I rely on my master's good judgment, who will consider that I have neither curds nor milk about me, nor anything like; and if I had I would rather put it into my stomach than in the helmet."

"It may be all so," quoth Don Quixote. And the gentleman in the Green Coat, who noted all, was utterly amazed, especially when, after Don Quixote had wiped dry his head, face, beard, and helmet, he put it on again, and settling himself firmly in his stirrups, reaching for his sword and grasping his lance, exclaimed—

"Now come what may, for here I stand to do battle with Satan himself in person."

The cart with the flags now approached, in which was nobody but the carter upon one of the mules and a man seated in front. Planting himself before it, Don Quixote exclaimed—

"Whither go ye, my brethren; what cart is this? What do you carry therein? And what flags are these?"

To which the carter replied, "The cart is mine; what go in it are two bold lions in a cage, which the General is sending from Oran to the capital as a present to his Majesty; the flags are the King's, our master, in token that something of his goes here."

"And are they large, the lions?" asked Don Quixote.

"So large," answered the man at the door of the van, "that none larger or so large have ever passed from Africa to Spain; and I am the lion-keeper, and have carried many, but none like these. They are male and female; the male goes in the first cage, and the female in the one behind, and they are now very hungry, for they have not eaten to-day; and so let your worship stand aside, for we must needs reach quickly the place where we are to give them their dinner."

On which said Don Quixote, with a little smile, "Lion-whelps to me? To me, lion-whelps? And at this time of day? Then by Heaven, those gentleman who send them here shall see whether I am a man who is frightened of lions. Alight, good fellow, and since you are the lion-keeper, open these cages, and turn me out these beasts, for in the middle of this open field I will teach them to know who Don Quixote of La Mancha is, in defiance and despite of the enchanters who send them to me."

"So, so," said he of the Green Coat to himself at this, "our good knight gives us a proof of what he is; the curds i' faith have softened his skull and mellowed his brain."

Here Sancho came up to him, and exclaimed, "For God's sake, sir, mind that my master, Don Quixote, does not fight with these lions, for if he fights them all we here will be torn to pieces."

"But is your master so mad," the gentleman answered, "that you fear and believe that he will fight with animals so fierce?"

"Not mad is he," replied Sancho, "but headstrong."

"I will make him desist," said the gentleman. And coming up to Don Quixote, who was pressing the keeper to open the cage, he said, "Sir Knight, Knights Errant have to engage in adventures which hold out some prospect of a good issue from them, and not in those that are wholly devoid of it, for the valour which enters within the bounds of temerity has more of madness than of fortitude; moreover, these lions come not against you, nor do they dream of doing so, but are going as a present to his Majesty, and it will not be right to detain them or hinder their journey."

"Get you gone, Sir Country-squire," replied Don Quixote, "and look after your quiet pointer and your saucy ferret, and leave every one to do his duty; this is mine, and I know whether they come against me or not, these gentlemen the lions." And, turning to the keeper, he said, "I swear, Don Rascal, that if you do not open the cage at once, instantly, I will pin you to the cart with this lance."

The carter, seeing that armed phantom's determination, said to him—

"Be pleased, dear sir, for charity, to let me unyoke the mules and place myself and them in safety before the lions are let loose, for if they are killed I shall be utterly ruined, for I have no other property but this cart and these mules."

"O man of little faith!" replied Don Quixote, "get down and unyoke, and do what thou wilt, for soon thou shalt see that thou toilest in vain, and might spare thyself these pains."

The carter alighted and in great haste unyoked, and the keeper cried in a loud voice, "Be witnesses as many as are here, how against my will and on compulsion I open the cages and let loose the lions, and that I protest to this gentleman, that all the evil and damage these beasts shall do will run and go to his account, with my wages and dues besides. Let you, sirs, make yourselves safe before I open; for myself, I am sure they will do me no harm."

Once more Don Diego entreated him not to commit such an act of madness, for to engage in such a freak were a tempting of Providence, to which Don Quixote replied that he knew what he was doing. The gentleman pressed him again to look well to it, for that he was surely mistaken.

"Nay, sir," quoth Don Quixote, "if your worship would not bear witness to this, which in your opinion is about to be a tragedy, spur your grey and put yourself in safety."

Sancho, on hearing this, prayed his master with tears in his eyes to desist from such an enterprise, compared to which that of the windmills, and the fearful one of the fulling-mills, and, in short, all the deeds his master had attempted in the course of his life, were but pleasuring and junketing.

"Look, sir," quoth Sancho, "here there is no enchantment, nor anything like it, for I have seen through the chinks and bars of the cage a claw of a real lion, and I gather from it that such a lion, to have such a claw, is bigger than a mountain."

"Fear, at least," said Don Quixote, "will make it seem bigger to thee than half the earth. Retire, Sancho, and leave me, and if I die here, thou knowest our old compact: thou wilt betake thee to Dulcinea. I say no more."

Other words he added to these which took away all hope of his giving up proceeding with his insane purpose. He of the Green Coat would have resisted him in it, but he saw himself unequal in arms, and judged it not wise to fight with a madman, for such he now appeared to him to be at all points. Don Quixote once more pressing the keeper and repeating his threats, caused the gentleman to urge his mare, and Sancho Dapple, and the carter his mules, all trying to get away from the cart as far as possible before the lions broke loose. Sancho wept over the death of his master, for this time he verily believed it had come from the lion's claws; he cursed his fortune and called it a fatal hour when it came into his mind once more to serve Don Quixote; but none the less, in weeping and lamenting, did he stop cudgelling Dapple to get him farther from the cart. The lion-keeper, seeing now that those who had fled were well away, again entreated and warned Don Quixote as he had entreated and warned him before, but the Knight replied that he heard him, and that he cared for no more warnings and entreaties, which would be fruitless, and bade him despatch. Whilst the keeper was engaged in opening the first cage, Don Quixote was considering whether it would be better to have the battle on foot or on horseback, and finally he decided to have it on foot, fearing lest Rozinante should be startled at the sight of the lions. Therefore, he leapt from his horse, threw away his lance, and buckling his shield and unsheathing his sword, leisurely, with a marvellous intrepidity and valiant heart advanced to post himself in front of the cart, commending his soul to God and then to his lady Dulcinea.

And it is to be known that, coming to this passage, the author of this truthful history breaks out into this exclamation, saying—

"O brave and beyond all commendation courageous Don Quixote of La Mancha! mirror wherein all the valiant may behold themselves, a second and new Don Manuel de Leon, who was the honour and glory of Spanish Knights! In what words shall I recount this dread exploit, or by what argument make it creditable to future ages? What praises can there be unfitting and unmeet for thee, be they ever such hyperboles upon hyperboles? Thou on foot, thou alone, thou fearless, thou great-hearted, with thy simple sword, and that not one of your trenchant dog blades; with a shield of no very bright and shining steel, standest watching and waiting for two of the fiercest lions that ever

"HE PUT HIS HEAD OUT OF THE CAGE AND GAZED ALL ABOUT WITH HIS EYES BLAZING LIKE LIVE COALS."

the African forests engendered! Let thy deeds themselves, valorous Manchegan, extol thee, for here I leave them at their height, failing words to glorify them."

Here the author breaks off from his apostrophe, and proceeds to take up the thread of his history, saying—

The keeper, seeing Don Quixote fixed in his position, and that it was impossible to avoid letting loose the male lion without falling under the resentment of the rageful and dauntless Knight, opened wide the door of the first cage where, as has been said, was the male lion, who looked to be of extraordinary size and of a hideous and terrible aspect. The first thing he did was to turn himself round in his cage, and to extend his claws and stretch himself to his full length. Then he opened his mouth and yawned very leisurely, and with about two hands'-breadth of tongue which he put out, he licked the dust from his eyes and bathed his face. This done, he put his head out of the cage and gazed all about with his eyes blazing like live coals, a spectacle and attitude to instil dread into daring itself. Don Quixote alone looked at him intently, longing for him to leap out of the cart and come within reach of his hands, between which he thought to rend him to pieces.

To this height did his unheard-of madness carry him; but the generous lion, more courteous than arrogant, taking no notice of these childish tricks and swaggerings, after having looked round about him, as has been said, turned his back and, showing to Don Quixote his hinder parts, with great calmness and nonchalance flung himself down again in the cage. Seeing this Don Quixote commanded him to give him some blows and tease him so that he might come out.

"That I will not do," answered the keeper, "for if I excite him the first he will tear in pieces will be myself. Let your worship, Sir Knight, be content with what has been done, which is all that one can tell of in point of valour, and seek not to tempt fortune a second time. The lion has his door open; it rests with him to come out or not; but since he has not come out up to now he will not come out all day. Your worship's greatness of heart is now made fully manifest. No champion fighter, as I take it, is bound to do more than defy his enemy and wait for him in the field; if the opponent does not appear the infamy rests upon him, and he who waits wins the crown of victory."

"That is true," said Don Quixote; "close the door, friend, and give in the best form thou canst a voucher of what thou hast seen me do: to wit, how that thou didst open to the lion; I awaited him; he did not come out; I waited for him again; again he did not come out, but turned to lie down. I am bound to do no more. Enchantments avaunt! and God prosper justice and truth and true chivalry! Shut the door, friend, whilst I signal to the fugitive and absent to return that they may learn of this exploit from thy mouth."

The keeper did so, and Don Quixote, placing on the point of his lance the cloth with which he had wiped the shower of curds off his face, began to hail those who had never ceased retreating all in a troop, looking round at every step, driven before him by the gentlemen in Green. Sancho happened to perceive the signal of the white cloth, and exclaimed, "May I die if my master has not conquered the wild beasts, for he is calling us!"

They all stopped, and seeing that it was Don Quixote who was making the signals, losing some of their fear, little by little they came nearer, until they clearly heard the voice of Don Quixote calling to them.

At length they returned to the cart, and on their approach Don Quixote said to the carter—

"Yoke your mules again, friend, and proceed on your journey, and thou, Sancho, give him two gold crowns for himself and for the keeper, towards amends for my having detained them."

"I will give them with all my heart," answered Sancho; "but what has been done with the lions? Are they dead or alive?"

Then the keeper recounted minutely and at his leisure the issue of the encounter, extolling, to the best of his power and skill, the valour of Don Quixote, at sight of whom the cowed lion cared not, or durst not, to come out of his cage, though he had held the door open a good while, and that it was through his having told the Knight that it was a tempting of Providence to provoke the lion so as to force him to come out, as he wanted him to do, that he had most unwillingly and against the grain permitted him to close the door."

"What is your judgment on this, Sancho?" quoth Don Quixote; "are there enchantments which avail against true valour? The enchanters may be able to rob me indeed of fortune, but of my resolution and courage, it is impossible."

Sancho gave the gold crowns; the carter yoked up; the keeper kissed Don Quixote's hands for the largess received, and promised to relate that valorous deed to the King himself when he should see him at Court.

"And if by chance his Majesty should ask who performed it," said Don Quixote, "you shall tell him, *The Knight of the Lions*; for henceforth I would that into this may be changed, altered, varied, and transferred, the name which till now I have borne, of the Knight of the Rueful Feature; and in this I follow the ancient usage of Knights Errant, who changed their names at their pleasure and according to the occasion."

The cart proceeded on its journey, and Don Quixote, Sancho, and he of the Green Coat, continued theirs.

Of the strange adventures which happened to Don Quixote in the Castle.

. . . With this she began to touch a harp very softly.

On hearing this Don Quixote was startled, for in that moment there came into his memory the infinite adventures similar to that, of windows, lattices, and gardens; of serenades, love-plaints, and languishments, which he had read of in his giddy books of chivalries. He at once conceived that some one of the Duchess's maidens was enamoured of him, and that modesty compelled her to keep her love in secret. He trembled lest he should yield, but resolved in his mind not to let himself be overcome; so, commending himself with all good heart and soul to his lady Dulcinea del Toboso, he determined to listen to the music; and to let them know he was there, he feigned to sneeze, at which the damsels were not a little rejoiced, for they desired nothing better than that Don Quixote should hear them. Then, the harp being set up and tuned, Altisidora struck up this ballad—

BALLAD.

Thou that all the night till morning
  Sleepest on thy downy bed;
Gaily with thy legs out-stretched,
  'Twixt two sheets of linen laid:

Valiant Knight! thou whom La Mancha
  Knows none greater or more bold;
Purer, blesseder, and chaster
  Than Arabia's sifted gold:

Hear a woful maid's complaining,
  Nurtured well but thriven ill,
Whose fond heart the burning sun-rays
  From thine eyes do scorch and kill.

Seekest thou thine own adventures;
  Others' ventures thou suppliest;
Dealest wounds, yet for their healing
  Salve of plaster thou deniest.

Tell me, lusty youth and valiant,
  May thy wishes all be sped !
Was't in Jaca's gloomy mountains,
  Or in Lybia thou wert bred ?

Say, didst suck thy milk from serpents ;
  Was thine infant babyhood
Nursed by the horrid mountain,
  Dandled by the rugged wood ?

Well may Dulcinea, thy charmer,
  Damsel plump and round, be proud,
Conquering that heart of tiger,
  Softening that bosom rude !

This shall make thy name e'er famous
  From Jarama to Henares ;
From Pisuerga to Arlanza ;
  From Tagus e'en to Manzanares.

Might I change with Dulcinea,
  I'd give her my best petticoat ;
Rarest silk, of pretty colours,
  Golden fringe and all to boot !

O to live within thine arms, and
  O to sit beside thy bed !
O that poll so sweet to scratch, and
  Brush the scurf from that dear head !

Much I ask, though undeserving
  Of so notable a grace,
Would that I thy feet were stroking,
  That's enough for maid so base.

What fine night-caps I would work thee ;
  What fine shiny silvern socks ;
Breeches of the rarest damask ;
  Lovely yellow Holland cloaks !

Precious milk-white pearls I'd give thee,
  Each as big as any gall,
Such as, having no companions,
  Orphans they are wont to call.

> Gaze not from thy rock Tarpeian
>   On the fire which scorches me,
> Nero of the world Manchegan!
>   Nor revive it cruelly.
>
> Child I am—a tender pullet—
>   Fifteen years I've never seen;
> I vow, by God and on my conscience,
>   I'm only three months past fourteen.
>
> Lame I am not, neither crooked,
>   Nothing in my body's wrong;
> Locks like lilies, when I stand up,
>   Sweep the ground, they are so long.
>
> Though my mouth is like an eagle's,
>   And a little flat my nose,
> With my topaz teeth,—of beauty
>   I've enough for Heaven, with those.
>
> And my voice is, if you listen,
>   Equal to the best, I trow;
> And I am of form and figure
>   Something less than middling too.
>
> Spoils of thy spear, thy bow and quiver,
>   These my charms and more, are;
> Maid am I of this here castle,
>   And my name Altisidora!

Here ended the lay of the sore-wounded Altisidora, and here began the terror of the courted Don Quixote, who, heaving a deep sigh, said to himself—

"How unhappy an Errant am I, that there is no maiden but looks upon me, who is not enamoured of me! How sad is the fate of the peerless Dulcinea, whom they will not leave free to enjoy my incomparable fidelity! Queens, what do ye want of her? Empresses, why do ye persecute her? Maidens of fourteen and fifteen, wherefore do ye molest her? Leave, O leave the unhappy one to triumph, to rejoice, to glory in the lot which love would assign her in the rendering her my heart, and delivering to her my soul! Know, ye amorous crew, that for Dulcinea alone am I dough and sugar-paste, and for all the rest of you flint. For her I am honey, and for you aloes. For me Dulcinea alone is the beautiful, the sensible, the chaste, the gay, and the well-bred; and the rest ugly, silly, wanton and base-born. To be her's and none other's Nature sent me into the world. Let Altisidora weep or sing; let the lady despair for whose sake they belaboured me in the castle of the enchanted Moor; for Dulcinea's I must be—roasted or boiled, clean, well-born, and chaste—in spite of all the powers of witchcraft in the world."

And with that he clapt the window to, and laid down on his bed; where for the present we will leave him, for the great Sancho calls, who is desirous of making a beginning with his famous Governorship.

Of the mode in which the great Sancho Panza began to govern, when he had taken possession of his Isle.

. . . At this moment there entered the justice-hall two men, one dressed as a labourer and the other as a tailor, for he bore a pair of scissors in his hand, and the tailor said—

"Sir Governor, I and this labouring man have come before your worship for the cause that this good fellow came to my shop yesterday, who, saving your presences, am a licensed tailor, blessed be God! and putting a piece of cloth in my hands, asked me: 'Sir, would there be enough in this cloth to make me a cap?' I, measuring the stuff, answered him '*Yes*.' He must have suspected, as I suspect, and suspected rightly, that without doubt I wished to rob him of some part of his cloth, founding his belief on his own roguery and the ill-opinion there is of tailors, and he replied that I should look and see if there were enough for two. I guessed his drift, and said, '*Yes*'; and he, riding away on his first damned intent, went on adding caps, and

I adding *reses*, till we reached five caps; and now at this moment he has come for them, and I am giving them to him; and he will not pay me for the making, but rather demands that I shall pay him, or give him back his cloth."

"Is all this so, brother?" inquired Sancho.

"Yes, sir," answered the man; "but let your worship make him show the five caps he has made me."

"With all my heart," said the tailor, and thrusting his hand suddenly under his cloak he showed five caps on it, placed on the five tops of his fingers, and said: "Here are the five caps which this good man wants of me, and on God and my conscience I have none of the cloth left for myself, and I will give the work to be examined by the inspectors of the trade."

All those present laughed at the number of caps, and at the novelty of the suit. Sancho set himself to consider a little while, and then said—

"Methinks there need be no long delays in this case, but that it may be decided, according to a wise man's judgment, off-hand; and so I decree that the tailor shall lose the making, and the countryman the stuff, the caps to be given to the prisoners in the gaol; and let no more be said."

This judgment provoked the laughter of the audience, but what the Governor commanded was done.

Of how Don Quixote fell sick, and of the will he made, and of his death.

. . . The Notary entered with the rest, and after having written the preamble to the will, and Don Quixote had disposed of his soul with all those Christian circumstances which are requisite, coming to the bequests he said—

"*Item, it is my will that of certain moneys which Sancho Panza, whom in my madness I made my squire, retains, that because there have been between him and me certain accounts, receipts, and disbursements, I wish that he be not charged with them, nor that any reckoning be asked from him, but that, if there should be any surplus after he has paid himself what I owe him, the residue should be his, which will be very little, and may it do him much good. And if I, being mad, was a party to giving him the governorship of the Isle, now, being sane, I would give him that of a Kingdom, were I able, for the simplicity of his nature and the fidelity of his behaviour deserve it."*

And turning to Sancho, he said to him—

"Pardon me, friend, that I have given thee occasion to appear mad like myself, making thee fall into the error into which I fell, that there were and are Knights Errant in the world."

"Alack!" responded Sancho, weeping, "don't you die, your worship, dear master, but take my advice and live many years, for the maddest thing a man can do in this life is to let himself die without more ado, without anybody killing him, nor other hands to finish him off than those of melancholy. Look you, do not be lazy, but get out of that bed, and we will go into the country, dressed like shepherds, as we have arranged. Mayhap behind some hedge we shall find the lady Donna Dulcinea disenchanted, and as fine as may be seen. If so be that you are dying of fretting at being conquered, put the fault on me, and say they overthrew you because I girthed Rozinante badly; more by token, as your worship must have seen in your books of chivalries, that it was a common thing for some Knights to overthrow others, and he who is conquered to-day may be conqueror to-morrow."

"It is so," said Samson, "and honest Sancho is very true about these matters."

"Gently, sirs," said Don Quixote, "for *in last year's nests you look not for birds of this year.* I was mad, and now I am sane. I was Don Quixote of La Mancha, and to-day I am, as I have said, Alonso Quixano the Good

May my repentance and my sincerity restore me to the esteem you once had for me, and so let Master Notary go on."

"*Item, I bequeath all my estate, without reserve, to Antonia Quixana, my Niece, who is present, there being first deducted from it, as may be most convenient, what is needed for the satisfaction of the bequests which I have made: and the first payment to be made I desire to be of the salary due to my Housekeeper from the time she has been in my service, with twenty ducats more for a dress. I leave as my executors Master Priest, and Master Bachelor Samson Carrasco, who are present. Item, it is my wish that if Antonia Quixana, my Niece, is inclined to marry, she should wed a man of whom she shall first have evidence that he knows not what books of chivalries are; and in case it shall be discovered that he does know, and yet my Niece wishes to marry with him and does so marry, that she shall forfeit all that I have bequeathed her, which my executors are empowered to distribute in pious works at their pleasure. Item, I beseech the said gentlemen, my executors, that if good fortune should bring them to know the author who, they say, wrote a history which is current hereabout under the title of Second Part of the Exploits of Don Quixote of La Mancha, that they will on my behalf beg him, as earnestly as they can, to pardon the occasion which I unwittingly gave him for writing so many and such enormous follies as therein be written, for I quit this life with some tenderness of conscience for having given him a motive for writing them.*"

With this he concluded his testament, and, being taken with a fainting fit, he lay extended at full length upon the bed. They were all alarmed, and ran to his assistance, and during the three days that he lived after the day on which he made his will he fainted very frequently. The house was all in confusion; however, the Niece ate, the Housekeeper drank, and Sancho Panza was cheerful; for this inheriting of something dulls or tempers in the inheritor the memory of the pain which the dead man naturally leaves behind.

At last came Don Quixote's end, after he had received all the sacraments, and after he had expressed with many and moving terms his horror at the books of chivalries. The Notary was present, and said that never had he read in any book of chivalries that any Knight Errant had died in his bed so tranquilly and so Christian-like as Don Quixote, who, amidst the tears and lamentations of all who stood by, gave up his spirit,—that is to say, died.

On seeing this, the Priest asked the Notary to give him a certificate that Alonso Quixano the Good, commonly called Don Quixote of La Mancha, had passed out of this present life, and had died a natural death; declaring that he sought such certificate in order to take away from any other author than Cid Hamet Benengeli the excuse falsely to resuscitate him, and write interminable histories of his deeds.

This was the end of the Ingenious Gentleman of La Mancha, whose village Cid Hamet desired not to indicate precisely, in order to let all the cities and towns of La Mancha contend among themselves for the honour of giving him birth and adopting him for their own, as the seven cities of Greece contended for Homer. The lamentations of Sancho, of the Niece, and the Housekeeper of Don Quixote are here omitted, as well as the new epitaphs upon his tomb; but this was what Samson Carrasco put there:—

> "A valiant gentleman here lies,
>   Whose courage reached to such a height,
> Of death itself he made a prize,
>   When against Death he lost the fight.
> He reck'd not of the world a jot,
>   The world's great bugbear and the dread;
> Strong was his arm, and strange his lot;
>   Stark mad in life,—when sober, dead."

"*Don Quixote de La Mancha.*" *Miguel Cervantes* (1547-1616). *Trans. H. E. Watts.*

CERVANTES TAKES A MERRY LEAVE OF LIFE.

IT happened afterwards, dear reader, that as two of my friends and myself were coming from Esquivias, a place famous for twenty reasons, more especially for its illustrious families and for its excellent wines, I heard a man behind me whipping his nag with all his might, and seemingly very desirous of overtaking us. Presently he called out to us, and begged us to stop, which we did; and when he came up, he turned out to be a country student, dressed in brown, with spatterdashes and round-toed shoes. He had a sword in a hugh sheath, and a band tied with tape. He had indeed but two tapes, so that his band got out of its place, which he took great pains to rectify. "Doubtless," said he, "Señors, you are in quest of some office or some prebendal stall at the court of my Lord of Toledo, or from the King, if I may judge from the celerity with which you journey; for, in good truth, my ass has hitherto had the fame of a good trotter, and yet he could not overtake you."

One of my companions answered, "It is the stout steed of Señor Miguel Cervantes that is the cause of it, for he is very quick in his paces."

Scarcely had the student heard the name of Cervantes, than, throwing himself off his ass, whilst his cloak-bag tumbled on one side and his portmanteau on the other, and his bands covered his face, he sprang towards me, and seizing me by the left hand, exclaimed: "This, then, is the famous one-handed author, the merriest of writers, the favourite of the Muses."

As for me, when I heard him pouring forth all these praises, I thought myself obliged in politeness to answer him; so embracing his neck, whereby I contrived to pull off his hands altogether, I said: "I am indeed Cervantes, Señor, but not the favourite of the Muses, nor any other of those fine things which you have said of me. Pray, sir, mount your ass again, and let us converse together for the small remainder of our journey."

The good student did as I desired. We then drew bit, and proceeded at a more moderate pace. As we rode on, we talked of my illness, but the student gave me little hope, saying: "It is an hydropsy, which all the water in the ocean, if you could drink it, would not cure; you must drink less, Señor Cervantes, and not neglect to eat, for this alone can cure you."

"Many other people," said I, "have told me the same thing; but it is as impossible for me not to drink, as if I had been born for nothing but drinking. My life is pretty nearly ended, and to judge by the quickness of my pulse, I cannot live longer than next Sunday. You have made acquaintance with me at a very unfortunate time, as I fear that I shall not live to show my gratitude to you for your obliging conduct."

Such was our conversation when we arrived at the bridge of Toledo, over which I was to pass, while he was bound another route by the bridge of Segovia.

"As to my future history, I leave that to the care of fame. My friends will, no doubt, be very anxious to narrate it, and I should have great pleasure in hearing it."

I embraced him anew, and repeated the offer of my services. He spurred his ass and left me as ill inclined to prosecute my journey, as he was well disposed to do so.

He had, however, supplied my pen with ample materials for pleasantry. But all times are not the same. Perhaps the time may yet arrive when, taking up the thread which I am now compelled to break, I may complete what is now wanting, and what I fain would tell. But adieu to gaiety, adieu to humour, adieu, my pleasant friends! I must now die, and I wish for nothing better than speedily to see you well contented in another world.

Preface (written a little time before the author's death) *to the "Labours of Persiles and Sigismunda." Miguel Cervantes* (1547–1616). *Trans. Roscoe.*

THE LOVERS' RUSE.

Theodora. Show more of gentleness and modesty;
Of gentleness in walking quietly,
Of modesty in looking only down
Upon the earth you tread.
   Belisa.   "Tis what I do.
   Theodora. What? When you're looking straight towards
     that man?
   Belisa. Did you not bid me look upon the earth?
And what is he but just a bit of it?
   Theodora. I said the earth whereon you tread, my
     niece.
   Belisa. But that whereon I tread is hidden quite
With my own petticoat and walking-dress.
   Theodora. Words such as these become no well-bred
     maid.
But by your mother's blessed memory,
I'll put an end to all your pretty tricks;—
What? You look back at him again?
   Belisa.   Who? I?

"'ELISA! "WHY, SURE YOU THINK IT WISE AND WARY TO NOTICE WELL THE PLACE I STUMBLED AT.'"

Theodora. Yes, you; and make him secret signs besides.
Belisa. Not I. 'Tis only that you troubled me
With teasing questions and perverse replies,
So that I stumbled and looked round to see
Who would prevent my fall.
    Riselo (to Lisardo).   She falls again.
Be quick and help her.
    Lisardo (to Belisa).   Pardon me lady,
And forgive my glove.
    Theodora.   Who ever saw the like?
    Belisa. Thank you, sir; you saved me from a fall.
    Lisardo. An angel, lady, might have fallen so;
Or stars that shine with Heaven's own blessèd light.
    Theodora. I, too, can fall; but this is but a trick.
Good gentleman, farewell to you!
    Lisardo.   Madam,
Your servants. (Heaven save us from such spleen!)
    Theodora. A pretty fall you made of it, and now I hope
You'll be content, since they assisted you.
    Belisa. And you no less content, since now you have
The means to tease me for a week to come.
    Theodora. But why again do you turn back your head?
    Belisa. Why, sure you think it wise and wary
To notice well the place I stumbled at,
Lest I should stumble there when next I pass.
    Theodora. Go to! Come home! come home!
    Belisa.   Now we shall have
A pretty scolding cook'd up out of this.

    "*El Acero de Madrid.*" Lope de Vega (1562-1635).
                                                 Trans. Ticknor.

AUNTS.

"THAT young creature whom you see there," said the God of Love, as he led me on, "is the chief captain of my war, the one that has brought most men under my banners. The elderly person that is leading her along by the hand is her aunt."

"Her *aunt*, did you say?" I replied; "her *aunt*? Then there is an end of all my love for her. That word '*aunt*' is a counter-poison that has disinfected me entirely, and quite healed the wound your well-planted arrow was beginning to make in my heart. For, however much a man may be in love, there can be no doubt an *aunt* will always be enough to purge him clean of it. Inquisitive, suspicious, envious,—one or the other she cannot fail to be,—and if the niece have the luck to escape, the lover never has; for if she is envious, she wants him for herself; and if she is only suspicious, she still spoils all comfort, so disconcerting every little project, and so disturbing every little nice plan, as to render pleasure itself unsavoury."

"Why, what a desperately bad opinion you have of aunts?" said Love.

"To be sure I have," said I. "If the state of innocence in which Adam and Eve were created had nothing else to recommend it, the simple fact that there could have been no *aunts* in Paradise would have been enough for me. Why, every morning, as soon as I get up, I cross myself and say, 'By the sign of the Holy Rood, from all aunts deliver us this day, good Lord.' And every time I repeat the *Pater Noster*, after 'Lead us not into temptation,' I always add, 'nor into the way of aunts either.'"

Jacinto Polo (?) (fl. 1630). Trans. Ticknor.

THE MISER CHASTISED.

IN this edifying manner did Don Marcos arrive at the age of thirty, with the reputation of a wealthy man; and with good reason, for he had gathered together, at the expense of every gentlemanly quality, and the starvation of his unfortunate carcase, a good round sum, which he always retained near him, for he dreaded every kind of speculation that might place in the slightest degree of jeopardy his darling treasure.

Now as Don Marcos was known to be neither a gambler nor a libertine, good opportunities of marriage continually presented themselves, of which, however, he did not avail himself always, considering it a speculation, and not unlikely to lead to some unfortunate result. Nevertheless, he wished to appear to advantage in the eyes of the ladies, some of whom, not knowing him, might have no objection to him as a husband. To them he appeared more in the light of a gallant than a miser. Amongst others who would have no objection to him, was a lady who had been married, but was not so well reconciled to her situation as a widow.

She was a lady of superior air and pretentions, although somewhat past the prime of life; but by the help of a little study and skill, no one would have supposed that she had arrived at so discreet an age as she certainly had. She was prettily enough called Donna Isidora, and was reported to be very rich; that she had actual property, at least according to those who knew her well, her manner of living clearly enough proved. Now this eligible match was proposed to Don Marcos; the lady was represented to him in such engaging colours, with such perfect assurance that she possessed more than fourteen or fifteen thousand ducats, that he was led into temptation—the temptation of Mammon. Her deceased husband was represented to have been a gentleman of one of the best families of Andalusia, and Donna Isidora was equally well born, and a native of the famous city of Seville.

These flattering communications so worked on the avarice and pride of our friend Don Marcos, that he almost wished himself already married, that he might be sure of the possession of so enviable a prize. He who first entangled Don Marcos in this notable affair was a cunning rogue of a dealer, who not only dealt in marriages, but in other descriptions of more sure traffic.

He promised therefore an introduction to Don Marcos that very evening, because, as he said, there was danger in delay.

Donna Isidora was profuse in her thanks to the obliging gentleman who had procured her the pleasure of such an acquaintance; and she finally established her triumph over Don Marcos, by inviting him to a costly entertainment, wherein she displayed the utmost luxury and wealth.

At this entertainment Don Marcos was introduced to a young man of a very gallant and prepossessing appearance, whom Donna Isidora honoured with the title of nephew. His name was Augustin, and he, in turn, seemed happy in the chance that gave him so delightful a relationship. The under servant, Ines, waited on them at table, because Marcella, the upper maid, by the order of her mistress, was engaged to entertain them with her guitar, in the management of which she was so perfect, that even the grandees of the court were seldom regaled with better music. Her voice, which she accompanied with the instrument, was so melodious, that it appeared more like that of an angel than a woman. The unaffected manner, too, without the slightest timidity, yet equally free from boldness, in which she sung, lent an additional charm; for without being entreated, she continued to amuse them, feeling confident that her performance would be well received.

Don Marcos felt himself so completely at ease with the well-bred, though generous hospitality of Donna Isidora and her nephew, that without the least scruple he amply indemnified himself for many a hungry day, as the sensible diminution of the luxuries of the table bore abundant, or rather scanty testimony. It may be said without exaggeration, that that evening's entertainment furnished him with as much as six days of his ordinary consumption; and the continual and repeated supplies, forced on him by his elegant and kind hostess, were in themselves sufficient to enable him to dispense with eating for a considerable time to come.

The pleasures of the conversation and of the table finished with the daylight, and four wax candles were placed in beautiful candelabras, by the light of which, and the sounds which Augustin drew from the instrument which Marcella had before touched so well, the two girls commenced a dance, in which they moved with such grace, as to excite the admiration of their superiors. After all this, Marcella, at the request of Don Marcos, again took her guitar, and closed the evening's amusement with an old chivalric romance.

On the conclusion of the song, the gentleman who had introduced Don Marcos gave him a hint that it was time to retire; who, though unwilling to leave such good company, and such good cheer, and at such little cost, took leave of his kind hostess with expressions of consideration and friendship, and took his road homewards, entertaining his friend by the way with expressions of admiration of Donna Isidora, or rather, more properly speaking, of her money. He begged him as soon as possible to have a deed drawn up which would ensure to him so enviable a treasure. His friend replied that he might already consider the marriage concluded, for that his opinion held such weight with Donna Isidora, that he would take an early opportunity of speaking with her to effect the arrangement, for he fully agreed with him, that delays were dangerous.

With this excellent maxim they separated, the one to recount to Donna Isidora what had passed, and the other to return to the house of his master.

It being very late, all the household had retired to rest. Don Marcos availing himself of the end of a candle, which he generally carried in his pocket for the purpose, withdrew to a small lamp, which lighted an image of the Virgin, at the corner of the street. There he placed it on the point of his sword and lighted it, making, at the same time, a very short but devout prayer that the very reasonable hopes he had framed might not be disappointed. Satisfied with this pious duty, he then retired to rest, waiting, however, impatiently for the day which should crown his expectations.

The next day he was visited by his friend Gamorre, such was the name of the gentleman who had recommended to him this tempting alliance. Don Marcos had risen by times that morning, for love and interest had conspired to banish sleep from his pillow. It was, therefore, with the utmost joy that he welcomed his visitor, who informed him that he had been successful in his mission to Donna Isidora, and that he was the bearer of an invitation to him from that lady to pass the day at her house, when he would have an opportunity of personally pressing his suit, and perhaps concluding the negociation which had so happily commenced.

Before they parted that night everything was arranged for their marriage, which in three days from that time was solemnised with all the splendour becoming people of rank and wealth. Don Marcos on this occasion so far overcame his parsimony as to present his wife with a rich wedding dress of great cost and fashion; calculating very wisely that the expense was but trifling in comparison with what he had to receive.

Behold, then, our friend Don Marcos, lord and master of this sumptuous dwelling, and its amiable inmates; and when the day of the auspicious union arrived, it found him in a state of the greatest possible contentment and happiness.

"Surely this is the happiest day of my life," he said to himself. The future domestic arrangements were all carefully discussed by the calculating mind of the bridegroom; and he already had disposed of his anticipated savings in a speculation; for he had begun even to think of speculating as to the greatest saving and profit.

Before retiring to rest, however, these flattering visions were a little disturbed by the sudden illness of Augustin. Whether it proceeded from mortification at his aunt's wedding, which threatened to curtail him of some of his fair proportions—his accustomed pleasures, or from some natural cause, it is impossible to say; but the house was suddenly thrown into a state of the greatest confusion; servants running about for remedies, and Donna Isidora in a state of the most violent agitation! However, the invalid became composed with the efforts which were made in his behalf; and Donna Isidora ventured to leave him and retire to rest, while the bridegroom went his round, taking care to see that the doors and windows were all fast, possessing himself of the keys for their better security.

This last act of caution seemed to be looked on with great distrust by the servants, who immediately attributed to jealousy that which was the result only of care and prudence; for Don Marcos had that morning removed to the house, with his own valuable person, and all his worldly possessions, including his six thousand ducats, which had not for a long time seen the light of day, and which he intended should still be consigned to solitary confinement, as far as locks and keys would ensure it.

Having arranged everything to his satisfaction, he retired to his bridal-chamber, leaving the servants to bewail their unhappy fortune, in having got a master whose habits threatened to curtail them of little liberties which the kindness of their mistress had so long indulged. Marcella spoke of her dissatisfaction at once; saying that rather than live like a nun, she should seek her fortune elsewhere, but Ines fancying that she heard a noise in the chamber of Don Augustin, and feeling he might require something in his illness, stepped lightly to his room to inquire in what she might assist him.

On the ensuing morning Ines was about the house earlier than usual, and to her surprise found the chamber of Marcella empty, and no appearance of her having slept there that night. Astonished at so strange a circumstance, she left the room to seek her, and was still more surprised on finding the outer door unlocked, which her master had so carefully fastened the night before, and which now, as if for the purpose of disturbing Don Marcos's ideas of security, had been left wide open.

On seeing this, Ines became terribly alarmed, and flew to the chamber of her mistress, raising an outcry that the house had been broken into. The bridegroom, half stupified with terror, leaped from the couch, calling for his wife to do the same; at the same time drawing aside all the curtains, and throwing open all the windows, in order that there might be no deficiency of light to see whether anything were missing. The first thing he beheld was what he supposed to be his wife, but so altered, that he could scarce believe her to be the same; instead of six-and-thirty years of age, which she professed to be, this sudden and unwelcome visitation of morning light added at least twenty years to her appearance; small locks of grey hair peeped from beneath her nightcap, which had been carefully concealed by the art of the hair-dresser, but the false hair had in the carelessness of sleep been unluckily transferred to the ground.

The suddenness of this morning's alarm had produced another no less unfortunate mischance; her teeth, which Don Marcos had so complimented for their regularity and whiteness, were now, alas! not to be seen, and the lady at least verified the old proverb of not casting pearls before swine. We will not attempt to describe the consternation of the poor hidalgo, or waste words which the imagination can so much better supply. We will only say that Donna Isidora was confounded. It was intolerable that her imperfections should be made thus manifest at so unseasonable an hour, and snatching up her strayed locks, she attempted to replace them, but with such little success, owing to her extreme hurry, that had not Don Marcos been overwhelmed with consternation, he would assuredly hardly have refrained from laughter. She then sought to lay hands on the dress she had worn the previous day; but, alas! nothing of the rich paraphernalia in which she had been attired by the gallantry of her husband—not one of the jewels and trinkets in which she had dazzled the spectators' eyes—remained.

Don Marcos, on his part, was struck dumb with horror, on finding that his own wedding suit was missing, and likewise a valuable gold chain which he had worn at the ceremony, and which he had drawn from his treasure for the purpose. No pen can describe the agony of Don Marcos upon this fatal discovery; he could not even console himself with the youthful graces of his wife, for turning towards her he saw nothing but age and ugliness, and turning his eyes again from her, he found his expensive clothes all vanished, and his chain gone.

Almost out of his wits, he ran out into the saloon, and throughout the apartments, attired only in his shirt, wring-ing his hands, and betraying every sign of a miser's lamentation and despair. While in this mood, Donna Isidora escaped to her dressing-room, without giving herself the trouble of inquiring into the minor catastrophe, and busied herself in repairing the personal injuries which the untoward event had produced. Don Augustin had by this time risen, and Ines recounted to him the adventures of the morning, and they both laughed heartily at the consternation of poor Don Marcos, the ridiculous accident of Donna Isidora, and the roguishness of Marcella.

Doña Maria de Zayas (fl. 1637).   Trans. Roscoe.

THE MARKET OF ANCESTORS.

THEY hereupon entered a fairly wide street, littered with coffins, amongst which walked several sextons, while a number of grave-diggers were breaking into various graves. Don Cleofas said to his companion—

"What street is this, it is the oddest I have ever seen?"

"This is more worldly and of the times than any other," replied the Limping Devil, "and the most useful. It is the old-clothes market of ancestors, where anybody in want of forefathers, his own not suiting him, or being somewhat shabby, comes to pick out the one he likes best for his money. Just look at that poor, deformed gentleman trying on a grandmother he badly wants, and the other, who has already chosen a father, putting on a grandfather as well, who's much too big for him. That fellow lower down is exchanging his grandfather for another, offering a sum of money into the bargain, but can't come to terms because the sexton, who is the dealer, would be a loser by it. The man over there has just turned his great-grandfather inside out and is patching him up with some-

"IT IS THE OLD-CLOTHES MARKET OF ANCESTORS."

body else's great grandmother. Here's another with a policeman to look for an ancestor of whom he has been robbed, and who is hanging up in the market. If you want an ancestor or two on credit, now's your chance; one of the dealers is a friend of mine."

"I could do with some money, but I'm not in want of ancestors," replied the student. So they continued their adventures.

"*The Limping Devil.*" *Velez de Guevara* (1644).

VISION OF THE LAST JUDGMENT.

HOMER, we find, represents Jupiter as the author or inspirer of dreams, more especially the dreams of princes and governors, granting always that the subject of them be of a religious and important character. It is stated, moreover, as the opinion of the learned Propertius, "that good dreams are sent from above, have their meaning, and ought not to be slighted." To give frankly my own idea upon this subject, I am inclined to his way of thinking, in particular as to the case of a certain dream I had the other night. As I was reading a sermon concerning the end of the world, it happened that I fell asleep over it, and pursuing the same line of thought, dreamed the following dream of the Last Judgment—a thing rarely admitted into the house of a poet, so much as in a dream. I was in this way reminded too of an observation in "Claudian," "that all creatures dream at night of what they have heard and seen in the day; as the hound," says Petronius Arbiter, "dreams of hunting the hare."

Well, methought I beheld a noble-looking youth towering in the air, and drawing loud and solemn tones from a mighty trumpet. The vehemence of his breath did certainly detract somewhat from the effect of his glorious beauty, yet even the monumental marbles, the earth-closed caverns—nay, the very dead within—obeyed his fearful call; for the ground was seen gradually to open, the bones to rise and unite together, and a mighty harvest of the living spring from the long-sown seed of the dead. The first that appeared were soldiers,—such as generals of armies, captains, lieutenants, and the common foot, who, thinking that a fresh charge had sounded, rose out of their graves with considerable boldness and alacrity, as if they had been preparing for combat, or a sudden assault. The misers next put their heads out, all pale and trembling, with the idea they were going to be again plundered. Cavaliers and boon companions came trooping along, supposing they were going to a horse-race, or a grand hunt. In short, though all heard the trumpet sound, not any one seemed to understand it, for their thoughts were plain enough to be read by the strangeness of their looks and gestures.

While the souls came trooping in on all sides, many were seen to approach their new bodies, not without signs of considerable aversion and difficulty. Others stood spellbound with wonder and horror, as if not venturing to come nearer to so dreadful a spectacle; for this wanted an arm, that an eye, and the other a head. Though, on the whole, I could not forbear smiling at so strange a variety of figures, I found yet greater matter for awe and admiration at the power of Providence, which drew order out of chaos, and restored every part and member to its particular owner. I dreamed that I was myself in a churchyard; that I saw numbers busied in changing heads, who were averse to make their appearance; and an attorney would have put in a demurrer, on the plea that he had got a soul that could be none of his, for that his soul and body belonged to some different ones elsewhere.

When it came at length to be generally understood that here at last was the Day of Judgment, it was curious to observe what strange evasions and excuses were made use of among the wicked. The man of pleasure, the betrayer of innocence, the epicure, and the hypocrite, would not own their eyes, nor the slanderer his tongue, because they were sure to appear in evidence against them. Pickpockets were seen running away as fast as possible from their own fingers, while an old usurer wandered about anxiously inquiring if the money-bags were not to rise as well as the bodies? I should have laughed outright at this, had not my attention been called away to a throng of cutpurses, hastening all speed from their own ears, now offered them, that they might not hear so many sad stories against themselves.

I was a witness to the whole scene, from a convenient station above it, when all at once there was uttered a loud outcry at my feet of "Withdraw, withdraw!" No sooner was it pronounced, than down I came, and forthwith a number of handsome women put out their heads and called me a base clown for not showing the respect and courtesy due to their high quality, not being a whit the less inclined to stand upon their etiquette,—although in Hell itself. They appeared half-naked, and as proud as Juno's peacock, whenever they happened to catch your eye; and, to say truth, they had a good complexion, and were well made. When they were informed, however, that it was no other than the Day of Judgment, they took the alarm, all their vivacity vanished, and slowly they took their way towards an adjacent valley, quite pensive and out of humour. Of these one among the rest had wedded seven husbands, and promised to each of them that she would never marry again, for she was unable to love any one like she had loved the last. Now the lady was eagerly inventing all manner of excuses, in order that she might return a proper answer when examined on this part of her conduct. Another, that had been common as the common air, affected to hum a tune, and delay the arrival on pretence of having forgotten some of her trickeries, as an eye brow, or a comb; but, spite of her art—for she could now neither lead nor drive—she was impelled on till she came within sight of the throne. There she beheld a vast throng, among whom were not a few she had brought far on their way to the worst place; and no sooner did they recognise her than they began to hoot after and pursue her, till she took refuge in a troop of city police.

Next appeared a number of persons driving before them a certain physician along the banks of a river, whither he had unfairly dispatched them considerably before their time. They assailed his ears all the way with cries of "*justice! justice!*" at the same time urging him forwards towards the seat of judgment, where they at length arrived. Meantime, I heard upon my left hand something like a paddling in the water, as if some one were trying to swim; and what should it all be but a judge, plunged into the middle of a river, and vainly trying to wash his hands of the foul matter that adhered to them. I inquired what he was employed about, and he told me, that in his lifetime he had often had them oiled so as to let the business slip the better through them, and he would gladly get out the stains before he came to hold up his hand before the bar. What was yet more horrible, I saw coming under guard of a legion of devils, all armed with rods, scourges, and clubs, a whole posse of vintners and tailors, suffering no little correction; and many pretended to be deaf, being unwilling to leave the grave under dread of a far worse lodging.

As they were proceeding, however, up started a little dapper lawyer, and inquired whither they were going; to which it was replied, that they were going to give an account of their works. On hearing this, the lawyer threw himself down flat on his face in his hole again, exclaiming at the same time, "If down I must without a plea, I am at least so far on my way." An innkeeper seemed in a great sweat as he walked along, while a demon at his elbow jeering at him cried,—"Well done, my brave fellow, get rid of the water, that we may have no more of it in our wine." But a poor little tailor, well bolstered up, with crooked fingers, and bandy legged, had not a word to say for himself all the way he went, except, "Alas! alas! how can any man be a thief that dies for want of bread!" As he cried, his companions, however, rebuked him for running down his own trade. Next followed a gang of highwaymen, treading upon the heels of one another, and in no little dread of treachery and cheating among each other. These were brought up by a party of devils in the turning of a hand, and were quartered along with the tailors; for, as was observed by one of the company, your real highwayman is but a wild sort of tailor. To be sure, they were a little quarrelsome at the first, but in a short time they went together down into the valley, and took up their quarters very quietly together. A little behind them came Folly, Bells, and Co., with their band of poets, fiddlers, lovers, and fencers—that kind of people, in short, that last dream of a day of reckoning. These were chiefly distributed among the hangmen, Jews, scribes, and philosophers. There were also a great many solicitors, greatly wondering among themselves how they could have so much conscience when dead, and none at all in their lifetime. In short, the catch-word "silence" was the order of the day.

The throne of the Eternal being at length elevated, and the mighty day of days at hand which spake of comfort to the good, and of terror to the wicked; the sun and the stars, like satraps, cast their glory round the footstool of the Supreme Judge—the avenger of the innocent, and the

Judge of the greatest monarchs and judges of the earth. The wind was stilled; the waters were quiet in their ocean-sleep—the earth being in suspense and anguish for fear of her human offspring. The whole creation looked about to yield up its trust in huge confusion and dismay. The just and righteous were employed in prayer and thanksgiving; the impious and wicked were vainly busy in weaving fresh webs of sophistry and deceit, the better to mitigate their sentence. On one side stood the guardian angels ready to show how they had fulfilled the part entrusted to them; and on the other frowned the evil genii, or the devils who had eagerly contended with the former, and fomented the worst human passions, attending now to aggravate every matter of charge against their unfortunate victims. The Ten Commandments held the guard of a narrow gate, so straight indeed, that the most subdued and extenuated body could not get through without leaving the better part of his skin behind.

In one portion of this vast theatre were thronged together Disgrace, Misfortune, Plague, Grief, and Trouble, and all were in a general clamour against the doctors. The plague admitted fairly that she had smitten many, but it was the doctor at last who did their business. Black Grief and Shame both said the same; and human calamities of all kinds made open declaration that they never brought any man to his grave without the help and abetting of a doctor. It was thus the gentlemen of the faculty were called to account for the number of fellow-men they had killed, and which were found to exceed by far those who had fallen by the sword. They accordingly took their station upon the scaffold, provided with pen, ink, and paper; and always as the dead were called, some or other of them made answer to the name, and quoted the year and day when such or such a patient passed from time to eternity through his hands.

They began the inquiry as far back as Adam, who, to say the truth, was rather roughly handled about biting an apple. "Alas!" cried one Judas that stood by, "if that were such a fault, what must be the end of me, who sold and betrayed my own Lord and Master?" Then next approached the race of patriarchs; and next the Apostles, who took up their places by the side of St. Peter. It was well worth observing that on this day there was not a whit distinction between kings and beggars: all were equal before the judgment-seat. Herod and Pilate had no sooner put out their heads, than they found it was likely to go hard with them. "My judgment, however, is just," exclaimed Pilate. "But alas!" cried Herod, "what have I to confide in? Heaven is no abiding place for me, and in Limbo I shall fall among the very innocents whom I murdered; I have no choice, therefore, but must e'en take up my quarters in Hell—the general refuge for the most notorious malefactors." After this, a rough sort of sour, ill-grained fellow, made his appearance: "See here," he cried, "here are my credentials—take these letters." The company, surprised at his odd humour, inquired of the porter who he was? "Who am I?" quoth he, "I am master of the noble science of defence": then pulling out a number of sealed parchments, "These will bear witness to my exploits." As he said these words, the testimonials fell out of his hand, and two devils near him were just going to pick them up, to keep as evidence against him at his trial, but the fencer was too nimble for them, and seized on them. An angel, however, now offered him his hand to help him in; while he, as if fearing an attack, leapt a step back, throwing himself into an attitude of defence. "Now," he exclaimed, "if you like, I will give you a taste of my skill"; upon which the company set a-laughing, and this sentence was pronounced against him: "That since by his art he had caused so many duels and murders, he should himself be allowed to go to the devil in a perpendicular line." He pleaded he was no mathematician, and knew no such a line; but with that word a devil came up, and gave him a twirl or two round, and down he tumbled before he could bring his sentence to an end.

The public treasurers came after him, pursued by such a hooting at their heels, that some supposed the whole band of thieves themselves were coming; which others denying, the company fell into a dispute upon it. They were greatly troubled at the word "thieves," and one and all requested they might be permitted to have the benefit of counsel. "For a very good reason," said one of the devils. "Here's a discarded apostle, a Judas, that played into both hands at once; seize him!"

On hearing this, the treasurers turned away; but a vast roll of accusations against them, held in another devil's hand, met their eyes, and one of them exclaimed, "For mercy's sake, away with those informations! We will one and all submit to any penalty; to remain in purgatory a thousand years, if you will only remove them from our sight." "Is it so?" quoth the cunning devil that had drawn out the charges—"you are hard put to it to think of compounding on terms like these." The treasurers had no more to say; but, finding they must make the best of a bad case, they very quietly followed the dancing-master.

Close upon the last came an unfortunate pastryman, and on being asked if he wished to be tried, he replied that he did, and with the help of the Lord would stand the venture. The counsel against him then prest the charge; namely, that he had roasted cats for hares, and filled his pies with bones in place of meat, and sold nothing but horse-flesh, dogs, and foxes, in lieu of good beef and mutton. It turned out, in fact, that Noah had never had so many animals in his ark as this ingenious fellow had put in his pies (for we hear of no rats and mice in the former);

so that, in utter despair, he threw up his cause, and went to be baked in his turn with other sinners like himself.

"Next came and next did go" a company of barefoot philosophers with their syllogisms, and it was amusing enough to hear them chop logic, and try all manner of questions in mood and figure, at the expense of their own souls. Yet the most entertaining of them all were the poets, who refused to be tried at any lesser tribunal than that of Jupiter himself. Virgil, with his *Sicelides Musæ*, made an eloquent defence of himself, declaring that he had prophecied the Nativity. But up jumped a devil with a long story about Mæcenas and Octavius, declaring that he was no better than an idolater of the old school. Orpheus then put in a word, asserting that, as he was the elder, he ought to be allowed to speak for all, commanding the poet to repeat his experiment of going into hell, and trying to get out again, with as many of the company as he could take along with him.

They were no sooner gone, than a churlish old miser knocked at the gate, but was informed that it was guarded by the Ten Commandments, to which he had always been an utter stranger. Yet he contended that if he had not kept, he had never broken, any of them, and proceeded to justify his conduct from point to point. His quirks, however, were not admitted—his works were made the rule of decision—and he was marched off to receive a due reward.

He was succeeded by a gang of housebreakers and others of the same stamp, some of whom were so fortunate as to be saved just in the nick of time. The usurers and attorneys, seeing this, thought they too had a good chance, and put so good a face on the matter that Judas and Mahomet began to look about them, and advanced rather confidently to meet their trial, a movement which made the devils themselves fall to laughing.

It was now the accusing demons of the usurers and attorneys proceeded with their accusations, which they took not from the bills of indictment made out, but from the acts of their lives, insisting upon the plain matter of fact, so as to leave them without the possibility of an excuse. Addressing the Judge—"The great crime of which these men were guilty was their being attorneys at all;"—to which it was ingeniously answered by the men of law—"No, not so; we only acted as the secretaries of other men." They nearly all denied their own calling; and the result was that, after much cross-questioning and pleading, two or three only were acquitted, while to the rest their accusers cried out, "You here! you are wanted elsewhere;" and they then proceeded to swear against some other people, some bribing the witnesses, making them say things which they had never heard, and see things they had never seen, in order to leave innocence no chance of escape. The lie was concocted in all its labyrinths; and I saw Judas, Mahomet, and Luther draw back, while the former prest his money-bag closer to him. Luther observed that he did just the same thing in his writings (*i.e.*, draw back); but the doctor interrupted him, declaring that, compelled by those who had betrayed him, *he* now appeared with the apothecary and the barber to defend himself. On this a demon with the accusations in his hand turned sharp round on him, asking, "Who it was had sent the greater part of the dead then present, and with the aid of his worthy *aide-de-camps*, had, in fact, occasioned the whole proceedings of that day." But the apothecary's advocate put in a plea for him, asserting that he had dosed the poor people for nothing. "No matter," retorted a devil, "I have him down on my list; two of his pill-boxes despatched more than ten thousand pikes could do in a battle, such was the virulence of his poisonous drugs, with which indeed he entered into a partnership with the plague, and destroyed two entire villages." The physician defended himself from any participation in these exploits, and at last the apothecary was obliged to succumb, the physician and the barber each taking the deaths that respectively belonged to them.

A lawyer was next condemned for taking bribes from both sides, and betraying both; and lurking behind him was discovered a fellow who seemed very desirous of concealing himself, and who, on being asked his name, replied that he was a player. "And a very comic player indeed," rejoined a devil, "who had done better not to appear on that stage to-day." The poor wretch promised to retire, and was as good as his word. A tribe of vintners next took their station, accused of having assassinated numbers of thirsty souls by substituting bad water for good wine. They tried to defend themselves on the plea of compensation, having supplied a hospital gratis with wine for the sacred ceremonies; but this was overruled, as was that preferred by the tailors, of having clothed some charity boys on the same terms, and they were all sent to the same place.

Three or four rich merchants next appeared, who had got wealth by defrauding their correspondents and creditors, but the accusing demon now informed them they would find it more difficult to make a composition; and turning towards Jupiter, he said, "Other men, my Lord Judge, have to give account of their own affairs, but these have had to do with everybody's." Sentence was forthwith pronounced, but I could not well catch it, so speedily they all disappeared. A cavalier now came forward with so good a face, and so upright, as to challenge even justice itself. He made a very lowly obeisance on entering, but his collar was of such a size as to defy you to say whether he had got any head in it at all. A messenger inquired, on the part of Jupiter, if he was a man, to which he courteously replied in the affirmative, adding that his name was Don Fulano, on the faith of a cavalier. At this one of the devils laughed, and he was then asked what it was he wanted? To which

"A BEVY OF FINE LADIES, TRICKED OUT IN CAP AND FEATHER."

he replied that he wanted to be saved. He was delivered over to the demons, whom he entreated to use him gently, lest they should chance to disorder his mustachios and ruff. Behind him came a man uttering great lamentations, which he himself interrupted by saying, "Though I cry, I am none so badly off, for I have shaken the dust off the saints themselves before now." Every one looked round, thinking to see a hero, or a Diocletian, from his brushing the ears of the saints; but he turned out to be a poor wretch whose highest office was to sweep the pictures, statues, and other ornaments of the church. His cause seemed safe, when all at once he was accused by one of the devils of drinking the oil out of the lamps, but which he again laid to the charge of an owl; that he had moreover clothed himself out of the church suits, that he drank the wine, ate the bread, and even laid a duty on the fees. He made but a lame defence, and was ordered to take the left hand road in his descent.

He made way for a bevy of fine ladies, tricked out in cap and feather, and so full of merriment that they fell to amuse themselves with the odd figures of the demons themselves. It was stated by their advocate that they had been excellent devotees." "True," retorted the demon, "devoted to anything but chastity and virtue." "Yes, certainly," replied one that had taken her full fling in life, and whose trial now came on. She was accused of making religion itself a cloak, and even marrying, the better to conceal the enormities of her conduct. When condemned she retired, bitterly complaining that, had she known the result, she would have taken care not to have done any of the charitable things, and said so many masses as she had.

Next, after some delay, appeared Judas, Mahomet, and Martin Luther, of whom a messenger inquired which of the three was Judas? To this both Mahomet and Luther replied that he was the man; on which Judas cried out in a rage that they were both liars, for that he was the true Judas, and that they only affected to be so, in order to escape a worse fate than his, for though he had indeed sold his Master, the world had been the better of it, while the other rascals, by selling both themselves and his Master, had well-nigh ruined it. They were all sent to the place they deserved.

An attorney who held the evidence in his hand now called on the alguazils and runners to answer the accusations brought against them. They cut a woful figure, and so clear was the case against them, that they were condemned without more ado.

An astrologer now entered with his astrolobes, globes, and other quackery, crying out that there was some mistake, for that that was not the Day of Judgment, as Saturn had not yet completed his course, nor he out of sheer fear his own. But a devil turned round on him, and seeing him loaded with wooden instruments and maps, exclaimed, "Well done, friend, you have brought firewood along with you, though it is a hard thing, methinks, after making so many heavens as are here, you should be sent to the wrong place at last for the want of a single one. "I will not go, not I," said the astrologer." "Then carry him," said the devil, and away he went.

The whole court after this broke up: the shadows and clouds withdrew, the air grew refreshing, flowers scented once more the breezes, the sunny sky reappeared, while I methought remained in the valley; and wandering about, heard a good deal of noise and voices of lamentation, as if rising out of the ground. I pressed forward to inquire what it could be, and I saw in a hollow cavern (a fit mouth to hell) a number of persons in pain. Among these was a *Letrado*, but busied not so much with dead laws as with live coals,—and an *Escrivano*, devouring only letters. A miser was there, counting more pangs than pieces; a physician contemplating a dead patient; and an apothecary steeped in his own mixtures.

I laughed so outright at this that I started wide awake, and was withal more merry than sad to find myself on my bed.

The foregoing indeed are dreams, but such as if your excellency will sleep upon them, it will come to pass, that in order to see the things as I see them, you will pray for them to turn out as I say they are.

Gomez de Quevedo (1580–1645).   *Trans. Roscoe.*

THE REVENGE OF DON LUCAS.

Don Lucas, *a rich, fat, ugly little man, betrothed to his ward,* Doña Isabel, *against her will.*
Don Pedro, *young cousin to* Don Lucas, *and in love with* Isabel.
Don Luis, *a gaunt old bachelor, also in love with* Isabel.
Doña Isabel.
Doña Alfonsa, *an old maid, sister to* Don Lucas, *and in love with* Don Pedro.
Periwig, *valet to* Don Lucas.

Don Lucas *and* Don Luis.

Don Luis. I tell you—yesterday at Illescas she departed from her mute coyness and, quitting her chamber, came to discourse with me under the porch, where she told me she would be my bride with all her heart, and that her hand was bestowed upon you against her will. If this be truth, why separate two loving souls? . . . I hold you for a man of mind, and therefore come to demand. . . .

Don Lucas. No more, for by the devil, I'll pay you out . . .

D. Alfonsa. (*knocking without*). Is my brother here?

Don Lucas. Into my bedroom, quick, I must see my sister.

Don Luis. Let me know first if my life and liberty are secure!

Don Lucas. Be off with you, there's time enough to look after your life and liberty.

[*Exit* Don Luis.

Don Lucas *and* Doña Alfonsa.

D. Alfonsa. Brother?

Don Lucas. Well, sister Alfonsa?

D. Alfonsa. I have something to tell you.

Don Lucas. Deuce take it, everybody has something to tell me. But it's my own fault for listening.

D. Alfonsa. Are we alone?

Don Lucas. Yes, sister.

D. Alfonsa. Will you be angry at what I'm going to tell you?

Don Lucas. How do I know?

D. Alfonsa. Well, you know . . .

Don Lucas. I don't know.

D. Alfonsa. . . . That I am a woman . . .

Don Lucas. I don't know anything of the kind.

D. Alfonsa. Brother? . . .

Don Lucas. Do be quick and have done with it. You'll all be the death of me.

D. Alfonsa. Well, I am a woman, and in love . . .

Don Lucas. The point at last.

D. Alfonsa. And with Don Pedro.

Don Lucas. All right.

D. Alfonsa. But he doesn't love me; the treacherous wretch is courting Doña Isabel, and betraying both of us.

Don Lucas. I say, I don't believe it.

D. Alfonsa. Well, you know, I often have fainting fits.

Don Lucas. Yes!

D. Alfonsa. And do you remember that I also had one at the inn at Illescas?

Don Lucas. Well, what of that?

D. Alfonsa. You must know it was feigned.

Don Lucas. And now who'll believe you when you really have one?

D. Alfonsa. I did it with a motive. Don Pedro, the traitor, thinking it was real, seized the opportunity to say a thousand tender things to Doña Isabel. I would have given vent to my rage, but he is so far gone, he even makes love to her before *you*.

Don Lucas. A pretty how-d'ye-do!

D. Alfonsa. Last—night—he—met—her—in—the—parlour—secretly . . . And now you know my wrongs. Make haste and avenge both yourself and me on that treacherous Don Pedro.

Don Lucas. A pretty kettle of fish. But, devil take it, Don Luis has just been to tell me that Isabel is in love with *him*. Perhaps she loves them both, she seems to have a great facility that way. But if Don Pedro is her accepted lover, I'll pay them both out! I shall have such a revenge as shall last their whole lives! To kill them would be too poor a vengeance.

D. Alfonsa. What do you mean to do?

Don Lucas. (*calling*). Don Pedro!

D. Alfonsa. There, he's just come in.

Don Lucas. (*calling*). Doña Isabel!

D. Alfonsa. Here she is.

Enter DOÑA ISABEL, DON PEDRO, *and* PERIWIG.

D. Isabel. Why are you calling me?

Don Pedro. What can I do for you?

Don Lucas. Just wait for a bit. Periwig, shut that door.

Periwig. Yes, sir. (*Shuts it.*)

Don Lucas. Lock it.

Periwig. Certainly, sir. (*Locks it.*)

Don Lucas. Give me the key.

Periwig. Here it is, your honour. (*Hands him the key.*)

Don Lucas. (*opening his bedroom door*). Come out, Don Luis.

Don Luis. Here I am. (*Comes out.*)

D. Isabel. What are you going to do?

Don Pedro. }
Don Luis.   } What's all this?

Don Lucas. Listen, all of you. Señor Don Luis, whom you here behold, has told me he is Doña Isabel's lover, and that he must marry her, for she gave him her word at Illescas and . . .

Periwig. Oh no, beg pardon, sir. I saw the gent knock at a door at Illescas and palaver with Doña Alfonsa, whom he took for the young lady. Don't you remember, sir, you heard a noise, and came out with a light and your sword? Well, it was him, sir.

Don Luis. I will not deny it. You came forth, and I discreetly hid, but I thought I was speaking with Isabel, not with Alfonsa.

D. Alfonsa. Wait, it was I with whom you spoke, but I took you for Don Pedro.

Don Pedro. (*aside*). Blessings upon Cupid and my lucky star.

Don Lucas. Well, that's one gallant done with. But to proceed (*to Don Pedro*), my sister, Doña Alfonsa, tells me treacherous and unloyal fellow, that you love Isabel.

Don Pedro. Yes, it is so. I confess I have long loved her, before you even thought of her; and who can blame my impotence to stifle a love so great that . . .

Don Lucas. Hold your tongue, young cousin, for by h——, but no, I won't swear. . . . I must have fierce and fatal vengeance.

Don Pedro. Plunge your poniard into this my throat.

Don Lucas. No, I won't do that; I don't want to kill you: that's what you'd like.

Don Pedro. Then what will you do?

Don Lucas. You shall know. You, Don Pedro, are a pauper, and but for me would have starved.

Don Pedro. It is true.

Don Lucas. Doña Isabel is a beggar. I was going to marry her for her looks only, for she hasn't a farthing for a dowry.

Don Pedro. But she is virtuous and beautiful.

Don Lucas. Well, then, give her your hand, for this is my vengeance. You are very poor, and she is very poor; no more happiness for you. Love flies out of the window when poverty enters the door. On your wedding-day you may laugh at me, but on the morrow when breakfasting on kisses, with vows on the table for victuals, and constancy for supper, Love instead of a silk frock, and "Darling" to keep you warm, you will see who laughs longest and last.

Don Pedro. Cousin . . .

Don Lucas. I say, you shall marry her.

Periwig. (*aside*). The punishment is *too* severe!

Don Lucas. (*joins* Don Pedro's *and* Doña Isabel's *hands*).

    Join hands, you fond and pretty fools,
      By vengeance is the nuptial knot:
    Too soon you'll learn what Love is like
      When there is nothing in the Pot.

"*Entre Bobos anda el Juego.*" *Francesco Rojas de Zorrilla*
      (*fl.* 1670).

THE MAYOR OF ZALAMEA.

DRAMATIS PERSONÆ.

KING PHILIP II.[1]
DON LOPE DE FIGUEROA.
DON ALVARO DE ATAIDE.

PEDRO CRESPO, *a Farmer of Zalamea.*
JUAN, *his Son.*
ISABEL, *his Daughter.*
INES, *his Niece.*

DON MENDO, *a poor Hidalgo.*
NUÑO, *his Servant.*

REBOLLEDO, *a Soldier.*
CHISPA, *his Sweetheart.*

A SERGEANT, A NOTARY, SOLDIERS, LABOURERS, CONSTABLES, ROYAL SUITE, &c.

ACT I.

SCENE I.—*Country near Zalamea.* Enter REBOLLEDO, CHISPA, *and Soldiers.*

Reb. Confound, say I, these forced marches from place to place, without halt or bait; what say you, friends?

All. Amen!

Reb. To be trailed over the country like a pack of gipsies, after a little scrap of flag upon a pole, eh?

1st. Soldier. Rebolledo's off!

Reb. And that infernal drum, which has at last been good enough to stop a moment, stunning us.

2nd. Sold. Come, come, Rebolledo, don't storm; we shall soon be at Zalamea.

Reb. And where will be the good of that if I'm dead

---

[1] Does not appear in this extract.

before I get there? And if not, 'twill only be from bad to worse: for if we all reach the place alive, as sure as death up comes Mr. Mayor to persuade the Commissary we had better march on to the next town. At first Mr. Commissary replies very virtuously, "Impossible! the men are fagged to death." But after a little pocket persuasion, then it's all "Gentlemen, I'm very sorry, but orders have come for us to march forward, and immediately," and away we have to trot, foot-weary, dust bedraggled, and starved as we are. Well, I swear if I do get alive to Zalamea to-day, I'll not leave it this side o' sunrise for love, lash, or money. It won't be the first time in my life I've given 'em the slip.

1st. *Sold.* Nor the first time a poor fellow has had the slip given him for doing so. And more likely than ever now that Don Lope de Figuerroa has taken the command, a fine brave fellow they say, but a devil of a tartar, who'll have every inch of duty done, or take the change out of his own son, without waiting for trial either.[1]

Reb. Listen to this now, gentlemen! By Heaven, I'll be beforehand with him.

2nd. *Sold.* Come, come, a soldier shouldn't talk so.

Reb. I tell you it isn't for myself I care so much, as for this poor little thing that follows me.

Chis. Signor Rebolledo, don't you fret about me: you know I was born with a beard on my heart if not on my chin, if ever girl was: and your fearing for me is as bad as if I was afeard myself. Why, when I came along with you I made up my mind to hardship and danger for honour's

---

[1] Don Lope de Figuerroa, who figures also in the *Amar despues de la Muerte*, was (says Mr. Ticknor) "the commander under whom Cervantes served in Italy, and probably in Portugal, when he was in the *Tercio de Flandes*, the Flanders regiment, one of the best bodies of troops in the armies of Philip II.," and the very one now advancing, with perhaps Cervantes in it, to Zalamea.

sake; else if I'd wanted to live in clover, I never should have left the Alderman who kept such a table as all aldermen don't, I promise you. Well, what's the odds? I chose to leave him and follow the drum, and here I am, and if I don't flinch, why should you?

Reb. 'Fore Heaven, you're the crown of womankind!

Soldiers. So she is, so she is, *Viva la Chispa*!

Reb. And so she is, and one cheer more for her Hurrah! especially if she'll give us a song to lighten the way.

Chis. The castanet shall answer for me.

Reb. I'll join in—and do you, comrades, bear a hand in the chorus.

Soldiers. Fire away!

Chispa sings.

I.

"Titiri tiri, marching is weary,
    Weary, weary, and long is the way:
Titiri tiri, hither, my deary,
    What meat have you got for the soldier to-day?
'Meat have I none, my merry men,'
Titiri tiri, then kill the old hen.
'Alas and a day! the old hen is dead!'
Then give us a cake from the oven instead.
        Titiri titiri titiri tiri,
Give us a cake from the oven instead.

II.

Admiral, admiral, where have you been-a?
    'I've been fighting where the waves roar.'
Ensign, ensign, what have you seen-a?
    'Glory and honour and gunshot galore;
Fighting the Moors in column and line,
Poor fellows, they never hurt me or mine —
        Titiri titiri titiri tina . . .'"

1st Sold. Look, look, comrades—what between singing and grumbling we never noticed yonder church among the trees.

Reb. Is that Zalamea?

Chis. Yes, that it is, I know the steeple. Hoorah! we'll finish the song when we get into quarters, or have another as good: for you know I have 'em of all sorts and sizes.

Reb. Halt a moment, here's the sergeant.

2nd. Sold. And the captain, too.

Enter CAPTAIN *and* SERGEANT.

Capt. Good news, men, no more marching for to-day at least; we halt at Zalamea till Don Lope joins with the rest of the regiment from Llerena. So who knows but you may have a several days' rest here?

Reb. and Solds. Hurrah for our captain!

Capt. Your quarters are ready, and the Commissary will give every one his billet on marching in.

Chis. (*singing*). Now then for

"Titiri tiri, hither, my deary,
Heat the oven and kill the old hen."

[*Exit with Soldiers.*

Capt. Well, Mr. Sergeant, have you my billet?

Serg. Yes, sir.

Capt. And where am I to be put up?

Serg. With the richest man in Zalamea, a farmer, as proud as Lucifer's heir apparent.

Capt. Ah, the old story of an upstart.

Serg. However, sir, you have the best quarters in the place, including his daughter, who is, they say, the prettiest woman in Zalamea.

Capt. Pooh! a pretty peasant! splay hands and feet.

Serg. Shame! shame!

Capt. Isn't it true, puppy?

Serg. What would a man on march have better than a pretty country lass to toy with?

Capt. Well, I never saw one I cared for, even on march. I can't call a woman a woman unless she's clean about the hands and fetlocks, and otherwise well appointed—a lady, in short.

Serg. Well, any one for me who'll let me kiss her. Come, sir, let us be going, for if you won't be at her, I will.

Capt. Look, look yonder!

Serg. Why, it must be Don Quixote himself, with his very Rosinante too, that Michel Cervantes writes of.

Capt. And his Sancho at his side. Well, carry you my kit on before to quarters, and then come and tell me when all's ready.

[*Exeunt.*

SCENE II.—*Zalamea, before* CRESPO's *House. Enter* DON MENDO *and* NUÑO.

Men. How's the grey horse?

Nuñ. You may as well call him the *Dun;* so screw'd he can't move a leg.

Men. Did you have him walk'd gently about?

Nuñ. Walk'd about! when it's corn he wants, poor devil!

Men. And the dogs?

Nuñ. Ah, now, they might do if you'd give them the horse to eat.

Men. Enough, enough—it has struck three. My gloves and tooth-pick.

Nuñ. That sinecure tooth pick?

Men. I tell you I would brain anybody who insinuated to me I had not dined—and on game too. But tell me, Nuño, havn't the soldiers come into Zalamea this afternoon?

Nuñ. Yes, sir.

Men. What a nuisance for the commonalty who have to quarter them.

Nuñ. But worse for those who havn't.

Men. What do you mean, sir?

Nuñ. I mean the squires. Ah, sir; if the soldiers aren't billeted on them, do you know why?

Men. Well, why?

Nuñ. For fear of being starved—which would be a bad job for the king's service.

Men. God rest my father's soul, says I, who left me a pedigree and patent all blazon'd in gold and azure, that exempts me from such impositions.

Nuñ. I wish he'd left you the gold in a more available shape, however.

Men. Though, indeed, when I come to think of it, I don't know if I owe him any thanks; considering that, unless he had consented to beget me an Hidalgo at once, I wouldn't have been born at all, for him or any one.

Nuñ. Humph! Could you have help'd it?

Men. Easily.

Nuñ. How, sir.

Men. You must know that every one that is born is the essence of the food his parents eat——

Nuñ. Oh! Your parents did eat, then, sir? You have not inherited *that* of them, at all events.

Men. Knave, do you insinuate——

Nuñ. I only know it is now three o'clock, and we have neither of us yet had anything but our own spittle to chew.

Men. Perhaps so, but there are distinctions of rank. An Hidalgo, sir, has no belly.

Nuñ. Oh, Lord! that I were an Hidalgo!

Men. Possibly; servants must learn moderation in all things. But let me hear no more of the matter; we are under Isabel's window.

Nun. There again — If you are so devoted an admirer, why on earth, sir, don't you ask her in marriage of her father; by doing which you would kill two birds with one stone: get yourself something to eat, and his grandchildren squires.

Men. Hold your tongue, sir, it is impious. Am I, an Hidalgo with such a pedigree, to demean myself with a plebeian connection just for money's sake?

Nun. Well, I've always heard say a mean father-in-law is best; better stumble on a pebble than run your head again a post. But, however, if you don't mean marriage, sir, what do you mean?

Men. And pray, sir, what business is that of yours? But go directly, and tell me if you can get a sight of her?

Nun. I'm afraid lest her father should get a sight of me.

Men. And what if he do, being my man? Go and do as I bid you.

Nun. (*after going to look*). Come, sir, you owe one meal at least now—she's at the window with her cousin.

Men. Go again and tell her something about her window being another East, and she a second Sun dawning from it in the afternoon.

(ISABEL *and* INES *come to the window.*)

Ines. For heaven's sake, cousin, let's stand here and see the soldiers march in.

Isab. Not I, while that man is in the way, Ines; you know how I hate the sight of him.

Ines. With all his devotion to you!

Isab. I wish he would spare himself and me the trouble.

Ines. I think you are wrong to take it as an affront.

Isab. How would you have me take it?

Ines. Why, as a compliment.

Isab. What, when I hate the man?

Men. Ah! 'pon the honour of an Hidalgo (which is a sacred oath), I could have sworn that till this moment the sun had not risen. But why should I wonder? When indeed a second Aurora —

Isab. Signor Don Mendo, how often have I told you not to waste your time playing these fool's antics before my window day after day.

Men. If a pretty woman only knew, la! how anger improves its beauty! her complexion needs no other paint than indignation. Go on, go on, lovely one, grow angrier and lovelier still.

Isab. You shan't have even that consolation; come, Ines. [*Exit.*

Ines. Beware of the portcullis, sir knight.

(*Shuts down the blind in his face.*)

Men. Ines, beauty must be ever victorious, whether advancing or retreating.

Enter CRESPO.

Cres. That I can never go in or out of my house without that squireen haunting it!

Nuñ. Pedro Crespo, sir!

Men. Oh—ah—let us turn another way; 'tis an ill-conditioned fellow.

As he turns, enter JUAN.

Juan. That I never can come home but this ghost of an Hidalgo is there to spoil my appetite.

Nuñ. His son, sir!

Men. He's worse. (*Turning back.*) Oh, Pedro Crespo, good-day, Crespo, good man, good day.

[*Exit with* NUÑO.

Cres. Good-day, indeed; I'll make it bad day one of these days with you, if you don't take care. But how now, Juanito, my boy?

Juan. I was looking for you, sir, but could not find you; where have you been?

Cres. To the barn, where high and dry
The jolly sheaves of corn do lie,
Which the sun, arch chemist of old,
Turn'd from black earth into gold,
And the swinging flail one day
On the barn-floor shall assay,
Separating the pure ore
From the drossy chaff away.
This I've been about.   And now,
Juanito, what hast thou?

Juan. Alas, sir, I can't answer in so good rhyme or reason.   I have been playing at fives, and lost every bout.

Cres. What signifies if you paid?

Juan. But I could not, and have come to you for the money.

Cres. Before I give it you, listen to me.
There are things two
Thou never must do;
Swear to more than thou knowest,
Play for more than thou owest;
And never mind cost,
So credit's not lost.

Juan. Good advice, sir, no doubt, that I shall lay by for its own sake as well as for yours.   Meanwhile I have also heard say—

"Preach not to a beggar till
The beggar's empty hide you fill."

Cres. 'Fore Heaven, thou pay'st me in my own coin. But——

Enter SERGEANT.

Serg. Pray, does one Pedro Crespo live hereabout?
Cres. Have you any commands for him, if he does?
Serg. Yes, to tell him of the arrival of Don Alvaro de

Ataide, captain of the troop that has just marched into Zalamea, and quartered upon him.

Cres. Say no more; my house and all I have is ever at the service of the king, and of all who have authority under him. If you will leave his things here, I will see his room is got ready directly; and do you tell his Honour that, come when he will, he shall find me and mine at his service.

Serg. Good—he will be here directly. [*Exit.*

Juan. I wonder, father, that, rich as you are, you still submit yourself to these nuisances.

Cres. Why, boy, how could I help them?

Juan. You know; by buying a patent of Gentility.

Cres. A patent of Gentility! upon thy life now dost think there's a soul who doesn't know that I'm no gentleman at all, but just a plain farmer? What's the use of my buying a patent of Gentility, if I can't buy the gentle blood along with it? will any one think me a bit more of a gentleman for buying fifty patents? Not a whit; I should only prove I was worth so many thousand royals, not that I had gentle blood in my veins, which can't be bought at any price. If a fellow's been bald ever so long, and buys him a fine wig and claps it on, will his neighbours think it is his own hair a bit the more? No, they will say, "So-and-so has a fine wig; and, what's more, he must have paid handsomely for it too." But they know his bald pate is safe under it all the while. That's all he gets by it.

Juan. Nay, sir, he gets to look younger and handsomer, and keeps off sun and cold.

Cres. Tut! I'll have none of your wig honour at any price. My grandfather was a farmer, so was my father, so is yours, and so shall you be after him. Go, call your sister.

Enter ISABEL *and* INES.

Oh, here she is. Daughter, our gracious king (whose life God save these thousand years!) is on his way to be crowned at Lisbon; thither the troops are marching from all quarters, and among others that fine veteran Flanders regiment, commanded by the famous Don Lope de Figuerroa, will march into Zalamea, and be quartered here to-day; some of the soldiers in my house. Is it not as well you should be out of the way?

Isab. Sir, 'twas upon this very errand I came to you, knowing what nonsense I shall have to hear if I stay below. My cousin and I can go up to the garret, and there keep so close, the very sun shall not know of our whereabout.

Cres. That's my good girl. Juanito, you wait here to receive them in case they come while I am out looking after their entertainment.

Isab. Come, Ines.

Ines. Very well —

"Though I've heard in a song what folly 'twould be
To try keep in a loft what won't keep on the tree."

[*Exeunt.*

Enter CAPTAIN *and* SERGEANT.

Serg. This is the house, sir.

Capt. Is my kit come?

Serg. Yes, sir, and (*aside*) I'll be the first to take an inventory of the pretty daughter. [*Exit.*

Juan. Welcome, sir, to our house; we count it a great honour to have such a cavalier as yourself for a guest, I assure you. (*Aside.*) What a fine fellow! what an air! I long to try the uniform, somehow.

Capt. Thank you, my lad.

Juan. You must forgive our poor house, which we devoutly wish was a palace for your sake. My father is gone after your supper, sir; may I go and see that your chamber is got ready for you?

Capt. Thank you, thank you.

Juan. Your servant, sir. [*Exit.*

Enter SERGEANT.

Capt. Well, sergeant, where's the Dulcinea you told me of?

Serg. Deuce take me, sir, if I haven't been looking everywhere—in parlour, bedroom, kitchen, and scullery, upstairs and downstairs, and can't find her out.

Capt. Oh, no doubt the old fellow has hid her away for fear of us.

Serg. Yes, I ask'd a serving wench, and she confess'd her master had lock'd the girl up in the attic, with strict orders not even to look out so long as we were in the place.

Capt. Ah! these clodpoles are all so jealous of the service. And what is the upshot? Why, I, who didn't care a pin to see her before, shall never rest till I get at her now.

Serg. But how, without a blow-up?

Capt. Let me see; how shall we manage it?

Serg. The more difficult the enterprise, the more glory in success, you know, in love as in war.

Capt. I have it!

Serg. Well, sir?

Capt. You shall pretend—but no, here comes one will serve my turn better.

Enter REBOLLEDO *and* CHISPA.

Reb. (*to* CHISPA). There he is; now if I can get him into a good humour.

Chis. Speak up then, like a man.

Reb. I wish I'd some of your courage; but don't you leave me while I tackle him. Please, your Honour —

Capt. (*to* SERGEANT). I tell you I've my eye on Rebolledo to do him a good turn; I like his spirit.

Serg. Ah, he's one of a thousand.

Reb. (*aside*). Here's luck! Please, your Honour——

Capt. Oh, Rebolledo— Well, Rebolledo, what is it?

Reb. You may know I am a gentleman who has, by ill-luck, lost all his estate; all that ever I had, have, shall have, may have, or can have, through all the conjugations of the verb "*to have.*" And I want your Honour —

Capt. Well?

Reb. To desire the ensign to appoint me roulette-master to the regiment, so I may pay my liabilities like a man of honour.

Capt. Quite right, quite right; I will see it done.

Chis. (*aside*). Oh, brave captain! Oh, if I only live to hear them all call me Madame Roulette!

Reb. Shall I go at once and tell him?

Capt. Wait. I want you first to help me in a little plan I have.

Reb. Out with it, noble captain. Slow said slow sped, you know.

Capt. You are a good fellow; listen. I want to get into that attic there, for a particular purpose.

Reb. And why doesn't your Honour go up at once?

Capt. I don't like to do it in a strange house without an excuse. Now look here; you and I will pretend to quarrel; I get angry and draw my sword, and you run away upstairs, and I after you, to the attic, that's all; I'll manage the rest.

Chis. (*aside*). Ah, he seems to be getting on famously.

Reb. I understand. When are we to begin?

Capt. Now directly.

Reb. Very good. (*In a loud voice.*) This is the reward of my services—a rascal, a pitiful, scoundrel, is preferred, when a man of honour—a man who has seen service——

Chis. (*aside*). Halloa! Rebolledo up? All is not so well.

Reb. Who has led you to victory?

Capt. This language to me, sir?

Reb. Yes, to you, who have so grossly insulted and defrauded ——

Capt. Silence! and think yourself lucky if I take no further notice of your insolence.

Reb. If I restrain myself, it is only because you are my captain, and as such—but 'fore God, if my cane were in my hand ——

Chis. (advancing.) Hold! hold!

Capt. I'll show you, sir, how to talk to me in this way. (*Draws his sword.*)

Reb. It is before your commission, not you, I retreat.

Capt. That sha'n't save you, rascal!

(*Pursues* REBOLLEDO *out.*)

Chis. Oh! I sha'n't be Madame Roulette after all. Murder! murder!

[*Exit calling.*

SCENE III.—ISABEL'S *Garret.* ISABEL *and* INES.

Isab. What noise is that on the stairs?

Enter REBOLLEDO.

Reb. Sanctuary! Sanctuary!

Isab. Who are you, sir?

Enter CAPTAIN.

Capt. Where is the rascal?

Isab. A moment, sir! This poor man has flown to our feet for protection; I appeal to you for it; and no man, and least of all an officer, will refuse that to any woman.

Capt. I swear no other arm than that of beauty, and beauty such as yours, could have withheld me. (*To*

Rebolledo.) You may thank the deity that has saved you, rascal.

Isab. And I thank you, sir.

Capt. And yet ungratefully slay me with your eyes in return for sparing him with my sword.

Isab. Oh, sir, do not mar the grace of a good deed by poor compliment, and so make me less mindful of the real thanks I owe you.

Capt. Wit and modesty kiss each other, as well they may, in that lovely face. (*Kneels.*)

Isab. Heavens! my father!

Enter Crespo *and* Juan *with swords.*

Cres. How is this, sir? I am alarmed by cries of murder in my house—am told you have pursued a poor man up to my daughter's room; and, when I get here expecting to find you killing a man, I find you courting a woman.

Capt. We are all born subjects to some dominion—soldiers especially to beauty. My sword, though justly raised against this man, as justly fell at this lady's bidding.

Cres. No lady, sir, if you please; but a plain peasant girl—my daughter.

Juan. (*aside*). All a trick to get at her. My blood boils. (*Aloud to Captain.*) I think, sir, you might have seen enough of my father's desire to serve you to prevent your requiting him by such an affront as this.

Cres. And, pray, who bid thee meddle, boy? Affront! what affront? The soldier affronted his captain; and if the captain has spared him for thy sister's sake, pray what hast thou to say against it?

Capt. I think, young man, you had best consider before you impute ill intention to an officer.

Juan. I know what I do know.

Cres. What! you will go on, will you?

Capt. It is out of regard for you I do not chastise him.

Cres. Wait a bit: if that were wanting, 'twould be from his father, not from you.

Juan. And what's more, I wouldn't endure it from any one but my father.

Capt. You would not?

Juan. No! death rather than such dishonour!

Capt. What, pray, is a clodpole's idea of honour.

Juan. The same as a captain's—no clodpole no captain, I can tell you.

Capt. 'Fore Heaven, I must punish this insolence.
(About to strike him.)

Cres. You must do it through me, then.

Reb. Eyes right!—Don Lope!

Capt. Don Lope!

Enter DON LOPE.

Lope. How now? A riot the very first thing I find on joining the regiment? What is it all about?

Capt. (*aside*). Awkward enough!

Cres. (*aside*). By the lord, the boy would have held his own with the best of 'em.

Lope. Well! No one answer me? 'Fore God, I'll pitch the whole house, men, women, and children, out of windows, if you don't tell me at once. Here have I had to trail up your accursed stairs, and then no one will tell me what for.

Cres. Nothing, nothing at all, sir.

Lope. Nothing? that would be the worst excuse of all, but swords arn't drawn for nothing; come, the truth?

Capt. Well, the simple fact is this, Don Lope; I am quartered upon this house; and one of my soldiers——

Lope. Well, sir, go on.

Capt. Insulted me so grossly I was obliged to draw my sword on him. He ran up here, where it seems these two girls live: and I, not knowing there was any harm, after him; at which these men, their father or brother, or some such thing, take affront. This is the whole business.

Lope. I am just come in time then to settle it. First, who is the soldier that began it with an act of insubordination?

Reb. What, am I to pay the piper?

Isab. (*pointing to* REBOLLEDO). This, sir, was the man who ran up first.

Lope. This? handcuff him!

Reb. Me! my lord?

Capt. (*aside to* REBOLLEDO). Don't blab, I'll bear you harmless.

Reb. Oh, I dare say, after being marched off with my hands behind me like a coward. Noble commander, 'twas the captain's own doing; he made me pretend a quarrel, that he might get up here to see the women.

Cres. I *had* some cause for quarrel, you see.

Lope. Not enough to peril the peace of the town for. Halloa there! beat all to quarters on pain of death. And, to prevent further ill blood here, do you (*to the* CAPTAIN) quarter yourself elsewhere till we march. I'll stop here.

Capt. I shall of course obey you, sir.

Cres. (*to* ISABEL). Get you in. (*Exeunt* ISABEL *and* INES.) I really ought to thank you heartily for coming just as you did, sir; else, I'd have done for myself.

Lope. How so?

Cres. I should have killed this popinjay.

Lope. What, sir, a captain in his Majesty's service?

Cres. Aye, a general, if he insulted me.

Lope. I tell you, whoever lays his little finger on the humblest private in the regiment, I'll hang him.

Cres. And I tell you, whoever points his little finger at my honour, I'll cut him down before hanging.

Lope. Know you not, you are bound by your allegiance to submit.

Cres. To all cost of property, yes; but of honour, no, no, no! My goods and chattels, aye, and my life—are the king's; but my honour is my own soul's, and that is God Almighty's.

Lope. 'Fore God, there's some truth in what you say.

Cres. 'Fore God, there ought to be, for I've been some years saying it.

Lope. Well, well. I've come a long way, and this leg of mine, which I wish the devil who gave it would carry [*sic*] away with him! cries for rest.

Cres. And who prevents its taking some? the same devil I suppose who gave you your leg, gave me a bed, which I don't want him to take away again, however, on which your leg may lie if it like.

Lope. But did the devil, when he was about it, make your bed as well as give it?

Cres. To be sure he did.

Lope. Then I'll unmake it—Heaven knows I'm weary enough.

Cres. Heaven rest you then.

Lope. (*aside*). Devil or saint alike he echoes me!

Calderon de la Barca (1600-1681).
Trans. Edward Fitzgerald.

THE SIMPLE GROOMS.

"LOOK," said Juanillo, "we have now arrived at the Puerta del Sol, one of the chief resorts in Madrid. This site of beautiful things, rightly called the Sol or Sun, is renowned not only in Madrid, but throughout the whole world." Just then the cries and loud sobs of a lad made them turn to inquire the cause, and Onofre, asking a boy close by, was told it was a doctor's groom who had gone out to sell a mule too slow for his master, who, on account of his large practice, required one with more go.

"Are there so many sick in Madrid?" asked Onofre: to which the boy replied: "He lives in a suburb of delicate people, who dress richly, lie a long time in bed, have all their windows shut to keep out the air, and if their chocolate is too sweet or too highly spiced, say it has done them harm, and then they send for the doctor, who, to feel the pulses and purses of all, needs a lively mule, and so he wanted to sell his slow one."

The boy went on to relate how the groom soon found a buyer in the servant of a country doctor, just arrived on horseback between the panniers of bread, a trick worthy of the devil himself, since that they might not suspect Death was entering the gates of Madrid, he came cloaked with the chief support of life; for they say he was abandoning his last residence, since it had lost half its population during the one year of his stay, and was, therefore, coming to Madrid, where, on account of its size, he hoped his work would not be so noticeable. With this executioner's servant . . . a bargain was struck, and the buyer allowed to try the mule, after entertaining and bribing the groom; whereupon he vanished down the street of Alcalá.

Onofre smiled at the youth's humour, and approaching

the blubbering groom, heard the crowd trying to advise and console him in various ways: to look in all the hostries, where the thief might have taken the mule to give it a feed; that his master would easily earn his value in four days; that it was no good crying over spilt milk, to all of which the groom wept loudly, the big tears running down his cheeks, which, as well as his nose, he wiped with his cape and shirt-sleeves. Onofre felt sorry for the poor fellow, but Juanillo, calling him, told him such things often happened market days, and he knew another case, which showed the astuteness of some thieves.

A groom went, like this one, to sell a mule, which was, however, so young and wild, his master could not ride it. He arrived at the market and straightway found a buyer, for those simple fellows always come across crafty rogues, up to all kinds of tricks. They quickly came to terms, and the thief asked the lad to come for his money astride his mule to a surgeon-barber, for whom it was purchased. He then lead him to a shop where he had been shaved once or twice, and, leaving him outside on the mule, inquired for the master, and after the customary salutations, told him he had brought a sick groom whom he wished to be examined, and cured if possible, but that, as he was very shy and embarrassed, and had put off coming to a doctor for a long time, he must try not to frighten him, and ask the lad to wait a while inside till he could see him, lest he should run away. He then paid half the fee and said he would pay the rest afterwards. The barber, highly pleased, went out and asked the groom to come in and wait, and his business would soon be despatched.

"You know my business?" said the lad.

"Certainly," said the barber.

The cheat, telling the groom that the barber would give him a dozen reals for himself beside the price for the mule, mounted, clapped spurs to the mule, and made off.

The groom, after waiting some little time, found out the fraud as soon as the barber began questioning him as to his health, and set up a great hullabaloo, whereupon the police hastened by, but could only warn him to be more prudent next time, with the hope that God would console him meanwhile.

"*Day and Night in Madrid.*" *Santos (fl.* 1697).

PORTUGUESE EPITAPHS AND SAYINGS.

A NOBLE Portugee lies here,
By name Don Vasco Cid Figuere,
Not in bloodshed
Died he, he fled
From wars and Moors, and did all he could
To die in bed as a gentleman should.

Here lies who once lived and is now dead, and although he died, he lives, for the world trembles at the sound of his name.

Here lies the body of Senhor Vasco Barreto,
He died by God's will and much against his own.
Breathe an *Ave Maria* for the repose of his soul.

Here lies Alfonso Galego. He died for the glory of God in spite of the Devil.

A Portuguese preacher once said: "The Moors are our neighbours, and the Jews are our neighbours, and even the Castilians are also our neighbours."

Another time a Portuguese friar, preaching on the anniversary of a great battle, said: "The Christians were on one side of the river, and the Castilians on the other."

(*Seventeenth Century*).

LA TARASCA AND THE CARRIERS.

A TOWN in Spain on the banks of the Tagus, just about to celebrate Corpus Christi, sent to a neighbouring town for the giants and the huge serpent, called La Tarasca. On the eve of the festival the bearers, in order to arrive in good time to join the procession, set out at dusk, with the intention of reaching their destination at break of day. They were inside the huge effigies, which were borne on their shoulders exactly as when they dance through the streets. The moon rose during their journey and shone down on the strange figures, to the great amazement and alarm of some carriers with loads of wine, who, becoming aware of the serpent and the giants behind, only screwed together enough courage to take to their heels as fast as they could. The bearers cried after them to come back and look after their teams, but in vain, the more they shouted, the faster they fled. Thereupon the porters of La Tarasca set her down and repaired to the mules, and when they perceived the sweet spoils they had won without any bloodshed, called to the bearers of the giants, and they all drank to each other's health in such long draughts and hearty quaffs, that the liquor rose to their heads and laid them full length on the road.

The carriers, who were great braggarts, returned home and told their Alcalde how they had encountered such giant thieves; and the whole township, armed with crossbows, lances and cudgels, sallied out in quest of these odd fish. They arrived at the spot, making so great a din, they almost awakened their foes, whom they found stretched on the ground.

The Alcalde, much amused at the jest, gave judgment that the carriers were to pay with wine those who had come to their help; upon which all drank to their heart's content

"THE MORE THEY SHOUTED, THE FASTER THEY FLED."

till the citizens and soldiers returned homewards and the porters again shouldered their burdens.

"*Truth on the Rack.*" Santos (*fl.* 1697).

PEDIGREE OF FOOLS.

THEY say Lost Time married Ignorance, and had a son called I Thought, who married Youth, and had the following children: I Didn't Know, I Didn't Think, Who Would Have Expected.

Who Would Have Expected married Heedlessness, and had for children It's All Right, To-morrow Will Do, There's Plenty of Time, Next Opportunity.

There's Plenty of Time married Doña I Didn't Think, and had for family I Forgot, I Know All About It, Nobody Can Deceive Me.

I Know All About It espoused Vanity, and begat Pleasure, who, marrying That's Not Likely, became father to Let Us Enjoy Ourselves and Bad Luck.

Bad Luck took to wife Little Sense, and had a very large family, among whom were This Will Do, What Business Is It Of Theirs, It Seems To Me, It's Not Possible.

Pleasure was widowed, and, marrying again, espoused Folly. Consuming their inheritance, they said one to the other, "Have Patience, let us spend our capital and enjoy ourselves this year, for God will provide for the next." But Deception took them to prison, and Poverty to the workhouse, where they died.

Strange obsequies were performed at their funeral, at which were present the five Senses, Intellect, Memory, and Will, although in a pitiful condition. Repentance, who came somewhat late, found no seat, and had to stand the whole time, while Consolation and Contentment were represented by Desolation and Melancholy, daughters of Memory.

Despair, grandchild of the deceased, went about begging for several days, in which he could only collect six maravedies, with which he bought a rope and hanged himself from a turret, which is the end of the family of Fools.

Anon. (*Seventeenth Century*).

THE FAMOUS PREACHER, FRIAR BLAS.

HE was in the full perfection of his strength, just about three-and-thirty years old, tall, robust, and stout; his limbs well set and well proportioned; manly in gait, inclining to corpulence, with an erect carriage of his head, and the circle of hair round his tonsure studiously and exactly combed and shaven. His clerical dress was always neat, and fell round his person in ample and regular folds. His shoes fitted him with the greatest nicety, and, above all, his silken cap was adorned with much curious embroidery and a fanciful tassel—the work of certain female devotees who were dying with admiration of their favourite preacher. In short, he had a very youthful, gallant look; and, adding to this a clear, rich voice, a slight fashionable lisp, a peculiar grace in telling a story, a talent at mimicry, an easy action, a taking manner, a high-sounding style, and not a little effrontery—never forgetting to sprinkle jests, proverbs, and homely phrases along his discourses with a most agreeable aptness—he won golden opinions in his public discourses, and carried everything before him in the drawing-rooms he frequented.

It was well known that he always began his sermons with some proverb, some jest, some pothouse witticism, or some strange fragment, which, taken from its proper connections

FRIAR BLAS.

and relations, would seem, at first blush, to be an inconsequence, a blasphemy, or an impiety; until at last, having kept his audience waiting a moment in wonder, he finished the clause, or came out with an explanation which reduced the whole to a sort of miserable trifling. Thus, preaching one day on the mystery of the Trinity, he began his sermon by saying, "I deny that God exists a Unity in essence and a Trinity in person," and then stopped short for an instant. The hearers, of course, looked round on one another scandalised, or, at least, wondering what would be the end of this heretical blasphemy. At length, when the preacher thought he had fairly caught them, he went on, "Thus says the Ebionite, the Marcionite, the Arian, the Manichean, the Socinian; but I prove it against them all from the Scriptures, the Councils, and the Fathers."

In another sermon, which was on the Incarnation, he began by crying out, "Your health, cavaliers!" and, as the audience burst into a broad laugh at the free manner in which he had said it, he went on, "This is no joking matter, however; for it was for your health and for mine, and for that of all men, that Christ descended from heaven and became incarnate in the Virgin Mary. It is an article of faith, and I prove it thus: '*Propter nos, homines et nostram salutem descendit de cælo et incarnatus est,*'"—whereat they all remained in delighted astonishment, and such a murmur of applause ran round the church that it wanted little of breaking out into open acclamation.

Trans. Ticknor.

THE MUSICAL ASS.

THE fable which I now present
Occurr'd to me by accident;
And whether bad or excellent,
Is merely so by accident.

A stupid Ass this morning went
Into a field by accident
And cropp'd his food and was content,
Until he spied by accident
A flute, which some oblivious gent
Had left behind by accident;
When, sniffing it with eager scent,
He breathed on it by accident,
And made the hollow instrument
Emit a sound by accident.
"Hurrah, hurrah!" exclaimed the brute,
"How cleverly I play the flute!"

A fool, in spite of nature's bent,
May shine for once—by accident.

  Yriarte (1750-1791).   *Trans. R. Rockliff.*

THE BASHFUL SHEPHERDESS.

THE BASHFUL SHEPHERDESS.

NO shady fruit tree
　In the early year
Deck'd with blossoms sweet
In the day dawn clear
So gladdens my eyes,
And raises my heart,
As when I catch sight
Of my own sweetheart.
He says, if I like,
In the fair springtime
We will married be,
For his love I see.
But to tell him yes
I feel such shame,
And no to answer
Gives still more pain.
But a thousand times yes,
The very first time
That he asks again,
Is the answer mine.

Iglesias (d. 1791).

THE BEAR, THE APE, AND THE PIG.

A BEAR, whose dancing help'd to gain
　　His own and owner's livelihood,
And whose success had made him vain
　As any petit-maître, stood
Upon his hinder legs to try
　The figure of a new quadrille,
When, seeing that an Ape was nigh,
　He stump'd about with all his skill,

And, "Tell me how you like," he cried,
　"My dancing, for I'm always glad
To hear the truth." The Ape replied,
　"I really think it very bad."
"'Tis plain enough," rejoin'd the Bear,
　"That envy makes you censure so ;
For have I not a graceful air,
　A slender shape and limber toe?"
But here a tasteless Pig began
　To grunt applause, and said, "I vow
I've never met, in brute or man,
　With one who danced so well as thou."
The bear, on hearing this, became
　Sedate and pensive for awhile ;
And then, as if abash'd with shame,
　Replied, in a more humble style :
"The agile Ape's rebuke might be
　Inspired by jealousy or spleen ;
But, since the Pig commends, I see
　How bad my dancing must have been."

Let every author think on this,
　And hold the maxim for a rule—
The worst that can befall him is
　The approbation of a fool."
　　　　Yriarte (1750-1791). *Trans. R. Rockliff.*

THE FROG AND THE HEN.

AS once a Frog,
　Who all day long had chatter'd from his bog,
　　　　Began to close
His mouth and eyes, and drop into a doze,
　　　　He chanced just then
To hear the sudden cackle of a hen.

"What sound is this?"
He cried. "Dear madam, what can be amiss,
    That thus you scream,
And keep a quiet neighbour from his dream?"
    The Hen replied,
Her feather's fluttering with maternal pride,
    "I humbly beg
Your pardon, sir: but, having laid an egg,
    I could not chuse
To let you sleep in ignorance of the news."
    "What! all this clatter
About a single egg!—so small a matter!"
    "True, neighbour, true;
'Tis but a single egg—a small one, too;
    But if you blame
The rout that I have made about the same,
    'Tis doubly wrong
In you to croak for nothing all day long.
    The egg's of use,
And therefore I may brag with some excuse;
    But the dull brute
That's unproductive should be also mute."

Yriarte. Trans. R. Rockliff.

MARIQUITA THE BALD.

(A TALE AFTER THE STYLE OF AN OLD CHRONICLE.)

IT is as sorry a matter to use the words of which one ignores the meaning as it is a blemish for a man of sense to speak of what he knows nothing about. I say this to those of you who may have the present story in your hands, however often you may have happened to have heard *Mariquita the Bald* mentioned, and I swear by my

doublet that you shall soon know who Mariquita the Bald
was, as well as I know who ate the Christmas turkey,
setting aside the surmise that it certainly must have been a
mouth.

I desire, therefore, to enlighten your ignorance of this
subject, and beg to inform you that the said noted Maria
(Mariquita is a diminutive of Maria) was born in the
District of Segovia, and in the town of Sant Garcia, the
which town is famed for the beauty of the maidens reared
within its walls, who for the most part have such gentle and
lovely faces, that may I behold such around me at the hour
of my death. Maria's father was an honest farmer, by
name Juan Lanas, a Christian old man, and much beloved,
and who had inherited no mean estate from his forefathers,
though with but little wit in his crown, a lack which was the
cause of much calamity to both the father and the daughter,
for in the times to which we have attained, God forgive me
if it is not necessary to have more of the knave than of the
fool in one's composition. Now it came to pass that Juan
Lanas, for the castigation of his sins, must needs commit himself to a lawsuit with one of his neighbours about a vine stock
which was worth about fifty maravedis; and Juan was in the
right, and the judges gave the verdict in his favour, so that
he won his case, excepting that the suit lasted no less than
ten years and the costs amounted to nothing less than fifty
thousand maravedies, not to speak of a disease of the eyes
which after all was over left him blind. When he found
himself with diminished property and without his eyesight,
in sorrow and disgust he turned into money such part of his
patrimony as sufficed to rid him of the hungry herd of
scribeners and lawyers, and took his way to Toledo with his
daughter, who was already entering upon her sixteenth
year, and had matured into one of the most beautiful,
graceful, and lovable damsels to be found throughout all
Castile and the kingdoms beyond. For she was white as

the lily and red like the rose, straight and tall of stature, and slender in the waist, with fair, shapely hips ; and again her foot and hand were plump and small to a marvel, and she possessed a head of hair which reached to her knees. For I knew the widow Sarmiento who was their housekeeper, and she told me how she could scarcely clasp Mariquita's hair with both hands, and that she could not comb the hair unless Maria stood up and the housekeeper mounted on a footstool, for if Maria sat down, the long tresses swept the ground, and therefore became all entangled.

And do not imagine her beauty and grace being such that she sinned greatly in pride and levity, as is the wont of girls in this age. She was as humble as a cloistered laysister, and as silent as if she were not a woman, and patient as the sucking lamb, and industrious as the ant, clean as the ermine, and pure as a saint of those times in which, by the grace of the Most High, saintly women were born into the world. But I must confide to you in friendship that our Mariquita was not a little vain about her hair, and loved to display it, and for this reason, now in the streets, now when on a visit, now when at mass, it is said she used to subtilely loosen her mantilla so that her tresses streamed down her back, the while feigning forgetfulness and carelessness. She never wore a hood, for she said it annoyed her and choked her ; and every time that her father reproached her for some deed deserving of punishment and threatened to cut off her hair, I warrant you she suffered three times more than after a lash from the whip, and would then be good for three weeks successively ; so much so that Juan Lanas, perceiving her amendment, would laugh under his cloak, and when saying his say to his gossips would tell them that his daughter, like the other saint of Sicily, would reach heaven by her hair. Having read so far, you must now know that Juan Lanas, the blind man, with the change of district and dwelling did not change his judgment, and if he was crack-brained at Sant Garcia, he remained crack-brained at Toledo, consuming in this resort his monies upon worthless drugs and quacks which did not cure his blindness and impoverished him more and more every day, so that if his daughter had not been so dexterous with her fingers in making and broidering garments of linen, wool, and silk, I promise you that this miserable Juan would have to have gone for more than four Sundays without a clean shirt to put on or a mouthful to eat, unless he had begged for it from door to door. The years passed by to find Maria every day more beautiful, and her father every day more blind and more desirous to see, until his affliction and trouble took such forcible possession of his breast and mind, that Maria saw as clear as daylight that if her father did not recover his sight, he would die of grief. Maria thereupon straightway took her father and led him to the house of an Arabian physician of great learning who dwelt at Toledo, and told the Moor to see if there were any cure for the old man's sight. The Arabian examined and touched Juan, and made this and that experiment with him, and everything was concerted in that the physician swore great oaths by the heel-bone of Mohammed that there was a complete certainty of curing Juan and making him to see his daughter again, if only he, the physician, were paid for the cure with five hundred maravedies all in gold. A sad termination for such a welcome beginning, for the two unhappy creatures, Juan and Maria, had neither maravedi nor cuarto in their money box! So they went thence all downcast, and Maria never ceased praying to his Holiness Saint John and his Holiness Saint James (the patron saint of Spain) to repair to their assistance in this sad predicament.

"In what way," conjectured she inwardly—"in what way can I raise fifty maravedies to be quits with the worthy Moor who will give back his sight to my poor old father?

Ah! I have it. I am a pretty maid, and suitors innumerable, commoners and nobles, pay their addresses and compliments to me. But all are trifling youths who only care for love-making and who seek light o' loves rather than spouses according to the law of the Lord Jesus Christ. I remember, notwithstanding, that opposite our house lives the sword-cutler, Master Palomo, who is always looking at me and never speaks to me, and the Virgin assist me, he appears a man of very good condition for a husband; but what maiden, unless she were cross-eyed or hunch-backed, could like a man with such a flat nose, with that skin the colour of a ripe date, with those eyes like a dead calf's, and with those huge hands, which are more like the paws of a wild beast than the belongings of a person who with them should softly caress the woman whom Destiny bestows upon him for a companion? 'Tis said that he is no drunkard, nor cudgeller, nor dallier with woman, nor a liar, and that he is besides possessed of much property and very rich. Pity 'tis that one who is so ugly and stiff-necked should unite such parts."

Thus turning the matter over and over in her mind, Maria together with Juan reached their home, where was awaiting them an esquire in a long mourning robe, who told Maria that the aunt of the Mayor of the city had died in an honest estate and in the flower of her age, for she had not yet completed her seventy years, and that the obsequies of this sexagenarian damsel were to be performed the following day, on which occasion her coffin would be carried to the church by maidens, and he was come to ask Maria if she would please to be one of the bearers of the dead woman, for which she would receive a white robe, and to eat, and a ducat, and thanks into the bargain.

Maria, since she was a well brought up maid, replied that if it seemed well to her father, it would also seem well to her.

Juan accepted, and Maria was rejoiced to be able to make a display of her hair, for it is well known that the maidens who bear another to the grave walk with dishevelled locks. And when on the morrow the tiring-women of the Mayoress arrayed Maria in a robe white as the driven snow and fine as the skin of an onion; and when they girt her slender waist with a sash of crimson silk, the ends of which hung down to the broad hem of the skirt; and when they crowned her smooth and white forehead with a wreath of white flowers, I warrant you that, what with the robe and the sash and the wreath, and the beautiful streaming hair and her lovely countenance and gracious mien, she seemed no female formed of flesh and blood, but a superhuman creature or blessed resident of those shining circles in which dwell the celestial hierarchies. The Mayor and the other mourners stepped forth to see her, and all unceasingly praised God, who was pleased to perform such miracles for the consolation and solace of those living in this world. And there in a corner of the hall, motionless like a heap of broken stones, stood one of the mutes with the hood of his long cloak covering his head, so that nothing could be seen but his eyes, the which he kept fixed on the fair damsel. The latter modestly lowered her eyes to the ground with her head a little bent and her cheeks red for bashfulness, although it pleased her no little to hear the praises of her beauty. At this moment a screen was pushed aside, and there began to appear a huge bulk of petticoats, which was nothing less than the person of the Mayoress, for she was with child and drawing near to her time. And when she saw Maria, she started, opened her eyes a hand's-breadth wide, bit her lips, and called hurriedly for her husband. They stepped aside for a good while, and then hied them thence, and when they returned the mutes and maidens had all gone.

While they are burying the defunct lady I must tell you,

curious readers, that the Mayor and Mayoress had been married for many years without having any children, and they longed for them like the countryman for rain in the month of May, and at last her hour of bliss came to the Mayoress, to the great content of her husband. Now, it was whispered that the said lady had always been somewhat capricious; judge for yourselves what she would be now in the time of her pregnancy! And as she was already on the way to fifty, she was more than mediocrely bald and hairless, and on these very same days had commissioned a woman barber, who lived in the odour of witchcraft, to prepare for her some false hair, but it was not to be that of a dead woman, for the Mayoress said very sensibly that if the hair belonged to a dead woman who rejoiced in supreme glory, or was suffering for her sins in purgatory, it would be profanation to wear any pledge of theirs, and if they were in hell, it was a terrible thing to wear on one's person relics of one of the damned. And when the Mayoress saw the abundant locks of Maria, she coveted them for herself, and it was for this reason that she called to the Mayor to speak to her in private and besought him eagerly to persuade Maria to allow herself to be shorn upon the return from the burial.

"I warn you," said the Mayor, "that you are desirous of entering upon a very knotty bargain, for the dishevelled girl idolises her hair in such wise, that she would sooner lose a finger than suffer one of her tresses to be cut off."

"I warn you," replied the Mayoress, "that if on this very day the head of this young girl is not shorn smooth beneath my hand as a melon, the child to which I am about to give birth will have a head of hair on its face, and if it happens to be a female, look you, a pretty daughter is in store for you!"

"But bethink yourself that Maria will ask, who knows, a good few crowns for this shaving."

"Bethink yourself, that if not, your heir or heiress, begotten after so many years' marriage, will come amiss; and bear in mind, by the way, that we are not so young as to hope to replace this by another."

Upon this she turned her back to the Mayor, and went to her apartment crying out: "I want the hair, I must have the hair, and if I do not get the hair, by my halidom I shall never become a mother."

In the meantime the funeral had taken place without any novelty to mention, excepting that if in the streets any loose fellow in the crowd assayed to annoy the fair Maria, the hooded mute, of whom we made mention before, quickly drew from beneath his cloak a strap, with which he gave a lash to the insolent rogue without addressing one word to him, and then walked straight on as if nothing had happened. When all the mourners returned, the Mayor seized hold of Maria's hand and said to her—

"And now, fair maid, let us withdraw for a little while into this other apartment," and thus talking whilst in motion he brought her into his wife's private tiring-room, and sat himself down in a chair and bent his head and stroked his beard with the mien of one who is studying what beginning to give to his speech. Maria, a little foolish and confused, remained standing in front of the Mayor, and she also humbly lowered before him her eyes, black as the sloe; and to occupy herself with something, gently fingered the ends of the sash which girded her waist and hung down over her skirt, not knowing what to expect from the grave mien and long silence of the Mayor, who, raising his eyes and looking up at Maria, when he beheld her in so modest a posture, devised thence a motive with which to begin, saying—

"Forsooth, Maria, so modest and sanctimonious is thy bearing, that it is easy to see thou art preparing thyself to become a black wimpled nun. And if it be so, as I presume it to be, I now offer of my own accord to dispose of thy entry into the cloisters without any dowry, on condition that thou dost give me something that thou hast on thy head, and which then wilt not be necessary for thee."

"Nay, beshrew me, Sir Mayor," replied Maria, "for I durst not think that the Lord calls upon me to take that step, for then my poor father would remain in the world without the staff of his old age."

"Then, now, I desire to give thee some wise counsel, maid Maria. Thou dost gain thy bread with great fatigue, thou shouldst make use of thy time as much as is possible. Now one of thy neighbours hath told me, that in the dressing of thy hair, thou doth waste every day more than an hour. It would be better far if thou didst spend this hour on thy work rather than in the dressing and braiding which thou dost to thy hair."

"That is true, Sir Mayor," replied Maria, turning as red as a carnation, "but, look you, it is not my fault if I have a wealth of tresses, the combing and plaiting of which necessitates so long a time every morning."

"I tell thee it is thy fault," retorted the Mayor, "for if thou didst cut off this mane, thou would save thyself all this combing and plaiting, and thus would have more time for work, and so gain more money, and would also give no occasion to people to call thee vain. They even say that the Devil will some day carry thee off by thy hair. Nay, do not be distressed, for I already perceive the tears gathering in thy eyes, for thou hast them indeed very ready at hand ; I admonish thee for thine own good without any self-interest. Cut thy hair off, shear thyself, shave thyself, good Maria, and to allay the bitterness of the shearing, I will give fifty maravedies, always on condition that thou dost hand me over the hair."

When Maria at first heard this offer of so reasonable a sum for this her hair, it seemed to her a jest of the

Mayor's, and she smiled right sweetly while she dried her tears, repeating—

"You will give me fifty maravedies if I shave myself?"

Now it appeared to the Mayor (who, it is said, was not gifted with all the prudence of Ulysses) that that smile signified that the maid was not satisfied with so small a price, and he added—

"If thou wilt not be content with fifty maravedies, I will give thee a hundred."

Then Maria saw some hangings of the apartment moving in front of her, and perceiving a bulky protuberance, she immediately divined that the Mayoress was hiding behind there, and that the protuberance was caused by her portly form. She now discovered the Mayor's design, and that it was probably a caprice of his spouse, and she made a vow not to suffer herself to be shorn unless she acquired by these means the five hundred maravedies needful to pay the Arabian physician who would give her father back his eyesight.

Then the Mayor raised his price from a hundred maravedies to a hundred and fifty, and afterwards to two hundred, and Maria continued her sweet smiling, shaking of the head and gestures, and every time that the Mayor bid higher and Maria feigned to be reluctant, she almost hoped that the Mayor would withdraw from his proposition, for the great grief it caused her to despoil herself of that precious ornament, notwithstanding that by means of it she might gain her father's health. Finally the Mayor, anxious to conclude the treaty, for he saw the stirring of the curtains, and knew by them the anxiety and state of mind of the listener, closed by saying—

"Go to, hussy, I will give thee five hundred maravedies, see, once and for all, if thou canst agree to these terms."

"Be it so," replied Maria, sighing as if her soul would

flee from her flesh with these words—"be it so, so long that nobody doth know that I remain bald."

"I will give my word for it," said the Mayoress, stepping from behind the curtains with a pair of sharp shears in her hands and a wrapper over her arm.

When Maria saw the scissors she turned as yellow as wax, and when they told her to sit down on the sacrificial chair, she felt herself grow faint and had to ask for a drink of water ; and when they tied the wrapper round her throat it is related that she would have immediately torn it asunder if her courage had not failed her. And when at the first movement of the shears she felt the cold iron against her skull, I tell you it seemed to her as if they were piercing her heart with a bright dagger. It is possible that she did not keep her head still for a moment while this tonsuring was taking place ; she moved it in spite of herself, now to one side, now to another, to flee from the clipping scissors, of which the rude cuts and the creaking axis wounded her ears. Her posture and movements, however, were of no avail to the poor shorn maiden, and the pertinacious shearer, with the anxiety and covetousness of a pregnant woman satisfying a caprice, seized the hair well, or ill, by handsful, and went on bravely clipping, and the locks fell on to the white wrapper, slipping down thence till they reached the ground.

At last the business came to an end, and the Mayoress, who was beside herself with joy, caressingly passed the palm of her hand again and again over the maid's bald head from the front to the back, saying—

"By my mother's soul, I have shorn you so regularly and close to root, that the most skilful barber could not have shorn you better. Get up and braid the hair while my husband goes to get the money and I your clothes, so that you can leave the house without any one perceiving it."

The Mayor and Mayoress went out of the room, and

"AT THE FIRST MOVEMENT OF THE SHEARS . . . IT SEEMED TO HER AS IF THEY WERE PIERCING HER HEART WITH A BRIGHT DAGGER."

Maria, as soon as she found herself alone, went to look at herself in a mirror that hung there; and when she saw herself bald she lost the patience she had had until then, and groaned with rage and struck herself, and even tried to wrench off her ears, which appeared to her now outrageously large, although they were not so in reality. She stamped upon her hair and cursed herself for having ever consented to lose it, without remembering her father, and just as if she had no father at all. But as it is a quality of human nature to accept what cannot be altered, poor angry Maria calmed down little by little, and she picked up the hair from the ground and bound it together and braided it into great ropes, not without kissing it and lamenting over it many times. The Mayor and the Mayoress returned, he with the money and she with the every-day clothes of Maria, who undressed and folded her white robe in a kerchief, put on her old gown, hid herself with her shawl to the eyes, and walked, moaning, to the house of the Moor, without noticing that the man with the hood over his head was following behind her, and that when she, in a moment of forgetfulness, lowered her shawl through the habit she had of displaying her tresses, her bald head could be plainly seen. The Moor received the five hundred maravedies with that good will with which money is always received, and told Maria to bring Juan Lanas to his house to stay there so long as there was any risk in the cure. Maria went to fetch the old man, and kept silence as to her shorn head so as not to grieve him, and whilst Juan remained the physician's guest, Maria durst not leave her home except after nightfall and then well enveloped; this, however, did not hinder her being followed by the muffled-up man.

One evening the Moor told her in secret that the next morning he would remove the bandages from Juan's eyes. Maria went to bed that night with great rejoicing, but thought to herself that when her father saw her (which would be with no little pleasure) he would be pleased three or four times more if he could see her with the pretty head-dress which she used to wear in her native town. Amidst such cavillation she donned the next day her best petticoat and ribands to hie to the Arabian's house : and while she was sitting down to shoe herself she of a sudden felt something like a hood closing over her head, and, turning round, she saw behind her the muffled-up man of before, who, throwing aside his cloak, discovered himself to be the sword-cutler, Master Palomo, who, without speaking, presented Maria with a little Venetian mirror, in which she looked and saw herself with her own hair and garb in such wise that she wondered for a good time if it were not a dream that the Mayoress had shorn her. The fact was, that Master Palomo was a great crony of the old woman barber, and had seen in her house Maria's tresses on the very same afternoon of the morning in which he saw Maria was bald, and keeping silence upon the matter, had wheedled the old woman into keeping Maria's hair for him, and dressing for the Mayoress some other hair of the same hue which the crone had from a dead woman—a bargain by which the crafty old dame acquired many a bright crown. And the story relates that as soon as Maria regained her much-lamented and sighed-for hair by the hands of the gallant sword-cutler, the Master appeared to her much less ugly than before, and I do not know if it tells that from that moment she began to look on him with more favourable eyes, but i'sooth it is a fact that upon his asking her to accept his escort to the Moor's house, she gave her assent, and the two set out hand in hand, the maiden holding her head up free from mufflers. As they both entered the physician's apartment her father threw himself into Maria's arms, crying—

"Glory to God, I see thee now, my beloved daughter. How tall and beautiful thou art grown! Verily, it is worth while to become blind for five years to see one's daughter matured thus! Now that I see daylight again, it is only right that I should no longer be a burden to thee I shall work for myself, for as for thee it is already time for thee to marry."

"For this very purpose am I come," broke in at this opportune moment the silent sword-cutler; "I, as you will have already recognised by my voice, am your neighbour, Master Palomo. I love Maria, and ask you for her hand."

"Lack-a-day, Master, but your exterior is not very prepossessing. Howbeit, if Maria doth accept you, I am content."

"I," replied Maria, wholly abashed, and smoothing the false hair (which then weighed upon her head and heart like a burden of five hundred weight)—"I, so may God enlighten me, for I durst not venture to reply."

Palomo took her right hand without saying anything, and as he did so Maria looked at the Master's wrists, and observed the wristbands of his shirt, neatly embroidered, and with some suspicion and beating of her heart said to him—

"If you wish to please me, good neighbour, tell me by what sempstress is this work?"

"It is the work," replied the Master, jocularly—"the work of a pretty maiden who for five years has toiled for my person, albeit she hath not known it till now."

"Now I perceive," said Maria, "how that all the women who have come to give me linen to sew and embroider were sent by you, and that is why they paid me more than is customary."

The Master did not reply, but he smiled and held out his arms to Maria. Maria threw herself into them, embracing him very caressingly; and Juan himself said to the two—

"In good sooth, you are made one for the other."

"By my troth, my beloved one," continued the sword-cutler after a while, "if my countenance had only been more pleasing, I should not have been silent towards you for so many long days, nor would I have been content with gazing at you from afar. I should have spoken to you, you would have made me the confidant of your troubles, and I would have given you the five hundred maravedies for the cure of your good father." And whispering softly into her ear, he added, "And then you would not have passed that evil moment under the hands of the Mayoress. But if you fear that she may break the promise she made to you to keep silence as to your cropped head, let us, if it please you, set out for Seville, where nobody knows you, and thus——"

"No more," exclaimed Maria, resolutely throwing on the ground the hair, which Juan picked up all astonished; "Send this hair to the Mayoress, since it was for this and not for that of the dead woman that she paid so dearly. For I, to cure myself of my vanity, now make a vow, with your good permission, to go shorn all my life; such artificial adornments are little befitting to the wives of honest burghers."

"But rely upon it," replied the Master-cutler, "that as soon as it is known that you have no hair, the girls of the city, envious of your beauty, will give you the nickname of *Mariquita the Bald!*"

"They may do so," replied Maria, "and that they may see that I do not care a fig for this or any other nickname, I swear to you that from this day forth I will not suffer anybody to call me by another name than *Mariquita the Bald.*"

This was the event that rendered so famous throughout all Castille the beautiful daughter of good Juan Lanas, who in effect married Master Palomo, and became one of the most honourable and prolific women of the most illustrious city of Toledo.

Juan Eugenio Hartzenbusch (1806-1880).

PULPETE AND BALBEJA; OR, AN ANDALUSIAN DUEL.

THROUGH the little square of St. Anna, towards a certain tavern, where the best wine is to be quaffed in Seville, there walked in measured steps two men, whose demeanour clearly manifested the soil which gave them birth. He who walked in the middle of the street, taller than the other by about a finger's length, sported with affected carelessness the wide, slouched hat of Ecija, with tassels of glass beads and a ribbon as black as his sins. He wore his cloak gathered under his left arm; the right, emerging from a turquoise lining, exposed the merino lambskin with silver clasps. The herdsman's boots—white, with Turkish buttons,—the breeches gleaming red from below the cloak and covering the knee, and, above all, his strong and robust appearance, dark curly hair, and eye like a redhot coal, proclaimed at a distance that all this combination belonged to one of those men who put an end to horses between their knees and tire out the bull with their lance. He walked on, arguing with his companion, who was rather spare than prodigal in his person, but marvellously lithe and supple. The latter was shod with low shoes, garters united the stockings to the light-blue breeches, the waistcoat was cane-coloured, his sash light green, and jaunty shoulder-knots, lappets, and rows of buttons ornamented the camelite jacket. The open cloak, the hat drawn over his ear, his short, clean steps, and the manifestations in all his limbs and movements of agility and elasticity beyond trial plainly showed that in the arena, carmine cloth in hand, he would mock at the most frenzied of Jarama bulls, or the best horned beasts from Utrera.

I—who adore and die for such people, though the compliment be not returned—went slowly in the wake of their worships, and, unable to restrain myself, entered with them the same tavern, or rather eating-house, since there they serve certain provocatives as well as wine, and I, as my readers perceive, love to call things by their right name. I entered and sat down at once, and in such a manner as not to interrupt my Oliver and Roland, and that they might not notice me, when I saw that, as if believing themselves alone, they threw their arms with an amicable gesture round each other's neck, and thus began their discourse :—

"Pulpete," said the taller, "now that we are going to meet each other, knife in hand—you here, I there, . . . *one*, *two*, . . . *on your guard*, . . . *triz, traz*, . . . *have that*, . . . *take this and call it what you like* . . .—let us first drain a tankard to the music and measure of some songs.

"Señor Balbeja," replied Pulpete, drawing his face aside and spitting with the greatest neatness and pulchritude towards his shoe, "I am not the kind of man either for la Gorja or other similar earthly matters, or because a steel tongue is sheathed in my body, or my weasand slit, or for any other such trifle, to be provoked or vexed with such a friend as Balbeja. Let the wine be brought, and then we will sing; and afterwards blood—blood to the hilt."

The order was given, they clinked glasses, and, looking one at the other, sang a Sevillian song.

This done, they threw off their cloaks with an easy grace, and unsheathed their knives with which to prick one another, the one Flemish with a white haft, the other from Guadix, with a guard to the hilt, both blades dazzling in their brightness, and sharpened and ground enough for operating upon cataracts, much less ripping up bellies and bowels. The two had already cleft the air several times with the said lancets, their cloak wound round their left arm—first drawing closer, then back, now more boldly and in bounds—when Pulpete hoisted the flag for parley, and said—

"Balbeja, my friend, I only beg you to do me the favour

not to fan my face with *Juilon* your knife, since a slash might use it so ill that my mother who bore me would not know me, and I should not like to be considered ugly; neither is it right to mar and destroy what God made in His likeness."

"Agreed," replied Balbeja; "I will aim lower."

"Except—except my stomach also, for I was ever a friend to cleanliness, and I should not like to see myself fouled in a bad way, if your knife and arm played havoc with my liver and intestines."

"I will strike higher; but let us go on."

"Take care of my chest, it was always weak."

"Then just tell me, friend, *where* am I to sound or tap you?"

"My dear Balbeja, there's always plenty of time and space to hack at a man: I have here on my left arm a wen, of which you can make meat as much as you like."

"Here goes for it," said Balbeja, and he hurled himself like an arrow; the other warded off the thrust with his cloak, and both, like skilful penmen, began again tracing S's and signatures in the air with dashes and flourishes, without, however, raising a particle of skin.

I do not know what would have been the end of this onslaught, since my venerable, dry, and shrivelled person was not suitable for forming a point of exclamation between two combatants; and the tavern-keeper troubled so little about what was happening that he drowned the stamping of their feet and clatter of the tumbling stools and utensils by scraping street music on a guitar as loud as he could. Otherwise he was as calm as if he were entertaining two angels instead of two devils incarnate.

I do not know, I repeat, how this scene would have ended, when there crossed the threshold a personage who came to take a part in the development of the drama. There entered, I say, a woman of twenty to twenty-two years of age, diminutive in body, superlative in audacity

"INCREASED THEIR FEINTS, FLOURISHES, CURVETS, CROUCHINGS, AND BOUNDS."

and grace. Neat and clean hose and shoes, short, black flounced petticoat, a linked girdle, head-dress or mantilla of fringed taffeta caught together at the nape of her neck, and a corner of it over her shoulder, she passed before my eyes with swaying hips, arms akimbo, and moving her head to and fro as she looked about her on all sides.

Upon seeing her the tavern-keeper dropped his instrument, and I was overtaken by perturbation such as I had not experienced for thirty years (I am, after all, only flesh and blood); but, without halting for such lay-figures, she advanced to the field of battle.

There was a lively to-do here: Don Pulpete and Don Balbeja when they saw Doña Gorja appear, first cause of the disturbance and future prize for the victor, increased their feints, flourishes, curvets, onsets, crouching, and bounds —all, however, without touching a hair. Our Helen witnessed in silence for a long time this scene in history with that feminine pleasure which the daughters of Eve enjoy at such critical moments. But gradually her pretty brow clouded over, until, drawing from her delicate ear, not a flower or earring, but the stump of a cigar, she hurled it amidst the jousters. Not even Charles V.'s cane in the last duel in Spain produced such favourable effects. Both came forward immediately with formal respect, and each, by reason of the discomposure of his person and clothes, presumed to urge a title by which to recommend himself to the fair with the flounces. She, as though pensive, was going over the passage of arms in her mind, and then, with firm and confident resolution, spoke thus—

"And is this affair for me?"

"Who else should it be for? since I . . . since nobody—" they replied in the same breath.

"Listen, gentlemen," said she. "For females such as I and my parts, of my charms and descent—daughter of la Gatusa, niece of la Méndez, and granddaughter of la Astrosa—know that there are neither pacts nor compacts, nor any such futile things, nor are any of them worth a farthing. And when men challenge each other, let the knife do its work and the red blood flow, so as not to have my mother's daughter present without giving her the pleasure of snapping her fingers in the face of the other. If you pretend you are fighting for me, it's a lie; you are wholly mistaken, and that not by halves. I love neither of you. Mingalarios of Zafra is to my taste, and he and I look upon you with scorn and contempt. Good-bye, my braves; and, if you like, call my man to account."

She spoke, spat, smoothed the saliva with the point of her shoe, looking Pulpete and Balbeja full in the face, and went out with the same expressive movements with which she entered.

The two unvarnished braggarts followed the valorous Doña Gorja with their eyes; and then with a despicable gesture drew their knives across their sleeve as though wiping off the blood there might have been, sheathed them at one and the same time, and said together—

"'Through woman the world was lost, through a woman Spain was lost;'[1] but it has never been known, nor do ballads relate, nor the blind beggars sing,[2] nor is it heard in the square or markets, that two valiant men killed each other for another lover."

"Give me that fist, Don Pulpete:"

"Your hand, Don Balbeja."

They spoke and strode out into the street, the best friends in the world, leaving me all amazed at such whimsicality.

Estébanez Calderón (El Solitario) (1799–1867).

[1] Count Julian, governor of the provinces on both sides of the Straits of Gibraltar, to avenge himself on King Roderick for dishonouring his daughter, the famous La Cava (also called Florinda) of the Spanish ballads, invited (711 A.D.) the Moors into Spain.

[2] The street singers of Spain are invariably recruited from the large army of the blind.

SEVILLE.

WHO Naples fair has never seen
  never a marvel, sure, has seen;
Nor who to Seville's ever been
will ever wish to leave, I ween,
" See bella Napoli and die ! "
is the Neapolitan's cry.
The counsel the Sevillians give
is " Seville see and learn to live ! "

José Zorrilla (1817–1893).

AFTER THE BULL-FIGHT.

BEG pardon, Mr. Magistrate, but it wasn't as my husband tells it, for he stayed at home with Alfonsa and the baby, who was asleep, and he knew nothing about what happened."

" Then, do you tell me how it happened."

" I, sir? Well, you see, your Worship, I'm an honest woman and don't know how to explain myself well; but that gentleman there is my husband, and his conduct is such as your Honour sees, always drunk and out of work."

" Come to the point."

" Well, I'm coming; the cause of it all is a friend of the family and very intimate, as every one knows, and they call him Malgesto, and he can thrust a banderilla[1] into the morning star, much less into a bull; well, as I was saying, the same had told me: 'Paca, I won't have my lady

---

[1] A stick about a foot in length, wound round with gay ribbon or strips of coloured paper, and with a barbed dart at the point. The great feat is to stick a pair of banderillas, at one and the same time, one in each side of the bull, just above the shoulder.

friends look at el Chato, and if I see them do it, I'll cut off the little nose he has left.' All right!" said I, "but as you see, your Lordship or your Worship, taste is taste, and in no catechism have I seen it called a sin to look at somebody ; so la Curra, who evil tongues say is Malgesto's wife, and I paid no attention, you see, and . . ."

"Go on, you went to the bull-fight with the other man."

"That's just it, since he hired a fly and took me and la Curra, so that we might not go alone, and everybody would have done the same, and I . . ."

"To the point, to the point."

"The point is a needle's point, as one says, for take my word for it, the other from the arena never takes his eyes off us the whole time, and he placed the darts in a cross, and cursed them with gestures towards us, from which Heaven deliver us."

"But at last . . . "

"At last the last bull was despatched as usual, and we all went away in peace and the grace of God, when as we were going out el Chato disappeared somehow, and I who expected to meet him at the door of the fly, who do you think I met? nobody more nor less than the banderillero, who said, 'Ungrateful woman, is this how you obey my orders?' I said to him . . . but no, I said nothing to him then, as if I were afraid, but I just shrugged my shoulders, and I don't know if I did anything else. He answered nothing, except two or three oaths and a little blasphemy, and then seizing la Curra, he lifted her violently into the cab, and then he pushed me in, saying : 'If you don't go in I'll kill el Chato'; and I, you see, your Honour, I'm a decent woman, and don't want anybody's death."

"And so what did you do?"

"What could I do? I got in."

"And afterwards?"

"Afterwards came the row, for la Curra began to grumble, and so did I, he to keep us quiet gave us each two or three cuffs; and then we began to call him names and call each other names, for your Honour knows defence is only natural; to finish up, the horse took fright and nearly upset us; but at last we got out in the Calle del Barquillo; he set off running, la Curra after him, and that's the last I've seen of them."

"So that you have nothing more to allege?"

"Nothing more."

"And you swear to this?"

"I swear that I am a respectable woman, incapable of scandalous behaviour, though at times a poor female can't help . . . but now I want to complain to your Worship, for I too have my wrongs."

"Let us hear them."

"In the first place I complain of all my neighbours, for they have stolen all I had in the house, inside and outside."

"And how can you prove?"

"I can prove the things are gone, which is the principal thing; secondly, I complain of my husband, who doesn't protect me in my danger; thirdly, I complain of la Curra for fourteen scratches and ten pinches, not to mention some kicks; besides this I complain of the policeman, who took me to prison only because I pulled a face at him on St. Anthony's day,[1] when he tried to make love to me; lastly, I complain of your Worship, who are Justice of the Peace for this ward, and——"

"Silence, you baggage, or by Heavens I'll put a gag in your mouth which it won't be so easy to shake off."

* * *

[1] San Antonio is the patron saint of animals (St. Anthony and his pig), and reference to this saint is a favourite Spanish jest. To tell a youth his saint's day is St. Anthony is equal to saying, "You are a donkey."

"What is it, constable?"

"Notice has just been brought, sir, that two men have been fighting with knives in front of Mother Alfonsa's tavern, and are both badly wounded."

"Who are they?"

"El Chato and Malgesto."

"*Scenes in Madrid.*"   *Mesonero Romanos (El Curioso Parlante)* (1803-1882).

DELIGHTS OF A MADRID WINTER.

NO, sir, you cannot deny that the best season of the year is winter. The theatres fill up. Gastronomists return to the juicy oyster; and as soon as it begins to freeze still their appetites with the tasty sea-bream. The crown ministers can infringe the laws with impunity, fearless of tumults and insurrections, for the people's blood does not boil as in the month of July, and patriots prefer roasting chestnuts and toasting themselves over the brazier to haranguing in rain and snow. The shoeblacks dance with joy, for the mud is all in their favour. The doctors make their fortunes with colds and lung diseases. The apothecaries sell cough lozenges to their hearts' content. The maid-servants make a new conquest every day of the Savoyards who cross the Pyrenees to clean out our chimneys and purses with their monkeys and hurdy-gurdies. But besides these and other votaries, who have powerful reasons for liking winter, there are other admirers of this season dubbed *rigorous* by the ignorant vulgar. These devotees are the only really intelligent beings, and nobody will be able to deny they are right, when they patent the advantages of the months of November, December, and January over those of May, June, and July.

The monotony of summer is insipid. The sun shines upon everything with the very same rays. The flowers unceasingly diffuse the identical scent. The country is always green. ... It is unsupportable, horrrible! The votaries of summer say that all this makes the little birds charm with their trills and warbles every heart sensible to the delights of harmony. And we defenders of winter reply, who can compare the feeble song of the timid nightingale to the animated and piercing duets intoned by enamoured cats on our roofs in January? And the rain? Can anything be more delicious than rain? Oh, how I rave for the rain! Let us talk about the rain!

Some people say the rain is monotonous. Ignorant idiots! Let them apply that epithet to the sun, but the rain—monotonous? Bah! Could anybody adduce anything more varied and agreeable than rain? Clouds, mists, dew, hail, drizzle, showers, snow-storms ... what a charming mosaic of precious things!

Is there a more sublime spectacle than a shower? ... especially when contemplated from behind a well-glazed window? When the cataracts of heaven are opened on Sundays, it is worth while hiring a balcony in the Puerta del Sol. Those who have been so imprudent as to sally out without their wife and umbrella, recognise the advantage of the latter article over the former. But what a pleasing sight is the picturesque group of a married pair and their little children under the protection of one umbrella! And when the crystalline rain is accompanied by a strong sou'-wester, which the most impermeable of taffety cannot resist—that boisterous blast which removes hats and wigs. ... oh, then the respectable couple who have issued forth to air their Sunday-best present a marvellous and really romantic spectacle. The husband, fearful for his precious umbrella abandons the arm of his better-half, and presses his feet firmly to the ground to save the article in question, for the wind has turned it inside out like a stocking, and seems desirous of snatching it from his hands, in the same way that it has whirled off his hat just as a flower-pot falls from one of the houses and smashes his skull. The modest spouse pays no attention either to her husband's catastrophe, or to the gusts or downpour, but thinks only of her angelical prudicity, and how she may best avoid making a display of her person, for the wind against which she is struggling marks out all her contour, seeming to take a pleasure in exposing to the spectators the most hidden curves of his victim.

But I should never end if I gave a minute description of all the fascinations of my favourite season. I have said enough about the beauties of rain. In another article I hope to illustrate the pleasures of the cold, the charm of chilblains, and particularly all that's heroic in cerebral rheums, fully persuaded that once the reasons upon which I base my opinions are read, all my readers will agree with me that there is nothing to be compared with the delights of winter.

Wenceslao Ayguals de Izco.

IN THE EARLIER DAYS OF PHOTOGRAPHY.

"I TELL you it's not good at all," vociferated a newly-elected parliamentary representative of some rural locality. "Why my constituency wouldn't recognise me in that portrait. It's detestable!"

"It's excellent!" replied the exasperated photographer. "There's not a better photographer than myself in Madrid."

"I don't doubt it; but it's clear you have not been successful with me."

"But what's the matter with it?"

"The matter? ... Look at me! ... Haven't I two eyes?"

"Certainly."

"Well, in the photograph there's only one."

"But ..."

"Haven't I two ears?"

"Of course, but ..."

"Well, you've only given me one too."

"But you are taken in profile. ..."

"Tut, tut, tut. ... Do you take me for a simple rustic? However much I placed myself in profile, does that prevent my having two eyes and two ears?"

(*Aside*) "And very long ones. ..." (*Aloud*) "But ..."

"Again, is my neck black?"

"That is the shade. ..."

"No imputations, sir! there's nothing shady in me or my political life, and in my district they will tell you who I am; and if, though I am mayor, I never served my two years in the militia, why ..."

"But the photograph, the photograph!"

"The photograph is not like me."

"Then you won't take it?"

"No, sir."

"Good; then I shall put it in the window, with the inscription, 'The original of this is a cheat.'"

"You can do it. ..."

"Everybody who knows you ..."

"Who would recognise me? ... My electors know perfectly well that I have two eyes and two ears."

"Then go, sir, in Heaven's name."

'And to think that people say photography is so true to life!" growled, as he departed, this father of his country.

"Number 25," cried the manservant, putting his head in at the door of the waiting-room.

And Number 25, who is not a bad-looking lady, passes through the corridor and enters the studio.

The photographer bows, and the following conversation begins:—

"Sir," said the lady, "my happiness lies in your hands."

"I am very pleased, I'm sure; but I don't quite understand. . . ."

"I am a single lady, sir, as yet single. . . ."

"Been so long?"

"What?"

"I beg your pardon, I mean . . . I'm at your service."

"I must tell you that a gentleman I do not love wants to marry me perforce. . . . He resides at Havana, and I do not wish to have my husband so far away."

"I understand."

"Now, tell me, if a man persisted in marrying you from Havana . . ."

"The hypothesis is not admissible, ma'am."

"Ah, true! well, if a woman . . ."

"There are matters, madam, in which the person interested can alone . . ."

"It is true; for this reason, wishing at all costs to break off the projected marriage, I have determined to send my likeness to my suitor."

"Your looks, ma'am, will captivate him more than ever."

"That's why; . . . I wish my likeness not to be my likeness: I want to come out ugly, very ugly."

"That's impossible, madam; photography always tells the truth."

"Do you refuse?"

"Decidedly. Even if I tried you would not come out ugly."

"That's what my cousin the lieutenant says."

"And he's right."

"But I must carry out my plan, and if you will not do it

I shall go to a photographer I saw in the Calle de Francia, where some hideous women are exhibited."

"As you like, madam."

The lady withdraws, and the manservant calls out, "Number 26."

Number 26 is a stalwart country bumpkin in a russet suit, who, after entering the studio, is asked if he desires his photograph on a card or on glass.

"I want those that cost twelve reals by the notice," says he.

"Good. Sit down in that chair."

"But it must be exactly like me; I give you warning."

"You will see, sir."

"And I must appear in the fancy dress I wear at home in our village for the Carnival."

"Have you brought it with you?"

"No; ought I to have?"

"Most certainly."

"Take me now, and the first time I come to Madrid again I'll bring the dress."

"Impossible!"

"Well, I am surprised; to think that . . ."

"Come, come, it's getting late, and other people are waiting for me." [*Exit bumpkin.*

"Number 27."

"*Viaje crítico alrededor de la Puerta del Sol.*"
M. Ossorio y Bernard.

THE OLD CASTILIAN.

SINCE I have grown older I very seldom care to change the order of my way of living, which has now been settled a long time, and I base this repugnance upon the fact that I have never for a single day abandoned my Lares to break my system without being overtaken by a most sincere repentance as the presumption of my deluded hopes. Nevertheless a remnant of the old-fashioned courtesy adopted by our forefathers in their intercourse obliges me at times to accept certain invitations, which to refuse would be rudeness, or at least a ridiculous affectation of delicacy.

Some days ago I was walking through the streets in search of material for my articles. Buried in my thoughts, I surprised myself several times, laughing like a poor wretch at my own fancies, and mechanically moving my lips. A stumble or so reminded me now and again that to walk on the pavements of Madrid it is not the best of circumstances to be either poet or philosopher; more than one malicious smile, more than one look of wonder from the passers-by, made me reflect that soliloquies should not be made in public; and when turning corners not a few collisions with those who turned them as heedlessly as I made me recognise that the absent-minded are not among the number of elastic bodies, much less among glorious and impassable beings. Such being my frame of mind, imagine my sensations upon receiving a horrible smack which a huge hand attached (it seemed to me) to a brawny arm administered to one of my shoulders, which unfortunately bear not the slightest resemblance to those of Atlas!

Not wishing to make it understood that I would not recognise this energetic way of announcing one's self, nor to rebuff the goodwill, which doubtless wished to show itself to be more than mediocre by leaving me crooked for the rest of the day, I was merely about to turn round to see who was so much my friend as to treat me so badly. But my Old Castilian is a man who, when he is joking, does not stop half-way. What? my reader will ask. He gave further proofs of his intimacy and affection? He clasped his hands tightly over my eyes from behind, crying out, "Who am I?" bubbling over with delight at the success of his pretty trick. "Who you are? A brute," I was about to reply; but I suddenly remembered who it might be, and substituted the words, "It's Braulio." Upon hearing me he loosened his hands, held his sides for laughter, disturbing the whole street, and making us both very conspicuous.

"Good, good! How did you recognise me?"

"Who could it be but you? . . ."

"Well, so you've come from your dear Biscay?"

"No, Braulio, I have not come?"

"Always the same merry humour. What does it matter? It's a way we have of talking in Spain. . . . Do you know it's my birthday to-morrow?"

"I wish you many happy returns of the day."

"Oh, no formalities between us; you know I'm a plain fellow and an Old Castilian, and call a spade a spade : consequently I require no compliments from you, but consider yourself invited ——"

"To what?"

"To dine with me."

"Impossible."

"You must."

"I cannot," I insist, trembling.

"You can't?"

"Very many thanks——"

"Thanks? Very well, my dear friend; as I'm not the Duke of F., or Count P., of course——"

Who can resist an attack of this kind? Who cares to appear proud? "It is not that, but——"

"Well, if it's not that," he breaks in, "I shall expect you at two. We dine early at my house—Spanish style. I expect a lot of people; there will be the famous improvisor X.; T. will sing after dinner in his usual first-rate style; and in the evening J. will play and sing some trifles."

This consoled me somewhat, and I had to give way. "Everybody," said I to myself, "has an evil day sometimes.

In this world, if one wishes to preserve friends, one must endure their civilities."

"You won't fail, unless you want to quarrel with me?"

"I shall not fail," I said in a lifeless voice and low spirits, like a fox vainly revolving in the trap in which it has allowed itself to be caught.

"Then good-bye till to-morrow," and he gave me a parting slap.

I watched him go as the sower watches the decreasing cloud of his seed, and remained wondering how one should take such adverse and fatal friendships.

* * * * * *

Two o'clock arrived. As I knew my friend Braulio, I did not think it advisable to make myself too fine for his party; that, I am sure, would have annoyed him; nevertheless I could not dispense with a light frock-coat and a white pocket-handkerchief as essential for such birthday festivities. Above all, I dressed myself as slowly as possible, like the wretched criminal confessing at the foot of the gallows, who would like to have committed a hundred more sins the which to confess in order to gain more time. I was invited at two, and I entered the state-parlour at half-past two.

I will not dwell on the ceremonious calls made before dinner-time by an infinite number of visitors, among which were not least all the officials of his department with their spouses and children, their cloaks, umbrellas, galoshes, and house-dogs; I will be silent as to the foolish compliments paid to the head of the family on his birthday, nor describe the monstrous circle which was formed in the parlour by the assembly of so many heterogeneous people, discoursing upon how the weather was about to change, and how the winter is generally colder than the summer. Let us come to the point: four o'clock struck, and we, the invited guests, found ourselves alone. Unluckily for me, Señor X., who was to have entertained us, being a connoisseur of this class of invitation, had had the good idea to fall sick that morning; the celebrated T. found himself opportunely compromised by another invitation, and the young lady who was to sing and play so well was hoarse to such a degree that she was appalled lest a single word should drop from her lips, while she had a rag round one of her fingers. Alas, for my beguiled expectations!

"I suppose all who are to dine are here," exclaimed Don Braulio. "Let us go to table, my dear."

"Wait a bit," replied his wife in a loud whisper. "Such a lot of callers prevented my being in the kitchen, and . . ."

"But, look, it's five o'clock . . ."

"Dinner will be ready in a moment . . ."

It was five o'clock when we sat down.

"Ladies and gentleman," said our amphitryon, as we staggered into our respective chairs, "I insist upon your making yourselves quite at home; we don't stand upon ceremony in my house. Oh, Figaro! I want *you* to be quite comfortable; you are a poet, and besides, these gentlemen who know how intimate we are will not be offended if I make an exception of you; take off your coat: it won't do to stain it."

"Why should I stain it?" I replied, biting my lips.

"Oh, that's all right; I'll lend you a loose jacket; I'm sorry I haven't one for everybody."

"I'd sooner not, thank you."

"Nonsense! My jacket! Here it is; it will be a little large for you!"

"But, Braulio . . ."

"You must have it—bother etiquette!" and he thereupon pulled off my coat himself, *velis nolis*, and buried me in a great striped jacket, through which only my feet and head protruded, and the sleeves of which would probably not permit me to eat. I thanked him; he thought he was doing me a favour.

The days upon which my friend has no visitors he contents himself with a low table, little more than a cobbler's bench, because he and his wife, as he says, what should they want more? From this little table he carries his food, like water drawn up a well, to his mouth, where it arrives dripping after its long journey; for to imagine that these people keep a proper table and eat comfortably every day in the year is to expect too much. It is easy, therefore, to conceive that the installations of a large table for a dinner-party was an event in that house, so much so that a table at which scarcely eight people could have eaten comfortably had been considered capable of sitting the whole fourteen of us. We had to sit sideways with one shoulder towards the dinner, and the elbows of the guests entered on intimate relationship with each other in the most confiding fashion possible. They put me as in a place of honour between a child five years old, raised on some cushions, which I had to arrange every minute, as the natural restlessness of my youthful neighbour caused them to slip, and one of those men that occupy in this world the room of three, whose corpulency rose from the basis of the armchair (the only one) in which he was sitting as from the point of a needle. The table-napkins which we silently unfolded were new, for they were just as little commodities of daily use, and were pulled by these good gentlemen through a button-hole of their frock-coats to serve as intermediary bodies between the sauces and their broadcloth.

"You will have to do penance, gentlemen," exclaimed our amphitryon as soon as he had sat down.

"What ridiculous affectation if untrue," said I to myself; "and if it is true, what folly to invite one's friends to do penance." Unfortunately it was not long before I knew that there was in that expression more truth than my good Braulio imagined. Interminable and of poor taste were the compliments with which, upon passing and receiving each dish, we wearied one another. "Pray help yourself." "Do me the favour." "I couldn't think of it." "Pass it on to the lady." "Ah, that's right." "Pardon me." "Thank you."

"No ceremony, gentlemen," exclaimed Braulio, and was the first to dip his spoon into his plate.

The soup was followed by an olla, an assortment of the most savoury impertinences of that most annoying but excellent dish; here was some meat, there some green stuff; here the dried beans,[1] there the ham; the chicken to the right, the bacon in the middle, and the Estremaduran sausage to the left. Then came some larded veal, upon which may the curse of Heaven alight, and after this another dish, and another and another and another, half of which were brought over from an hotel, which will suffice to excuse our praising them, the other half made at home by their own maid and a Biscayan wench, a help hired for this festivity, and the mistress of the house, who on such occasions is supposed to have a hand in everything, and can consequently superintend nothing properly.

"You must be indulgent with this dish," said the latter of some pigeons, "they are a little burnt."

"But, my dear . . ."

"I only left them for a moment, and you know what servants are."

"What a pity this turkey was not half an hour longer before the fire! It was put down too late. And don't you think that stew is a little smoked?"

"What can you expect? A woman can't be everywhere at once."

"Oh, they're excellent!" we all exclaimed, leaving the pieces on our plates—"delicious!"

"This fish is bad."

"Well, they said in the office of the fresh fish delivery that it had only just arrived; the man there is so stupid!"

[1] Garbanzos—chick-peas.

"Where does this wine come from?"

"Now there you're wrong, for it's . . ."

"Detestable."

These short dialogues were accompanied by a number of furtive glances from the husband to acquaint his wife of some negligence, and both tried to give us to understand that they were quite at home in all those formulæ which in similar cases are reputed correct, and that all the blunders were the fault of the servants, who can never learn to wait. But these omissions were so numerous, and looks were of such little avail, that the husband had recourse to pinches and kicks, and his wife, who, until the present, had barely succeeded in rising superior to her spouse's persecution, now became inflamed in the face, and had tears in her eyes.

"Dear madam, do not distress yourself about such trifles," said her neighbour.

"Ah! I assure you I shall not do this kind of thing in the house again; you don't know what it means; another time, Braulio, we'll dine at the hotel, and then you'll not have . . ."

"You, madam, shall do what I . . ."

"Braulio! Braulio!"

A terrible storm was about to burst; however, all the guests vied with each other in settling these disputes born of the desire to demonstrate the greatest refinement, and of which not the smallest components were Braulio's mania, and the concluding remark which he again directed to the assembly with regard to the inutility of ceremony, by which he understood being properly served and knowing how to eat. Is there anything more ridiculous than those people who wish to pass for refined in the depths of the crassest ignorance of social usage, and who, to favour you, forcibly oblige you to eat and drink, and will not allow you to do what you like? And why are there people who only care to eat with a little more comfort on birthdays?

To add to all this, the child to my left violently knocked against a dish of ham and tomatoes a saucer of olives, of which one hit one of my eyes, and prevented me seeing clearly for the rest of the day; the stout gentleman to my right had taken the precaution to heap up on the cloth by the side of my bread the crumbs of his own and the bones of the birds which he had picked; and the guest opposite me, who piqued himself on his carving, had taken upon himself to make the autopsy of a capon, or cock, for nobody knew which, and whether by reason of the advanced age of the victim, or the lack of anatomical science of the executioner, the joints would not sever.

"This bird has no joints!" exclaimed the poor wretch, the drops of perspiration running down his face from his struggles, "for the carver is the labourer who digs that I may eat," and then a wonderful occurrence took place. Upon one of the attacks the fork, as if in resentment, slipped on the animal, which, thus violently despatched, took a flight as in its happier days, and then quietly alighted on the tablecloth, as on a roost in the poultry yard.

The fright was general, and the alarm reached its climax when a sauce-boat, impelled by the bird's wild career, upset, splashing my snow-white shirt. At this point the carver rose hastily, with a mind to chase the fugitive fowl, and as he precipitated himself upon it, a bottle to the right, which he knocked with his arm, abandoning its perpendicular position, poured out an abundant stream of Valdepeñas [1] over the capon and the cloth. The wine ran; the uproar increased; salt was abundantly sprinkled on the top of the wine to save the cloth; to save the table a napkin was inserted below the cloth, and an eminence arose on the site of so many ruins. A terrified maid-servant, who was bidden bear away the capon, now reposing in its own gravy, tilted the dish as she lifted it over me, and an accursed

[1] A generous red wine.

"TOOK A FLIGHT AS IN ITS HAPPIER DAYS."

shower of grease descended like the dew upon the meadows to leave lasting traces on my pearl-grey pantaloons. The anguish and confusion of the girl are beyond bounds; she withdraws, unsuccessful in her excuses, and, turning round, collides with the waiter, who is carrying a dozen clean plates and a salver for the dessert wines, and the whole machine comes to the ground with the most horrible clatter and commotion.

"By St. Peter!" roars our host, and a mortal pallor diffused itself over his features, while a fire broke out on his wife's face. "But no matter; let us continue, friends," said he, calming down.

Oh, honest homes where a modest olla and a single dish constitute the daily happiness of a family, shun the perturbation of a birthday dinner-party! The custom of eating well and being well served every day can alone avert similar discomfiture.

Are there any more disasters? Alas, there are for my miserable self! Doña Juana, the lady with the black and yellow teeth, holds out to me from her plate and with her own fork a dainty bit, which I am bound to accept and swallow; the child diverts himself by shooting cherry-stones at the eyes of the assembly; Don Leandro makes me taste the delicious orange, which I had refused, squeezed into his glass, which preserves the indelible traces of his greasy lips; my fat friend is smoking, and makes me the flue of his chimney; finally, oh last of miseries! the clamour and uproar increase, voices already hoarse demand couplets and stanzas, and Figaro is the only poet present.

"You must." "It's for you to say something," they all shout. "Start him with the first line; let him compose a couplet for each of us." "I'll start him:

'To Don Braulio on this day.'"

"Gentlemen, for Heaven's sake!"

"There's no getting out of it."
"I've never improvised in my life."
"Don't play the bashful."
"I shall go."
"Lock the door. He sha'n't leave the room till he recites something."

And so I repeat some verses at last, and vomit absurdities, which they praise, and the smoke, the hubbub, and the purgatory increases.

Thank Heavens, I succeed in escaping from this new pandemonium. At last I again breathe the pure air of the street; there are now no more lunatics, no more Old Castilians around me.

"Ye gods, I thank you!" I exclaimed, breathing freely like a stag who has just escaped a dozen dogs and can barely hear their distant barks. "Henceforward I do not pray for riches, office, or honours. But deliver me from those houses in which a dinner-party is an event, in which a decent table is only laid for visitors, in which they think they are doing you a good turn while they are doing you a bad one, in which they are over-polite, in which they recite verses, in which there are children, in which there are fat men, in which, finally, there reigns the brutal frankness of the Old Castilians! If I fall again by similar temptations, may I ever lack roast beef, may beefsteaks vanish from this world, may timbales of macaroni be annihilated, may there be no turkeys in Perigueux, nor pies in Perigord, may the wines of Bordeaux dry up, and everybody but myself drink the delicious foam of champagne!"

Mariano José de Larra (*Figaro*) (1809-1837).

A DEMAGOGIC JOURNALIST.

ELEVEN was striking by the nearest clock ; and as the last stroke vibrated upon Don Liberato Plebista's tympanum an instantaneous electric commotion was transmitted from it to his brain, which made him hastily sit up in bed and begin to dress. He violently rubbed his eyes with his knuckles, which, together with the use of his pocket-handkerchief and four or five loud hollow coughs, sufficed to cause him to regain entire possession of his senses and natural powers, and shook him out of that kind of lethargy, or state of doze, which between a deep sleep and being wide awake occupies the function of a scruple.

He had fallen asleep with a fixed idea that he must rise early to write a long, forcible, and brilliant article, and seeing the sun already so advanced on its course, he jumped out of bed, and made towards his study in a rich dressing-gown and canvas slippers delicately embroidered by some feminine hand. He leaned back in an armchair before a solid mahogany writing-table, pulled the bell loudly three times by a silken rope; a footman appeared, who placed upon the table the silver brazier with some large red-hot pieces of charcoal ; and then, when he had demanded breakfast with an imperative manner, and the man had withdrawn, Don Liberato lit a fragrant Havana, seized it between his teeth, grasped the pen with his right hand, rested his brow on his left, and leaning his elbow on the desk and gently tapping his right foot on the carpet, as if to excite ideas by this slight motion, remained in this attitude for five minutes, at the end of which he put his pen to paper and began to write to the following effect :—

" The incarnate enemies of the unhappy people—those wicked and egoistic men, who live under the shadow of privileges (*Don Liberato smiled to himself*) and grow fat with the substance of the poor—take very good care in all their writings and perorations to speak of nothing but principles and political questions, more or less metaphysical and vague, astutely keeping silence when there is any reference to social questions, upon which is actually based the revolution, which in this our age agitates Spain, disturbs Europe, and threatens the world."

(*Liberato, savouring the sonority of this rounded period, expelled from his cigar a dense cloud of azure and aromatic smoke . . . and continued writing.*)

" The priority of certain castes, the inequality with which property is distributed, the malign influence of priesthood, the tyranny of the rich and potential over the masses, and other thousand obstacles which oppose the felicity of the people, are those which must be destroyed, but with regard to which the partisans of abuses ever succeed in embroiling a discussion. You, unhappy day-labourers, unfortunate artisans, fathers of a numerous family, who to gain bread for your unfortunate offspring must abandon your narrow bed at break of day, . . . "

(*At this moment Don Liberato's clock struck a quarter to twelve, and the rays of the noonday sun, penetrating the green curtains, succeeded in bathing with light the richly furnished room of the journalist, who went on writing thus*) :—

" You will tell me if what interests you most is to discuss the preference for this or that method of electing representatives, or, on the contrary, the monstrous superiority of the potentate swimming in pleasures, of the sensual sybarite passing the night amidst the delicacies of the table, while you earn with the sweat of your brow the bread you must eat soaked in your tears."

(*The room door is opened, and Don Liberato's footman enters carrying an exquisite china tea-service, with a savoury dish, tea, milk, and buttered toast. Placing his burden on a small table, covered with a fine white embroidered cloth, he draws it in the greatest silence within reach of his master to the right of the desk, and retires stealthily, so as not to interrupt the sublime composition which continues multiplying sheets of paper thus wise*) :—

"Ye hungry and naked sons of the unfortunate Spanish people (*The writer throws away the stump of the Havana, and crams his mouth full with sweet-bread*) rear your naked and hungry children with anxiety and fatigue, and rear them to be the slaves of a rich, powerful, and proud aristocracy . . . "

(*Don Liberato again smiles to himself, and devours the rest of the sweet-bread.*)

"Rear them to till *their* land, to build *their* palaces, to weave *their* rich clothes, to wrench from the bowels of the earth the precious metals with which *their* ostentatious apparel is embroidered, and *their* ornaments and furniture covered in scandalous profusion."

(*The writer imbibes about a quart of tea, and attacks the buttered toast.*)

"Rear them that they may be dragged into misery with you, while the gilded chariots of the great, bearing their mistresses to shows and pageants, roll by, threatening to run over them, and bespattering them with mud . . . "

"Sir," said the Gallegan servant, entering timidly.

"What's the matter?" replied Don Liberato.

"They have brought this letter from the lady. It is urgent."

Having read the note, he replied thus—

"Say, 'very well'; and Domingo, remember to hire a carriage for this evening at five sharp: and I can't see anybody now, I must get on with my writing."

"This, this is the real evil of society, the pitiful state of which the present generation aspires to vary by a revolution as glorious as just. Let those monstrous fortunes be divided and subdivided, let them return in small capitals to the hands of the poor people who made them. Thus these terrible scenes of misery will not be seen which are augmented by the scandalous neglect of the Government for the widows and orphans of the best servants of the State."

" Sir ! "

" What is it now ? "

" The widow of that captain, who comes to see if you . . . "

" D—— you and the widow ; throw her downstairs, and don't open the door to every beggar."

" But there also came . . . "

" Who came ?—quickly."

" A man with cigars, the one who brought that other box."

" Here, take these twenty-five dollars, and go to the devil ! Let us see if I can finish my article."

" Meanwhile the vile aristocrats keep the people in the most humiliating servitude, and their condition and treatment is worse than that of cattle."

" Sir."

" If you don't shut that door, you brute, I'll throw the ink-bottle at your head."

" The habits of despotism which they have acquired through the course of centuries . . . "

" But, sir, only one word . . . "

(*Don Liberato hurls the salver at the poor Gallegan, and then continues scribbling with the greatest amenity until he comes to the following words*) :—

" And these errors, upheld by venal journalists . . . "

(*Domingo returns to the charge, preceded this time by a man of ugly appearance, who pays Don Liberato a large sum for a compilation. Having taken the money, and returned the receipt, he continues*) :—

" And who tells these calumniators that the defence

of the people is a propensity to anarchy ; that the severe censure of deeds of despotism is an act of rebellion ; and that the struggle against fanaticism is unbelief, impiety, and hatred of the sacred religion which we venerate more than they ? "

" May I go out, sir ? "

" No, no, hang you, and by heavens if you interrupt me again . . . "

" It is Sunday, sir, if you remember, and there is only late mass now."

" You must do without mass, I require you here."

" You must take it on your conscience, sir."

" And so I will, you rascal ; and I may take a stick too, and send you to hear mass in the infernal regions, that will stop your being such a confounded hypocrite."

*

With this last invective the scene ended between master and man, and with a few more lines the article of our journalist. The latter, after having dined sumptuously, passed the evening driving with his mistress, entered a café, where he spent a dollar or two, calling the waiter a scoundrel and stupid idiot ; went in the night to a gambling-house, where he parted with ten gold pieces, and returned to bed with the dawn, forming plans for heartrending articles on the lot of the poor, and furious declamations against the aristocracy, the rich, and the Government.

" *El Estudiante.*"   *Antonio Maria Segovia.*

A CAT CHASE DURING THE SIEGE OF GERONA.

"SISETA," I said suddenly, "it is a long time since I have seen Pussy, but I suppose she is wandering about somewhere with her three kittens."

"Oh!" she replied sorrowfully, "don't you know that Dr. Pablo has done for the whole family? Poor Pussy! He says the flesh is excellent; but I think I would rather die of hunger than eat her."

"What? he killed Pussy? I never heard about it; and the little kittens too?"

"I didn't like to tell you. The last few days that we have not been at home, the doctor often came in. One day he knelt down and implored me to give him something for his sick daughter, for he had no provisions left or money to buy them. While he was talking one of the kittens sprang on to my shoulder, and Don Pablo seized it quickly and put it into his pocket. The next day he came again and offered me his drawing-room furniture for another kitten, and without awaiting my answer went into the kitchen, then into the dark lobby, lay in wait and chased the kitten like a cat after a rat. I had to bathe the scratches on his face. The third perished in the same way, and then Pussy disappeared from the house, probably thinking she was not safe."

I was meditating upon the desertion of the poor animal, when Don Pablo suddenly presented himself. He was lean and cadaverous-looking, and had lost by physical and moral sufferings the kindly expression and gentle accent which distinguished him. His clothes were disorderly and torn, and he was carrying a large gun and a hunting-knife.

"Siseta," he said abruptly, and forgetting to greet me,

although we had not seen each other for several days. "I know now where that cunning cat is."

"Where is she, Don Pablo?"

"In the loft the other side of the yard where my corn and straw was stored when I kept a horse."

"Perhaps it is not our Pussy," said Siseta, in her generous desire to save the poor animal.

"Yes, it is, I tell you. She can't deceive me. The sly thing jumped in this morning through the pantry window and stole a kitten's leg hanging there. The audacity! and to eat her own children's flesh too. I must put an end to her, Siseta. I have already given you a good part of my furniture for the kittens. I have nothing valuable left except my books of medicine. Will you have them in exchange for the cat?"

"Don Pablo, I will take neither furniture nor books, catch Pussy, and, as we are reduced to such extremities, give part of her to my brothers."

"Good. Andres, do you dare chase the animal?"

"I don't think we want such a lot of arms," I replied.

"But I do. Let us go."

* * *

The doctor and I climbed to the loft, which we entered slowly and warily, for fear we might be attacked by the ravenous beast, probably maddened by hunger and the instinct of preservation. Don Pablo, lest our prey should escape us, closed the door from within and we remained in almost total darkness, since the feeble light which entered by a narrow slit of a window merely illumined the immediate obscurity. Gradually, however, our eyes got accustomed to the murkiness, and we saw that the room was lumbered with a lot of old and broken furniture; above our heads floated dense curtains of spider webs covered with the dust of a century. Then we began to look for the truant; but saw nothing nor in fact any indication of her presence. I expressed my doubt to Don Pablo; but he replied—

"Oh, she's here. I saw her enter a moment ago."

We moved some empty cases, threw on one side some bits of a broken armchair and a little barrel, and then saw a small body glide away and leap over the piled-up objects. It was Pussy. We could see in the dark background her two golden-green eyes, watching the movements of her persecutors with a fierce inquietude.

"Do you see her?" said the doctor. "Take my gun and shoot at her."

"No," I replied laughing. "It is not very easy to aim in the dark. The gun is of no good. Keep on one side and give me your hunting-knife."

The two eyes remained motionless in their first position, and that green and golden light, unlike the irradiation of any other gaze, or any gem, produced in me a strong impression of terror. I gradually distinguished the outline of the animal, and the grey and black stripes on her tawny coat multiplied in my eyes, increasing the size of her body till she had the proportions of a tiger. I was afraid, why deny it? and for a moment repented having undertaken such a difficult task. Don Pablo was more frightened than I, his teeth were chattering.

We held a council of war, the result of which was that we were to take the offensive; but when we had recovered a little valour, we heard a low rumbling, a noise between a dove's coo and a death-rattle, which announced Pussy's hostile disposition. The cat was saying to us in her language. "Come on, murderers of my children, I am ready for you!"

She had first adopted a sphinx-like posture, but now cowered together, her angular head resting on her fore paws, and her eyes changed, projecting a blue light in vertical rays. Her grim aspect seemed to glower at us. Then she raised her head, rubbed her paws over her face, cleaning her long whiskers, and took a few somersaults to descend to a nearer site, where she crouched in readiness to spring. The muscular force possessed by these animals in the articulation of their hind paws is immense, and she could have sprung upon us in one bound. I saw her looks were directed more especially towards Don Pablo than myself.

"Andres," he said, "if you are afraid, I shall attack her. It's disgraceful that such a little animal should make cowards like this of two men. Yes, Señora Pussy, we shall eat you."

It seemed as if the animal heard and understood the threatening words, for my friend had scarcely pronounced them when she precipitated herself with lightning speed upon him, alighting on his neck and shoulders. The struggle was short, and the cat had put into execution the whole of her offensive power, so that the rest of the combat could not be otherwise than favourable to us. I hastened to my ally's defence, and the animal fell to the ground, carrying away with her claws some particles of the good doctor's person and tattooing my right hand. She then doubled in different directions, but once as she sprang at me, I had the good luck to receive her on the point of the hunting-knife, which put an end to the unequal combat.

"The animal was more formidable than I thought," said Don Pablo, putting his hand to his beating heart.

"Well, doctor," said I, after a pause, "let us now divide the prey."

The doctor pulled a face of profound disgust, and, wiping the blood from his neck, said in the most aggressive tone I had heard from his lips—

"What's that about dividing? Siseta gave me the cat in exchange for my books. Do you know my daughter ate nothing yesterday?"

"Siseta and the children have also eaten nothing," I replied.

Don Pablo scratched his head, making ugly contractions with his mouth and nostrils—and taking the dead animal by the neck, said—

"Don't bother me, Andres. The children can live on any rubbish they pick up in the street; but my invalid needs better food; do me the favour not to touch the cat."

"Do you mean to say you won't divide the cat? Good, good," I said, and advanced towards him. Our hands met; we struggled for a short time and then the doctor fell and rolled along the floor, leaving me in full possession of our prey.

"Thief! thief!" he exclaimed. "Is this the way you rob me? Just wait a moment!"

I was picking up our victim to leave the loft. But the doctor ran, or rather leapt like a cat, to the gun, and aimed it full at me, crying with a hoarse and tremulous voice—

"Drop the cat, or I'll kill you."

*　　　*　　　*　　　　　　*

"Don Pablo," said I, "take the cat. You have become a wild beast."

Without reply, but showing the horrible agitation of his mind by a smothered groan, he seized the animal which I had hurled from me, and opening the door, disappeared.

Perez Galdos.

A WELL-WON DISH OF CHERRIES.

MANALET ran away, but he soon came back with a lot of other little boys, all barefoot, dirty, unkempt, and ragged, and amongst them his brother Badoret, with Gasparo pickapack, clinging tightly with arms and legs to his shoulders and waist. All seemed very pleased, especially Badoret, who was distributing cherries to his companions.

"Take one, Andres," said the boy, giving me a cherry. "How did you think I got them? Well, I'll tell you. I was going with Gasparo on my back down the calle del Lobo, when I saw open the gate of the Convent of the Capuchin Nuns, which is always shut. Gasparo would keep on asking me for bread and crying, and I gave him little slaps to make him keep quiet, telling him that if he wouldn't leave off I would tell his Excellency the Governor. But when I saw the convent gate open, I said to myself, 'there will be something to find here,' and I slipped in. I crossed the courtyard, and then entered the church and passed through the choir till I reached a long corridor with a lot of little rooms, and I didn't meet a soul. I looked carefully everywhere to see if I could get anything, but I only came across some candle-ends and two or three skeins of silk, which I began to chew to see if they gave any juice. I was thinking of returning to the street, when I heard behind me, '*Ss—t, Ss—t*,' as if somebody was calling me. I looked, but I saw nobody. Oh, how afraid I was, Andres! Down at the bottom of the corridor there was a huge print, in which was a devil with a long green tail. I thought it was the devil calling me, and began to run. But, oh dear! I could not find a door, and I went round and round that horrid corridor, and all the time, '*Ss—t!*' And then I heard some one say, 'Little boy, come here,' and I looked at the ceiling and the walls, until I at last saw behind some bars a white hand and a worn and wrinkled face. I was not afraid then, and went to it. The nun said to me, 'Come, don't be afraid, I have something to say to you.' I went close to the grating, and said to her, 'Pardon me, Señora, I thought you were the devil.'"

"Why, it must have been some poor sick nun who could not escape with the others."

"That's it. The lady said to me, 'Little boy, how did you come in here? God has sent you to do me a great service. All the sisters have gone away. I am ill and a cripple. They wanted to take me, but it grew late, and so they left me behind. I am very afraid. Is all the town burnt? Have the French entered? Just now, when I was half asleep, I dreamt that all the sisters had been beheaded in the slaughter-house, and that the French were eating them. Boy, would you venture to go, now at once, to the fort, and give this note to my nephew, Don Alonso Carrillo, captain of the regiment of Ultonia? If you do so, I will give you the dish of cherries you see here, and this half loaf.'

"Even if she hadn't offered them me I would have gone, you know. I seized the note, she told me where I could get out, and I ran towards the fort. Gasparo cried more than before, but I said to him, 'If you don't keep quiet, I'll put you in a cannon as if you were a ball, and shoot you away, and you'll go rolling amongst the French, who will cook you in a saucepan and eat you.'

"At last I reached the fort. What a lot of firing there! That down here is nothing to it. The cannon balls whizzed through the air like a flight of birds. And do you think I was afraid? Not I! Gasparo went on crying and screaming; but I showed him the flames bursting from the bombs, and the flashes from the powder-pans, and said, 'Look, how pretty! We are going to shoot cannons too now!'

"A soldier gave me a cuff to push me to one side, and I fell on a heap of dead, but I got up and went straight on. Then the Governor appeared, and grasping a large black banner he waved it in the air, and then he said that he would have the first coward hanged. What do you think of that? I went in front and shouted, 'Quite right, too!' Some soldiers told me to go away, and the women who were looking after the wounded began to abuse me, asking me why I had taken the baby there. What a crowd of sparks! They fell like flies, first one, then another. The French wanted to get in, but we wouldn't let them."

"What? You wouldn't?"

"Yes; the women and our men threw stones from the top of the wall at the scoundrels who wanted to climb them. I loosened Gasparo, putting him on the top of a box in which was some powder and cannon-balls, and I also began to throw stones. And what stones! I threw one which weighed at least six hundredweight, and hit a Frenchman, doubling him in two. You ought to have seen it. The French were many, and they wanted to do nothing else but come into the fort. You should have seen the Governor, Andresillo! Don Mariano, and I, we sprang in front . . . and always went where the soldiers were most hard pressed. I don't know what I did, but I did something, Andres. I could not see for the smoke, nor hear for the noise. Such terrible firing! Into your very ears, Andres. It makes one quite deaf. I began to shout, calling them blackguards, thieves, and telling them that Napoleon was a good-for-nothing. Maybe they didn't hear me for the noise, but I made them turn back and a-half. Rather! Well, Andres, not to tire you, I stayed there until they retreated. The Governor told me he was satisfied—no, he did not speak to me, he said it to the rest."

"But the letter."

"I looked for Captain Carrillo—I knew him by sight before—and I met him at last when all was over. I gave him the paper, and he gave me a message for the nun. Then, remembering Gasparo, I went to look for him where I had left him, but he wasn't there. I began to shout out, 'Gasparo, Gasparo!' but he didn't answer. At last I saw him under a gun carriage, rolled up like a little ball, with his fists in his mouth, looking between the spokes of the wheel, and a large tear in each eye. I put him on my back and ran to the convent. But now comes the best of it; as I was going along thinking of battles, and my head full of all I had seen, I forgot the message the Captain had given me for the nun. She scolded me, saying that I had torn up the letter, and wanted to deceive her, and that she couldn't think of giving me either the cherries or the bread she had promised. And then she began to grumble, and called me a bad boy and a beast. One of Gasparo's toes was bleeding, and the nun tied a rag round it; but the cherries —not a single one! At last all was settled, for Captain Carrillo came himself, and she gave me the cherries and the bread, and I ran out of the convent."

"Take the child home to your sister," I said, noticing that poor Gasparo's foot was still bleeding.

"I have kept some cherries for Siseta," he cried.

*   *

"Oh, I say, boys!" shouted Manalet, running back towards us, "the Governor is going through the town with a lot of people and banners; the ladies are singing in front, and the monks dancing, and the bishop smiling, and the nuns crying. Come along!"

And like a flock of birds the band of children ran down the street.

Gerona: "*Episodios Nacionales.*" *Perez Galdos.*

FIRST LOVE.

HOW old I was then? Eleven or twelve years? More probably thirteen, for before then is too early to be seriously in love; but I won't venture to be certain, considering that in Southern countries the heart matures early, if that organ is to blame for such perturbations.

If I do not remember well *when*, I can at least say exactly *how* my love first revealed itself. I was very fond— as soon as my aunt had gone to church to perform her evening devotions—of slipping into her bedroom and rummaging her chest of drawers, which she kept in admirable order. Those drawers were to me a museum; in them I always came across something rare or antique, which exhaled an archaic and mysterious scent, the aroma of the sandalwood fans which perfumed her white linen. Pincushions of satin now faded; knitted mittens, carefully wrapped in tissue paper; prints of saints; sewing materials; a reticule of blue velvet embroidered with bugles, an amber and silver rosary would appear from the corners: I used to ponder over them, and return them to their place. But one day—I remember as well as if it were to-day—in the corner of the top drawer, and lying on some collars of old lace, I saw something gold glittering. . . I put in my hand, unwittingly crumpled the lace, and drew out a portrait, an ivory miniature, about three inches long, in a frame of gold,

I was struck at first sight. A sunbeam streamed through the window and fell upon the alluring form, which seemed to wish to step out of its dark background and come towards me. It was a most lovely creature, such as I had never seen except in the dreams of my adolescence. The lady of the portrait must have been some twenty odd years; she was no simple maiden, no half-opened rosebud, but a woman in the full resplendency of her beauty. Her face was oval, but not too long, her lips full, half-open and smiling, her eyes cast a languishing side-glance, and she had a dimple on her chin as if formed by the tip of Cupid's playful finger. Her head-dress was strange but elegant; a compact group of curls plastered conewise one over the other covered her temples, and a basket of braided hair rose on the top of her head. This old-fashioned head-dress, which was trussed up from the nape of her neck, disclosed all the softness of her fresh young throat, on which the dimple of her chin was reduplicated more vaguely and delicately. As for the dress . . . I do not venture to consider whether our grandmothers were less modest than our wives are, or if the confessors of past times were more indulgent than those of the present; I am inclined to think the latter, for seventy years ago women prided themselves upon being Christianlike and devout, and would not have disobeyed the director of their conscience in so grave and important a matter. What is undeniable is, that if in the present day any lady were to present herself in the garb of the lady of the portrait, there would be a scandal; for from her waist (which began at her armpits) upwards, she was only veiled by light folds of diaphanous gauze, which marked out, rather than covered, two mountains of snow, between which meandered a thread of pearls. With further lack of modesty she stretched out two rounded arms worthy of Juno, ending in finely-moulded hands. . . when I say *hands* I am not exact, for, strictly speaking, only one hand could be seen, and that held a richly embroidered handkerchief.

Even to-day I am astonished at the startling effect which the contemplation of that miniature produced upon me, and how I remained in ecstasy, scarcely breathing, devouring the portrait with my eyes. I had already seen here and there prints representing beautiful women: it often happened that in the illustrated papers, in the mythological engravings of our dining-room, or in a shop-window, that a beautiful face, or a harmonious and graceful figure attracted my precociously artistic gaze; but the miniature encountered in my aunt's drawer, apart from its great beauty, appeared to me as if animated by a subtle and vital breath; you could see it was not the caprice of a painter, but the image of a real and actual person of flesh and blood. The warm and rich tone of the tints made you surmise that the blood was tepid beneath that mother-of-pearl skin. The lips were slightly parted to disclose the enamelled teeth; and to complete the illusion there ran round the frame a border of natural hair, chestnut in colour, wavy and silky, which had grown on the temples of the original. As I have said, it was more than a copy, it was the reflection of a living person from whom I was only separated by a wall of glass. . . . I seized it, breathed upon it, and it seemed to me that the warmth of the mysterious deity communicated itself to my lips and circulated through my veins. At this moment I heard footsteps in the corridor. It was my aunt returning from her prayers. I heard her asthmatic cough, and the dragging of her gouty feet. I had only just time to put the miniature into the drawer, shut it, and approach the window, adopting an innocent and indifferent attitude.

My aunt entered noisily, for the cold of the church had exasperated her catarrh, now chronic. Upon seeing me, her wrinkled little eyes brightened, and giving me a friendly tap with her withered hand, she asked me if I had been turning over her drawers as usual.

Then, with a chuckle—

"Wait a bit, wait a bit," she added, "I have something for you, something you will like."

And she pulled out of her vast pocket a paper bag, and out of the bag three or four gum lozenges, sticking together in a cake, which gave me a feeling of nausea.

My aunt's appearance did not invite one to open one's mouth and devour these sweets: the course of years, her loss of teeth, her eyes dimmed to an unusual degree, the sprouting of a moustache or bristles on her sunken-in mouth, which was three inches wide, dull grey locks fluttering above her sallow temples, a neck flaccid and livid as the crest of the turkey when in a good temper. . . . In short, I did not take the lozenges. Ugh! A feeling of indignation, a manly protest rose in me, and I said forcibly—

"I do not want it, I don't want it."

"You don't want it? What a wonder! You who are greedier than a cat!"

"I am not a little boy," I exclaimed, drawing myself up, and standing on tip-toes; "I don't care for sweets."

My aunt looked at me half good-humouredly and half ironically, and at last, giving way to the feeling of amusement I caused her, burst out laughing, by which she disfigured herself, and exposed the horrible anatomy of her jaws. She laughed so heartily that her chin and nose met, hiding her lips, and emphasising two wrinkles, or rather two deep furrows, and more than a dozen lines on her cheeks and eyelids; at the same time her head and body shook with the laughter, until at last her cough began to interrupt the bursts, and between laughing and coughing the old lady involuntarily spluttered all over my face. . . . Humiliated, and full of disgust, I escaped rapidly thence to my mother's room, where I washed myself with soap and water, and began to muse on the lady of the portrait.

And from that day and hour I could not keep my thoughts from her. As soon as my aunt went out, to slip into her room, open the drawer, bring out the miniature, and lose myself in contemplation, was the work of a minute. By dint of looking at it, I fancied that her languishing eyes, through the voluptuous veiling of her eyelashes, were fixed in mine, and that her white bosom heaved. I became ashamed to kiss her, imagining she would be annoyed at my audacity, and only pressed her to my heart or held her against my cheek. All my actions and thoughts referred to the lady; I behaved towards her with the most extraordinary refinement and super-delicacy. Before entering my aunt's room and opening the longed-for drawer, I washed, combed my hair, and tidied myself, as I have seen since is usually done before repairing to a love appointment. I often happened to meet in the street other boys of my age, very proud of their slip of a sweetheart, who would exultingly show me love-letters, photographs, and flowers, and who asked me if I hadn't a sweetheart with whom to correspond.

A feeling of inexplicable bashfulness tied my tongue, and I only replied with an enigmatic and haughty smile. And when they questioned me as to what I thought of the beauty of their little maidens, I would shrug my shoulders and disdainfully call them *ugly mugs*. One Sunday I went to play in the house of some little girl-cousins, really very pretty, and the elder of whom was not yet fifteen.

We were amusing ourselves looking into a stereoscope, when suddenly one of the little girls, the youngest, who counted twelve summers at most, secretly seized my hand, and in some confusion and blushing as red as a brazier, whispered in my ear—

"Take this."

At the same time I felt in the palm of my hand something soft and fresh, and saw that it was a rosebud with its green foliage. The little girl ran away smiling and casting a side-glance at me; but I, with a Puritanism worthy of Joseph, cried out in my turn—

"Take this!"

And I threw the rosebud at her nose, a rebuff which made her tearful and pettish with me the whole afternoon, and which she has not pardoned me even now, though she is married and has three children.

The two or three hours which my aunt spent morning and evening together at church being too short for my admiration of the entrancing portrait, I resolved at last to keep the miniature in my pocket, and went about all day hiding myself from people just as if I had committed a crime. I fancied that the portrait from the depth of its prison of cloth could see all my actions, and I arrived at such a ridiculous extremity, that if I wanted to scratch myself, pull up my sock, or do anything else not in keeping with the idealism of my chaste love, I first drew out the miniature, put it in a safe place, and then considered myself free to do whatever I wanted. In fact, since I had accomplished the theft, there was no limit to my vagaries ; at night I hid it under the pillow, and slept in an attitude of defence ; the portrait remained near the wall, I outside, and I awoke a thousand times, fearing somebody would come to bereave me of my treasure. At last I drew it from beneath the pillow and slipped it between my nightshirt and left breast, on which the following day could be seen the imprint of the chasing of the frame.

The contact of the dear miniature gave me delicious dreams. The lady of the portrait, not in effigy, but in her natural size and proportions, alive, graceful, affable, beautiful, would come towards me to conduct me to her palace by a rapid and flying train. With sweet authority she would make me sit on a stool at her feet, and would pass her beautifully moulded hand over my head, caressing my brow, my eyes, and loose curls. I read to her out of a big missal, or played the lute, and she deigned to smile, thanking me for the pleasure which my reading and songs gave her. At last romantic reminiscences overflowed in my brain, and sometimes I was a page, and sometimes a troubadour.

With all these fanciful ideas, the fact is, that I began to grow thin quite perceptibly, which was observed with great disquietude by my parents and my aunt.

"In this dangerous and critical age of development, everything is alarming," said my father, who used to read books of medicine, and anxiously studied my dark eyelids, my dull eyes, my contracted and pale lips, and above all, the complete lack of appetite which had taken possession of me.

"Play, boy ; eat, boy," he would say to me, and I replied to him dejectedly —

"I don't feel inclined."

They began to talk of distractions, offered to take me to the theatre ; stopped my studies, and gave me foaming new milk to drink. Afterwards they poured cold water over my head and back to fortify my nerves ; and I noticed that my father at table or in the morning when I went to his bedroom to bid him good morning, would gaze at me fixedly for some little time, and would sometimes pass his hand down my spine, feeling the vertebrae. I hypocritically lowered my eyes, resolved to die rather than confess my crime. As soon as I was free from the affectionate solicitude of my family, I found myself alone with my lady of the portrait. At last, to get nearer to her, I thought I would do away with the cold crystal. I trembled upon putting this into execution; but at last my love prevailed over the vague fear with which such a profanation filled me, and with skilful cunning I succeeded in pulling away the glass and exposing the ivory plate. As I pressed my lips to the painting and could scent the slight fragrance of the border of hair, I imagined to myself even more realistically that it was a living person whom I was grasping with my trembling hands. A feeling of faintness overpowered me, and I fell unconscious on the sofa, tightly holding the miniature.

When I came to my senses I saw my father, my mother, and my aunt, all bending anxiously over me; I read their terror and alarm in their faces: my father was feeling my pulse, shaking his head, and murmuring—

"His pulse is nothing but a flutter, you can scarcely feel it."

My aunt, with her claw-like fingers was trying to take the portrait from me, and I was mechanically hiding it and grasping it more firmly.

"But, my dear boy. . . . Let go, you are spoiling it!" she exclaimed. "Don't you see you are smudging it? I am not scolding you, my dear. . . . I will show it to you as often as you like, but don't destroy it; let go, you are injuring it."

"Let him have it," begged my mother, "the boy is not well."

"Of all things to ask!" replied the old maid. "Let him have it! And who will paint another like this . . . or make me as I was then? To day nobody paints miniatures . . . it is a thing of the past, and I also am a thing of the past, and I am not what is represented there!"

My eyes dilated with horror; my fingers released their hold on the picture. I don't know how I was able to articulate—

"You . . . the portrait . . . is you . . .?"

"Don't you think I am as pretty now, boy? Bah! one is better looking at twenty-three than at . . . than at . . . I don't know what, for I have forgotten how old I am!"

My head drooped and I almost fainted again; anyway, my father lifted me in his arms on to the bed, and made me swallow some tablespoons of port.

I recovered very quickly, and never wished to enter my aunt's room again.

Emilia Pardo Bazan (Nineteenth Century).

THE ACCOUNT BOOK.

A RURAL TALE.

GAFFER BUSCABEATAS was already beginning to stoop at the time when the events occurred which I am going to relate; for he was now sixty years old, and of these sixty years he had spent forty cultivating a garden bordering on the shore of La Costilla.

In the year in question he had cultivated in this garden some wonderful pumpkins, as large as the ornamental globes on the breastwork of some massive bridge, that at the time of our story were beginning to turn yellow, inside and out, which is the same as saying that it was the middle of June.

Old Buscabeatas knew by heart the particular form and the stage of maturity at which it had arrived of every one of these pumpkins, to each of which he had given a name, and especially of the forty largest and finest specimens, which were already crying out, "Cook me!" and he spent the days contemplating them affectionately, and saying in melancholy accents—

"Soon we shall have to part!"

At last, one evening, he made up his mind to the sacrifice, and marking out the best fruits of those beloved vines which had cost him so many anxieties, he pronounced the dreadful sentence—

"To-morrow," he said, "I shall cut from their stalks these forty pumpkins and take them to the market at Cadiz. Happy the man who shall eat of them!"

And he returned to his home with slow step and spent the night in such anguish as a father may be supposed to feel on the eve of his daughter's wedding-day.

"What a pity to have to part from my dear pumpkins!" he would sigh from time to time in his restless vigil. But presently he would reason with himself and end his reflections by saying, "And what else can I do but sell them? That is what I have raised them for. The least they will bring me is fifteen dollars!"

Judge, then, what was his consternation, what his rage and despair, on going into the garden on the following morning, to find that during the night he had been robbed of his forty pumpkins! Not to weary the reader, I will only say that his emotion, like that of Shakespeare's Jew, so admirably represented, it is said, by the actor Kemble, reached the sublimity of tragedy as he frantically cried—

"Oh, if I could but find the thief! If I could but find the thief!"

Poor old Buscabeatas presently began to reflect upon the matter with calmness, and comprehended that his beloved treasures could not be in Rota, where it would be impossible to expose them for sale without risk of their being recognised, and where, besides, vegetables bring a very low price.

"I know as well as if I saw them, that they are in Cadiz!" he ended. "The scoundrel! the villain! the thief must have stolen them between nine and ten o'clock last night, and got off with them at midnight on the freight-boat. I shall go to Cadiz this morning on the hour-boat, and it will surprise me greatly if I do not catch the thief there, and recover the children of my toil."

After he had thus spoken, he remained for some twenty minutes longer on the scene of the catastrophe, whether to caress the mutilated vines, to calculate the number of pumpkins that were missing, or to formulate a declaration of the loss sustained, for a possible suit; then, at about eight o'clock, he bent his steps in the direction of the wharf.

The hour-boat was just going to sail. This was a modest coaster which leaves Cadiz every morning at nine o'clock precisely, carrying passengers, as the freight-boat leaves Cadiz every night at twelve, laden with fruits and vegetables.

The former is called the hour-boat because in that space of time, and occasionally even in forty minutes, if the wind is favourable, it makes the three leagues which separate the ancient village of the Duke of Arcos from the ancient city of Hercules.

It was, then, half-past ten in the morning on the beforementioned day, when old Buscabeatas passed before a vegetable-stand in the market of Cadiz, and said to the bored policeman who was accompanying him—

"Those are my squashes! arrest that man!" and he pointed to the vendor.

"Arrest me!" cried the vendor, astonished and enraged. "These squashes are mine: I bought them!"

"You will have to prove that before the judge!" answered old Buscabeatas.

"I say No!"

"I say Yes!"

"Thief!"

"Vagabond!"

"Speak more civilly, you ill-mannered fellows! Decent men ought not to treat one another in that way!" said the policeman tranquilly, giving a blow with his closed fist to each of the disputants.

By this time a crowd had gathered, and there soon arrived also on the scene the inspector of public markets.

The policeman resigned his jurisdiction in the case to his Honour, and when this worthy official had learned all the circumstances relating to the affair, he said to the vendor majestically —

"From whom did you purchase those squashes?"

"From Gossip Fulano, a native of Rota," answered the person thus interrogated.

"It could be no one else!" cried old Buscabeatas. "He is just the one to do it! When his own garden, which is a very poor one, produces little, he takes to robbing the gardens of his neighbours!"

"But, admitting the supposition that forty pumpkins were stolen from you last night," said the inspector, turning to the old gardener and proceeding with his examination, "how do you know that these are precisely your pumpkins?"

"How?" replied old Buscabeatas. "Because I know them as well as you know your daughters, if you have any! Don't you see that they have grown up under my care? Look here: this one is called Roly-poly, this one Fat-cheeks, this one Big-belly, this one Ruddy-face, this

Manuela, because it reminded me of my youngest daughter."

And the poor old man began to cry bitterly.

"That may be all very well," replied the inspector; "but it is not enough for the law that you should recognise your pumpkins. It is necessary also that the authorities be convinced of the pre-existence of the article in dispute, and that you identify it with incontrovertible proofs; gentlemen, there is no occasion for you to smile—I know the law!"

"You shall see, then, that I will very soon prove to the satisfaction of everybody present, without stirring from this spot, that these pumpkins have grown in my garden!" said old Buscabeatas, to the no little surprise of the spectators of this scene. And laying down on the ground a bundle which he had been carrying in his hand, he bent his knees until he sat upon his heels, and quietly began to untie the knotted corners of the handkerchief.

The curiosity of the inspector, the vendor, and the chorus was now at its height.

"What is he going to take out of that handkerchief?" they said to themselves.

At this moment a new spectator joined the crowd, curious to see what was going on, whom the vendor had no sooner perceived than he exclaimed—

"I am very glad that you have come, Gossip Fulano! This man declares that the squashes which you sold me last night, and which are now here present, listening to what we are saying about them, were stolen. Answer, you!"

The newcomer turned as yellow as wax, and made a movement as if to escape, but the bystanders detained him by force, and the inspector himself ordered him to remain. As for Gaffer Buscabeatas, he had already confronted the supposed thief, saying to him—

"Now you are going to see something good."

Gossip Fulano, recovering his self-possession, answered—

"It is you who ought to see what you are talking about, for if you do not prove, as prove you cannot, your accusation, I shall have you put in prison for libel. These pumpkins were mine. I cultivated them, like all the others that I brought this year to Cadiz, in my garden, the Egido, and no one can prove to the contrary!"

"Now you shall see!" repeated old Buscabeatas, loosening the knots of the handkerchief and spreading out its contents on the ground.

And there were scattered over the floor a number of fragments of pumpkin stalks, still fresh and dripping sap, while the old gardener, seated on his heels and unable to control his laughter, addressed the following discourse to the inspector and the wondering bystanders.

"Gentlemen, have any of you ever paid taxes? If you have, you must have seen the big green book of the collector, from which he tears off your receipt, leaving the stub or end, so as to be able to prove afterward whether the receipt is genuine or not."

"The book you mean is called the account-book," said the inspector gravely.

"Well, that is what I have here—the account-book of my garden; that is to say, the stalks to which these pumpkins were attached before they were stolen from me. And in proof of what I say, look here! This stalk belongs to this pumpkin; no one can doubt it. This other—you can see for yourselves—belonged to this other. This is thicker—it must belong to this one. This to that one. This to that other."

And as he spoke he went fitting a stub or peduncle to the hole which had been made in each pumpkin as it was pulled from the stalk, and the spectators saw with surprise that the irregular and capricious shaped ends of the peduncles corresponded exactly with the whitish circles and the slight hollows presented by what we might call the cicatrices of the pumpkins.

Every one present, including the policeman, and even the inspector himself, then got down on their heels and began to help old Buscabeatas in his singular comprobation, crying out with childlike delight—

"He is right! he is right! There is not a doubt of it! Look! This belongs to this one. This to that one. That one there belongs to this. This belongs to that!" And the bursts of laughter of the grown people were mingled with the whistling of the boys, the abuse of the women, the tears of joy and triumph of the old gardener, and the pushes that the policeman gave to the convicted thief, as if they were impatient to carry him off to prison.

Needless to say that the policeman had that pleasure; that Gossip Fulano was immediately compelled to restore to the vendor the fifteen dollars he had received from him, that the vendor handed these over at once to Gaffer Buscabeatas, and that the latter departed for Rota, highly delighted, although he kept repeating all the way home—

"How handsome they looked in the market! I should have brought Manuela back with me to eat at supper tonight, and save the seeds."

"*Moors and Christians, and other Tales.*" *Pedro Antonio de Alarcon* (1833-1891). *Trans. Mary J. Serrano.*

SISTER SAINT SULPICE.

Sister Sulpice (Gloria, by her mundane name), a novice about to quit the convent for the world, against her mother, Doña Tula's, wish.
Sister Maria de la Luz, cousin to Sister Sulpice, and also a novice.
The Mother Superior Florentina.
Paca, Gloria's foster-sister.
Don Ceferino, native of Galicia.
Don Paco, landlord of the Fonda Continental.

I. AT THE MARMOLEYO SPA.

ALONG a gentle slope, over which was intended to be a high-road, we descended to the spring which gushes out in the very middle of the river Guadalquiver, which comes circling around the brow of the sierra. There is a gallery or bridge which leads from the shore to the spring. Across it were gravely walking two or three persons, who, by their wandering and vacant looks, showed that they were perhaps paying more attention to the contents of their stomachs than to the discourse and steps of their companions. From time to time they hastened to the spring, descended the steps, asked for a glass of water, and drank it eagerly, shutting their eyes with a kind of pleasurable emotion, suggesting the hope of health.

"Have you been taking much of the water, Mother?" asked my landlord, leaning over the railing of the well.

A short, plump nun, who appeared to be dropsical, and had a small red nose, raised her head just as she was about to put the glass to her lips.

"Good morning, Señor Paco. . . . I have had only four glasses so far. Would you like a little to increase your appetite?"

That greatly delighted my landlord.

"Increase my appetite, eh? Give me something to reduce it, rather! that's what I should prefer. . . . And the Sisters?"

Two young nuns, not at all ill-favoured, who were standing beside the other with their heads raised towards us, smiled politely.

"The same as always; two little sips," rejoined one of them, who had lively black eyes, and spoke with a downright Andalusian accent, and displayed an elegant set of teeth.

"How little!"

"Why, surely you would not wish to make our stomachs ponds for anchovies, would you, like the Mother's?"

"Anchovies?"

"Yes, Cadiz anchovies. You have only to cast the net."

The Mother's dropsical form was shaken violently by a laughing fit. The anchovies swimming in her stomach, according to the young nun, must have thought that they were exposed to an earthquake.

We all laughed and went down to the spring. As we came near the Mother, she greeted me with an affectionate smile. I bent low, took the crucifix which hung from her girdle, and kissed it. The nun smiled still more tenderly, and looked at me with an expression of generous sympathy.

Let us be explicit: if this book is to be an honest history or confession of my life, it is my duty to declare that by the act of bending over to kiss the metal crucifix, I do not think that I was actuated by any mystic impulse, rather, I suspect, that the pretty Sister's black eyes shrewdly fixed upon me had a very active part in it. Perhaps, without being aware of it, I desired to ingratiate myself with those eyes. And the truth is that I failed in my attempt; because, instead of showing that she was flattered by such an act of devotion, it seemed to me that they assumed a slight expression of mockery. I was a bit confused.

"Has the gentleman come to take the waters?" asked the Mother half directly, half indirectly.

"Yes, señora, I have just arrived from Madrid."

"They are wonderful! The Lord our God has given them a virtue which is almost beyond belief. You will see how they develop the appetite. You will eat as much as you possibly can, and it will not hurt you. . . . You see, I can say I am a different woman, and it is only a week since we came. . . . Just imagine! yesterday I ate pig's liver, and it did not hurt me at all. . . . Then this young girl," she added, pointing to the black-eyed Sister: "I can't tell you what a colour she had! She was as pale as ashes. To be sure she hasn't much colour yet, but, . . . there now, . . . that is another thing."

I looked at her closely, and noticed that she was blushing, though she instantly turned her back to get another glass of water.

She was a young woman of nineteen or twenty, of average height, with an oval face of a pale brunette, her nose slightly "tip-tilted," her teeth white and close, and her eyes, as I have already said, of an intense and velvety black, shaded by long lashes, and bordered by a slight pink circle. Her hair was entirely covered from sight by the hood that bound her forehead. She was dressed in black serge, with a girdle around her waist, from which hung a large bronze crucifix. On her head, beside the hood, she wore a great white *papalina*, or "coronet," with stiffly starched flaps. Her shoes were large and coarse, but could not wholly disguise the grace of her dainty Southern foot.

The other Sister was likewise young, perhaps even younger than the first, as well as shorter in stature, and with a lily-white face, showing under the transparent skin an exceedingly lymphatic temperament; her eyes were clear blue, her teeth somewhat faulty. By the purity and correctness of her features, and likewise by her quiet manners, she looked like a Virgin of painted wood. She kept her eyes constantly fixed upon the ground, and did not open her lips during the short moments that we were together there.

"Come, drink, señor, prove the Divine grace," said the Mother.

I took the glass which the Sister with the white teeth had just laid down, and proceeded to fill it with water, since the attendant had disappeared through a trap-door; but in doing so I had to lean on the rock, and when I bent over to dip the glass into the pool I slipped, and my foot went in above my ankle.

"Be careful!" simultaneously cried my landlord and the Mother, as is always said after one has met with any accident.

I drew out my foot with the water spurting from my shoe, and could not refrain from a rather energetic exclamation.

The Mother was disturbed, and hastened to ask me with a grave face—

"Did it hurt you?"

The little Sister of the transparent skin blushed up to her ears. The other began to laugh so heartily, that I gave her a quick and not very affectionate look. But she paid no heed to it; she continued to laugh, although, in order not to meet my eyes, she turned her face the other way.

"Sister San Sulpicio, remember that it is a sin to laugh at another's misfortunes," said the Mother. "Why do you not imitate Sister Maria de la Luz?"

The latter was blushing like a poppy.

"I can't help it, Mother, I cannot; excuse me," she replied, endeavouring, but without success, to contain herself.

"Let her laugh; the truth is, the thing is more ludicrous than serious," said I, affecting good-humour though angry at heart.

These words, instead of inciting the Sister, had the opposite effect, and she quickly grew calm. I looked at her now and then, with a curiosity mingled with annoyance. She returned my look with a frank and smiling eye, in which still lurked a trace of mockery.

"You must change your shoes and stockings as quick as you can; getting the feet wet is very bad," said the Mother with interest.

"Pshaw! I shall not change them till night. I am accustomed to go all day with my feet soaking," said I, in a scornful tone of voice, putting on a show of robustness, which, unfortunately, I am very far from being blessed with. But it pleased me to affect bravado before the smiling nun.

"By all means . . . go, go home and take off your stocking. We are going to walk across the gallery to see if the water is going down. May the Lord our God bless you!"

I once more made a low bow and kissed the Mother's crucifix. I did the same with Sister Maria's, who, of course, blushed again. As to Sister San Sulpicio's I refrained from touching it. I merely bowed low with a grave face. Thus should she learn not to laugh at people when they get wet.

II. IN SEVILLE.

. . . When I returned to my boarding-house to dinner, I found Paca waiting at the door to give me a letter. I did not care to open it before the messenger, and tried to dismiss her as soon as possible. But the worthy woman was too happy over her señorita's escape from the convent, not to chatter for a while. Both interested and impatient, I was treated to all the particulars; how Doña Tula had gone to get Gloria in her carriage; how abominably they had behaved towards her at the convent, no one except the chaplain coming to bid her good-bye; how happy her señorita felt to take off her nun's dress; how glad every one was to see her "so bright and chipper!" and all the insignificant words which they had exchanged in their talk.

At last she went away, and I hastened to my room, nervously lighted my candle, and opened the note.

"I am out of the convent," it read. "If you wish to receive the promised scolding, pass in front of my house at eleven o'clock. I will be at the grating, and we will have a talk."

The keen joy produced in me by that letter may be imagined. All my dreams were coming true at once. Gloria loved me, and was giving me a rendezvous, and this rendezvous was singularly attractive to a poet and a man of the North by being at the grating!

The grating—*la reja*![1] Does not this word exert a strange fascination? does it not awake in fancy a swarm of vague, sweet thoughts, as though it were the symbol and centre of love and poesy? Who is there with so little imagination as never to have dreamed of a talk with a loved one through the grating on a moonlight night? These talks and these nights have, moreover, the incalculable advantage that they can be described without an actual experience of them. There is not a lyrical mosquito among all those that hum and buzz in the central or septentrional provinces of Spain who has not given expression to his feelings concerning them, and framed a more or less harmonious structure with the sweet notes of the guitar, the scents of tuberoses, the moonlight scattering its delicate filaments of silver over the windows, the heavens bespangled with stars, the orange flowers, the maiden's fascinating eyes, her warm perfumed breath, &c.

I myself, as a descriptive poet and colourist, have on more than one occasion, to the applause of my friends, jumbled together these commonplaces of Andalusian aesthetics.

[1] "*La reja.*" In Spanish houses the large casements of the ground floor are all heavily barred, permitting the windows in the hot weather to be wide open without fear of intrusion. *La reja* is to Spain in aesthetic value (with regard to love scenes) what the balcony is to Italy.

But now the reality far exceeded and differed from this poetic conventionalism. For the time being, as I entered the Calle de Argote de Molina, at eleven o'clock, I failed to notice whether moon and stars were shining in the sky or not. It is quite possible that they were, for such things are natural; but I did not notice. What could be seen with perfect distinctness was the watchman with pike and lantern leaning up against a door not very far from Gloria's.

"Shall I have to wait till this fellow goes off?" I asked myself with a sudden pang of fear.

Fortunately, after a little while I saw him start away from that place and move up the street.

Moreover, I went to the trysting-place without guitar or cloak, merely with a jonquil in my hand, and wearing a plain and inoffensive jacket. Neither did I go mounted on a fiery steed, black, dappled, or sorrel; but on my own wretched legs, which certainly trembled all too violently as I approached the windows of the house. In one of them I saw the gleam of a white object, and I hastened to tap on the grating.

"Gloria!" I said in a very low voice.

"Here I am," replied the girl's voice.

At the same instant her graceful bare head bent over toward the grating, and I saw the gleam of her little white teeth with that same bewitching and mocking smile which was so delineated on my heart. I saw her dark velvety eyes shining. As though I were in the presence of a supernatural apparition, I stood motionless with both hands clenching the grating. I found nothing more to say than—

"Cómo sigue V." "How do you do?"

That ordinary formula of every-day courtesy did not seem to arouse any sad ideas in her, for I saw her put her hand to her mouth to hide a laugh. After a brief silence, she replied—

"Well; and you?"

"How I have longed for this moment to arrive!" I exclaimed, realising that I was not "in situation," as they say in the theatres. "Can you not imagine the eagerness with which I have been waiting for it, Gloria? . . ."

"And why should you have been anxious for it?"

"Because my heart was tormented with the desire to tell you how I worship you."

"That indeed is news! Why, my son, you have repeated it in the nine letters you have written me, forty-one times. . . . I counted them!"

"Then it was so as to tell you so the forty-second time. What is taking place between us, Gloria, seems to me just like a novel. It is not three months that I have known you, and yet it seems to me as if I had lived three years since then. What a change! How it has altered our lives! You were a nun, and now I see you transformed into a perfect young lady of the world."

"So you really find that I am perfect?"

"Exquisite!"

"A thousand thanks. What would it be if you were to see me!"

"I do see you . . . not very well, but sufficient to make me realise what a favourable change."

Up to a certain point that was true. Although the darkness that prevailed in that corner did not allow me to make out her features, I could see the outline of her graceful head, adorned with waving hair, and when she bent it over a little toward the grating, the dim light of the street shone into her face, which seemed to me paler than when she was at Marmolejo, though not less lovely.

A moment of silence ensued, and, embarrassed by it, I said at last—

"Is this your chamber?"

"This is not a chamber, it is the reception-room."

"Ah!"

And again silence fell.

I noticed that her eyes were fastened upon me, and, if the truth be told, I could not deceive myself into thinking that they were overflowing with love, but rather that they displayed a mischievous curiosity.

"O Gloria, if you only knew how sadly those days passed for me when I got no word from you! I believed that you had forgotten me."

"I never forget my good friends. Besides, I had promised you one thing, and I should certainly not wish to fail of fulfilling my promise."

"What was it?"

"Don't you remember?—the scolding. . . ."

"Oh, yes," I exclaimed, laughing.

And, encouraged by these words, I felt that I ought to have my love affairs put upon a definite basis, and I said—

"Well, then, Gloria, I have come for nothing else than to have you undeceive me if I am under a false impression, or else confirm my hopes of being loved if they have any foundation. Since I have already repeated forty-one times that I adore you, as you say, I need not say it again. Ever since I have seen you and talked with you at Marmolejo, you have kept me a willing prisoner of love and admiration. My fate is in your hands, and I wait with the greatest anxiety to hear my sentence."

Gloria paused a few moments before she answered; then she coughed a little, and finally said—

"The fatal moment has arrived. Prepare for the worst. . . . Señor Don Ceferino, I should not tell the truth if I gave you to understand that from the first day I talked with you at Marmolejo, I did not perceive that you were courting me. Further, I believe that the kiss which you gave Mother Florentina's crucifix, the first time we saw each other, you gave me in my honour. . . . You laugh? Well, it shows that I was not deceived. Those gallantries of yours have caused me some annoyances, but I cherish no hard feelings against you. Sooner or later I had to let the thunder burst, for I had made up my mind not to stay in the convent, even though I had to go out to service. Then you greatly aided me in accomplishing my wishes, and for this I am very grateful . . . But gratitude is one thing and love is another. So far I have not been able to reciprocate your love. I esteem you . . . I like you, and I shall never forget how kind you have been to me; but I speak frankly, I cannot have you live longer labouring under a mistake. I will be your sincere and affectionate friend. . . . Your betrothed I cannot be."

It is absolutely impossible for me to give any idea of my state of mind on hearing those words. They were spoken in an ironical tone, which might have left one open to think that they were in jest, but the reasoning was so natural and logical that they put an end to any such supposition. Nevertheless, by a supreme act of self-control, I burst into a laugh, exclaiming—

"Well, that is a well-fabricated refusal! I might think that you really meant it!"

"What! don't you believe what I say? . . . Child, have you not a very lofty opinion of your little self?"

"It is not a question of whether I have a high opinion of myself, Gloria," I replied, becoming grave; "it is that it is hard to believe that you would have waited so long to refuse me."

"But you have not given me a chance till now!"

"Are you speaking seriously, Gloria?"

"Why not? Come, now, you have imagined because I accepted your aid in getting out of the convent, that I was in so far bound to worship you, did you not?"

A wave of hot blood surged into my cheeks; my ears hummed. I suddenly realised the fact that I had been making a fool of myself in a most lamentable fashion, that this girl had most shamefully turned me into ridicule. Indignation and anger took complete possession of me; I poured out all my bile in a perfect torrent of words. I stood for some little time clutching the grating, gazing at her in silence with flaming eyes. Finally, in a voice hoarse with anger, I said,—

"The truth is, you are the veriest flirt,[1] unworthy of receiving the attentions of any decent man. I do not regret the time that I have wasted in loving you, but I do regret having wasted my love on you! I believed that under your apparent frivolity you had a good heart, but I see that it was nothing but vanity and giddiness. I rejoice that I have found it out in good time, for I will at one blow tear it out of my heart and my thoughts, where you ought never to have found a place. Good-bye! and for ever!"

As I withdrew my contracted hands from the iron bars I felt the pressure of hers, and I heard a compressed laugh, which entirely confused me.

"Bravo, bravo? I like you so, my dear! I was becoming weary of so much sweetness!"

"What does this mean, Gloria?"

"It means that you must not be so honey-like, for one gets tired of syrup, and incense is sickening. See here! You have advanced your cause more in one moment by saying impudent things to me, than in three months of flatteries. You will say that I like to have my knuckles rapped with the fire-shovel. It may be so. But I tell you that a little touch of genius never hurts a man!"

"Yes? Then wait a bit, and I will insult you some more," said I, laughing.

"No, no," she exclaimed, also laughing, "enough for to-day."

During that sweet and memorable interview, which was prolonged till one o'clock, our love was mutually confessed

---

[1] *Sed mai ima coquetuela.*

and agreed upon. Without any difficulty we began to address each other with the familiar "thee" and "thou," and we swore fidelity till death, no matter what might happen.

Not a soul passed through the street. The watchman, when he saw me glued to the grating, did not come near. I was afraid that Doña Tula might come into the room, but Gloria re-assured me by declaring that in Seville no one ever acted traitorously towards two lovers, and the watchmen still less interfered with these colloquies at the gratings, which they saw every night. She also had great confidence in the servants. Therefore the prospect of a series of delightful interviews was spread before us, filling my soul with joy.

"They will know about it sooner or later," said she. "But suppose they do. I will take it upon me to make them mind their own business if they attempt to interfere."

And in her handsome eyes I saw a flash of audacious mischief, which made it plain enough that it would not be an easy matter to lead her in paths where she did not wish to go.

"Now it is getting late. Mamma gets up very early for mass, and will wish me to go with her. Now you must go."

"A little while longer, sweetheart! It is not midnight yet."

"Yes, the clock in the Giralda[1] struck one."

"No, it is only a quarter-past twelve. . . ."

The slow, solemn stroke of the bell in the Giralda just then struck a quarter-past one.

"Do you hear? It is a quarter-past one. Adios! adios!"

"And are you going to send me off so, without giving me your hand?"

She reached it out to me, and I, naturally, was about to kiss it, but she snatched it away.

[1] The Giralda is the celebrated cathedral tower of Seville, built by a Moor 1196.

"No, no; wait a little, I will give you the crucifix, as in Marmolejo," she cried with a laugh.

"I prefer your hand."

"You heretic, begone!"

"God is everywhere. But still if you wish to give me the crucifix I will guard it carefully as a keepsake."

"Wait just a second. I have my dress here."

She withdrew from the window for a moment and came back with the bronze crucifix, which she handed out to me through the iron grating. In taking it from her I got possession of her brown, firm hand, and kissed it a number of times voraciously, gluttonously!

"That will do, little boy. Do you expect to keep it up till morning?"

I went away from that window grating intoxicated with love and bliss. So far gone was I that when I met the watchman a little distance away I gave him two pesetas. Afterwards I regretted it, for there was no need of doing so, according to what Gloria had said. This time, also, I noticed as little as before whether the stars were glittering on high with sweet brilliancy, or whether the moonlight filtered down into the dark labyrinthine streets, spotting them here and there with patines of bright silver. I carried in my own heart a radiant sun, which dazzled me and prevented me from seeing such petty details!

III. A VISIT TO THE CONVENT.

. . . During all this time neither the Mother Superior nor the sisters had asked who I was, or how and why Gloria happened to be in that place. They looked at me with quick glances of curiosity, showing that my presence embarrassed them. I had not opened my lips.

My wife, doubtless piqued by this neglect, suddenly said, "Did you not know that I was married?"

The sisters burst into a laugh.

"Ay! what a Sister!—always so full of spirit," exclaimed the Mother Superior.

"Yes, Mother, I have been married for a month and three days to this fine young man whom you see. He has only one defect," she added, growing grave, "and that is that he is a Gallegan! . . . But you would not think it, would you?"

"What a Sister!" again exclaimed some of the nuns. "How witty she is!—who would have said that she was married! Something has happened to her!"

"What! Don't you believe me?"

The Sisters still laughed, giving me keen and mysterious glances.

"Well, then, this very instant I will prove it to you!" exclaimed my wife with a sudden impulse. And at the same time she threw her arms around my neck and began to give me some ringing kisses on the cheek, saying,—

"*Rico mio!* Isn't it true that you are my husband? Isn't it true that I am your little wife? Isn't it true that we are married? Tell me, sweetheart! Tell me, my own life!"

While I, quite abashed, was trying to escape from her caresses, I heard exclamations of reproof, and saw that the nuns were flying in fright towards the portal. One of them, more intrepid, seized the cord of the curtain and pulled it with all her force. The curtain, as it shut together, likewise sent up a squeak of scandalised amazement.

I heard hurried steps and a sound of voices. Then nothing; it had grown silent.

My wife, laughing merrily and blushing at the same time, seized my hand and drew me out. We passed through the melancholy corridors in this way, ran down the stairs, passed through the great passageway, and when we found ourselves in the street I said to her, half vexed, "Child, how crazy you were! What got into you, to . . ."

"Forgive me, my dear," she replied, still laughing and

crimson. "They made me nervous. They might as well know that we were married as the priest who gave us his benediction."

A. Palacio Valdés (Nineteenth Century).
Trans. Nathan Haskell Dole.

PEPITA.

IN the past few days I have had occasion to practise patience in an extreme degree, and to mortify my self-love in the most cruel manner. My father, wishing to return Pepita's compliment of the garden-party, invited her to visit his villa at the Pozo de la Solana. The excursion took place on the 22nd of April. I shall not soon forget the date.

The Pozo de la Solana is about two leagues distant from the village, and the only road to it is a bridle-path. We all had to go on horseback. As I never learned to ride, I had on former occasions accompanied my father mounted on a pacing mule, gentle, and, according to the expression of Dientes the muleteer, as good as gold, and of easier motion than a carriage. On the journey to the Pozo de la Solana I went in the same manner.

My father, the notary, the apothecary, and my cousin Currito were mounted on good horses. My aunt, Doña Casilda, who weighs more than two hundred and fifty pounds, rode on a large and powerful donkey, seated in a commodious side-saddle. The reverend vicar rode a gentle and easy mule like mine.

As for Pepita Jiménez, who, I supposed, would go also mounted on a donkey, in the same sort of easy saddle as my aunt—for I was ignorant that she knew how to ride—she surprised me by making her appearance on a black and white horse full of fire and spirit. She wore a riding-habit, and managed her horse with admirable grace and skill.

"SHE WORE A RIDING-HABIT, AND MANAGED HER HORSE WITH ADMIRABLE GRACE AND SKILL."

I was pleased to see Pepita look so charming on horseback, but I soon began to foresee and to be mortified by the sorry part I would play, jogging on in the rear beside my corpulent Aunt Casilda and the vicar, all three as quiet and tranquil as if we were seated in a carriage, while the gay cavalcade in front would caracole, gallop, trot, and make a thousand other displays of their horsemanship.

I fancied on the instant that there was something of compassion in Pepita's glance as she noted the pitiable appearance I no doubt presented, seated on my mule. My cousin Currito looked at me with a mocking smile, and immediately began to make fun of me and to tease me.

Confess that I deserve credit for my resignation and courage. I submitted to everything with a good grace, and Currito's jests soon ceased when he saw that I was invulnerable to them. But what did I not suffer in secret! The others, now trotting, now galloping, rode in advance of us, both in going and returning. The vicar and I, with Doña Casilda between us, rode on, tranquil as the mules we were seated upon, without hastening or retarding our pace.

I had not even the consolation of chatting with the vicar, in whose conversation I find so much pleasure, nor of wrapping myself up in my own thoughts and giving the rein to my fancy, nor of silently admiring the beauty of the scenery around us. Doña Casilda is gifted with an abominable loquacity, and we were obliged to listen to her. She told us all there is to be told of the gossip of the village; she recounted to us all her accomplishments; she told us how to make sausages, brain-puddings, pastry, and innumerable other dishes and delicacies. There is no one, according to herself, who can rival her in matters pertaining to the kitchen, or to the dressing of hogs, but Antoñona, Pepita's nurse, and now her housekeeper and general manager. I am already acquainted with this Antoñona, for she goes back and forth between her mistress's house and ours with messages, and is in truth extremely handy—as loquacious as Aunt Casilda, but a great deal more discreet.

The scenery on the road to the Pozo de la Solana is charming, but my mind was so disturbed during our journey that I could not enjoy it. When we arrived at the villa and dismounted, I was relieved of a great load, as if it had been I who carried the mule, and not the mule who carried me.

We then proceeded on foot through the estate, which is magnificent, of varied character and extensive. There are vines, old and newly planted, all on the same property, producing more than five hundred bushels of grapes; olive-trees that yield to the same amount; and, finally, a grove of the most majestic oaks that are to be found in all Andalusia. The water of the Pozo de la Solana forms a clear and deep brook, at which all the birds of the neighbourhood come to drink, and on whose borders they are caught by hundreds, by means of reeds smeared with bird-lime, or of nets, in the centre of which are fastened a cord and a decoy. All this carried my thoughts back to the sports of my childhood, and to the many times that I too had gone to catch birds in the same manner.

Following the course of the brook, and especially in the ravines, are many poplars and other tall trees, which, together with the bushes and the shrubs, form a dark and labyrinthine wood. A thousand fragrant wild flowers grow there spontaneously, and it would, in truth, be difficult to imagine anything more secluded and sylvan, more solitary, peaceful, and silent than this spot. Even in the fervour of noonday, when the sun pours down his light in torrents from a heaven without a cloud, the mind experiences the same mysterious terror as visits it at times in the silent hours of the night. One can understand here the manner of life of the patriarchs of old, and of the primitive shepherds and heroes; and the visions and apparitions that appeared to them of nymphs, of gods, and of angels, in the midst of the noonday brightness.

As we walked through this thicket, there arrived a moment in which, I know not how, Pepita and I found ourselves alone together. The others had remained behind.

I felt a sudden thrill pass through me. For the first time, and in a place so solitary, I found myself alone with this woman; while my thoughts were still dwelling on the noontide apparitions, now sinister, now gracious, but always supernatural, vouchsafed to the men of remote ages.

Pepita had left the long skirt of her riding habit in the house, and now wore a short dress that did not interfere with the graceful ease of her movements. She had on her head a little Andalusian hat, which became her extremely. She carried in her hand her riding-whip, which I fancied to myself to be a magic wand, by means of which this enchantress might cast her spells over me.

I am not afraid to transcribe here these eulogies of her beauty. In this sylvan scene she appeared to me more beautiful than ever. The precaution recommended in similar cases by ascetics, to think of her beauty defaced by sickness and old age, to picture her to myself dead, the prey of corruption and of the worm, presented itself, against my will, to my imagination; and I say *against my will*, for I do not concur in the necessity for such a precaution. No thought of the material, no suggestion of the evil spirit, troubled my reason or infected my will or my senses.

What did occur to me was an argument—at least to my mind—in disproof of the efficacy of this precaution. Beauty, the creation of a Sovereign and Divine Power, may indeed be frail and ephemeral, may vanish in an instant; but the idea of beauty is eternal, and, once perceived by the mind, it lives there an immortal life. The beauty of this woman, such as it manifests itself to-day, will disappear in a few short years; the graceful form, those charming contours, the noble head that raises itself so proudly above her shoulders: all will be food for loathsome worms; but—though the material must of necessity be transformed—its idea, the creative thought—abstract beauty, in a word—what shall destroy this? Does it not exist in the Divine Mind? Once perceived and known by me, must it not continue to live in my soul, triumphing over age and even over death?

I was meditating thus, striving to tranquillise my spirit and to dissipate the doubts which you have succeeded in infusing into my mind, when Pepita and I encountered each other. I was pleased and at the same time troubled to find myself alone with her—hoping and yet fearing that the others would join us.

The silvery voice of Pepita broke the silence, and drew me from my meditations, saying—

"How silent you are, Don Luis, and how sad! I am pained to think that it is perhaps through my fault, or partly so at least, that your father has caused you to spend a disagreeable day in these solitudes, taking you away from a solitude more congenial, where there would be nothing to distract your attention from your prayers and pious books."

I know not what answer I made to this. It must have been something nonsensical, for my mind was troubled. I did not wish to flatter Pepita by paying her profane compliments, nor, on the other hand, did I wish to answer her rudely.

She continued—

"You must forgive me if I am wrong, but I fancy that, in addition to the annoyance of seeing yourself deprived to-day of your favourite occupation, there is something else that powerfully contributes to your ill-humour."

"And what is this something else?" I said, "since you have discovered it, or fancy you have done so."

"This something else," responded Pepita, "is a feeling not altogether becoming in one who is going to be a priest so soon, but very natural in a young man of twenty-two."

On hearing this I felt the blood mount to my face, and my face burn. I imagined a thousand absurdities; I thought myself beset by evil spirits; I fancied myself tempted by Pepita, who was doubtless about to let me understand that she knew I loved her. Then my timidity gave place to haughtiness, and I looked her steadily in the face. There must have been something laughable in my look, but either Pepita did not observe it, or, if she did, she concealed the fact with amiable discretion; for she exclaimed, in the most natural manner—

"Do not be offended because I find you are not without fault. This that I have observed seems to me a slight one. You are hurt by the jests of Currito, and by being compelled to play—speaking profanely—a not very dignified *rôle*, mounted, like the reverend vicar with his eighty years, on a placid mule, and not, as a youth of your age and condition should be, on a spirited horse. The fault is the reverend dean's, to whom it did not occur that you should learn to ride. To know how to manage a horse is not opposed to the career you intend to follow, and I think, now that you are here, that your father might in a few days give you the necessary instruction to enable you to do so. If you should go to Persia or to China, where there are no railroads yet, you will make but a sorry figure in those countries as a bad horseman. It is possible even that, by this oversight, the missionary himself may come to lose prestige in the eyes of those barbarians, which will make it all the more difficult for him to reap the fruits of his labours."

This and other arguments Pepita adduced in order to

persuade me to learn to ride on horseback; and I was so convinced of the necessity of a missionary's being a good horseman, that I promised her to learn at once, taking my father as a teacher.

"On the very next expedition we make," I said, "I shall ride the most spirited horse my father has, instead of the mule I am riding to-day."

"I shall be very glad of it," responded Pepita, with a smile of indescribable sweetness.

At this moment we were joined by the rest of the party, at which I was secretly rejoiced, though for no other reason than the fear of not being able to sustain the conversation, and of saying a great many foolish things, on account of the little experience I have had in conversing with women.

After our walk my father's servants spread before us on the fresh grass, in the most charming spot beside the brook, a rural and abundant collation.

The conversation was very animated, and Pepita sustained her part in it with much discretion and intelligence. My cousin Currito returned to his jests about my manner of riding and the meekness of my mule. He called me a theologian, and said that, seated on mule-back, I looked as if I were dispensing blessings. This time, however, being now firmly resolved to learn to ride, I answered his jests with sarcastic indifference. I was silent, nevertheless, with respect to the promise I had just made Pepita. The latter, doubtless thinking as I did—although we had come to no understanding in the matter—that silence for the present was necessary to insure the complete success of the surprise that I would create afterward by my knowledge of horsemanship, said nothing of our conversation. Thus it happened, naturally and in the simplest manner, that a secret existed between us; and it produced in my mind a singular effect.

Nothing else worth telling occurred during the day.

In the afternoon we returned to the village in the same manner in which we had left it. Yet, seated on my easy-going mule and at the side of my aunt Casilda, I did not experience the same fatigue or sadness as before.

During the whole journey I listened without weariness to my aunt's stories, amusing myself at times in conjuring up idle fancies. Nothing of what passes in my soul shall be concealed from you. I confess, then, that the figure of Pepita was, as it were, the centre, or rather the nucleus and focus, of these idle fancies.

The noonday vision in which she had appeared to me, in the shadiest and most sequestered part of the grove, brought to my memory all the visions, holy and unholy, of wondrous beings, of a condition superior to ours, that I had read of in sacred authors and in the profane classics. Pepita appeared to the eyes and on the stage of my fancy in the leafy seclusion of the grove, not as she rode before us on horseback, but in an ideal and ethereal fashion—as Venus to Æneas, as Minerva to Callimachus, as the sylph who afterward became the mother of Libusa to the Bohemian Kroco, as Diana to the son of Aristæus, as the angels in the valley of Mamre to the Patriarch, as the hippocentaur to St. Anthony in the solitude of the wilderness.

That the vision of Pepita should assume in my mind something of a supernatural character, seems to me no more to be wondered at than any of these. For an instant, seeing the consistency of the illusion, I thought myself tempted by evil spirits; but I reflected that in the few moments during which I had been alone with Pepita near the brook of the Solana, nothing had occurred that was not natural or commonplace; that it was afterward, as I rode along quietly on my mule, that some demon, hovering invisible around me, had suggested these extravagant fancies.

That night I told my father of my desire to learn to ride. I did not wish to conceal from him that it was Pepita who had suggested this desire. My father was greatly rejoiced; he embraced me, he kissed me, he said that now not you only would be my teacher, but that he also would have the pleasure of teaching me something. He ended by assuring me that in two or three weeks he would make me the best horseman of all Andalusia; able to go to Gibraltar for contraband goods, and come back laden with tobacco and cotton, after eluding the vigilance of the Custom-house officers; fit, in a word, to astonish the riders who show off their horsemanship in the fairs of Seville and Mairena, and worthy to press the flanks of Babieca,[1] Bucephalus, or even of the horses of the sun themselves, if they should by chance descend to earth, and I could catch them by the bridle.

I don't know what you will think of this notion of my learning to ride, but I take it for granted you will see nothing wrong in it.

If you could but see how happy my father is, and how he delights in teaching me! Since the day after the excursion I told you of, I take two lessons daily. There are days on which the lesson is continuous, for we spend from morning till night on horseback. During the first week the lessons took place in the courtyard of the house, which is unpaved, and which served as a riding-school.

We now ride out into the country, but manage so that no one shall see us. My father does not want me to show myself on horseback in public until I am able to astonish every one by my fine appearance in the saddle, as he says. If the vanity natural to a father does not deceive him, this, it seems, will be very soon, for I have a wonderful aptitude for riding.

[1] The Cid's famous charger.

"It is easy to see that you are my son!" my father exclaims with joy, as he watches my progress.

My father is so good that I hope you will pardon him the profane language and irreverent jests in which he indulges at times. I grieve for this at the bottom of my soul, but I endure it with patience. These constant and long-continued lessons have reduced me to a pitiable condition with blisters. My father enjoins me to write to you that they are caused by mortification of the flesh.

As he declares that within a few weeks I shall be an accomplished horseman, and he does not desire to be superannuated as a master, he proposes to teach me other accomplishments of a somewhat irregular character, and sufficiently unsuited to a future priest. At times he proposes to train me in throwing the bull, in order that he may take me afterwards to Seville, where, with lance in hand, on the plains of Tablada, I shall make the braggarts and the bullies stare. Then he recalls his own youthful days, when he belonged to the body-guard, and declares that he will look up his foils, gloves, and masks, and teach me to fence. And, finally, as my father flatters himself that he can wield the Sevillian knife better than any one else, he has offered to teach me even this accomplishment also.

You can already imagine the answer I make to all this nonsense. My father replies that, in the good old times, not only the priests, but even the bishops themselves, rode about the country on horseback, putting infidels to the sword. I rejoin that this might happen in the Dark Ages, but then in our days the ministers of the Most High should know how to wield no other weapons than those of persuasion. "And what if persuasion be not enough?" rejoins my father. "Do you think it would be amiss to re-enforce argument with a few good blows of a cudgel?" The complete missionary, according to my father's opinion, should know how on occasion to have recourse to these heroic measures, and as my father has read a great many tales and romances he cites various examples in support of his opinion. He cites, in the first place, St. James, who on his white horse, without ceasing to be an apostle, put more Moors to the sword than he preached to or convinced; he cites a certain Señor de la Vera, who, being sent on an embassy to Boabdil by Ferdinand and Isabella, became entangled in a theological discussion with the Moors in the courtyard of the Lions, and, being at the end of his arguments, drew his sword and fell upon them with fury in order to complete their conversion: and he finally cites the Biscayan hidalgo, Don Inigo de Loyola, who, in a controversy he had with a Moor regarding the purity of the Holy Virgin, growing weary at last of the impious and horrible blasphemies with which the aforesaid Moor contradicted him, fell upon him, sword in hand, and, if he had not taken to his heels, would have enforced conviction upon his soul in a terrible fashion. In regard to the incident relating to St. Ignatius, I answer my father that this was before the saint became a priest; and in regard to the other examples, I answer that historians are not agreed.

In short, I defend myself as best I can against my father's jests, and I content myself with being a good horseman, without learning other accomplishments unsuited to the clergy, although my father assures me that not a few of the Spanish clergy understand and practise them with frequency in Spain, even in our own day, with a view to contributing to the triumph of the faith, and to the preservation or the restoration of the unity of the Church.

I am grieved to the soul by this levity of my father's, and that he should speak with irreverence and jestingly about the most serious things; but a respectful son is not called upon to go further than I do in repressing his somewhat Voltairean freedom of speech. I say *Voltairean,* because I am not able to describe it by any other word. At heart my father is a good Catholic, and this thought consoles me.

Yesterday was the Feast of the Cross, and the village presented a very animated appearance. In each street were six or seven May-crosses covered with flowers, but none of them was so beautiful as that placed by Pepita at the door of her house. It was adorned by a perfect cascade of flowers.

In the evening we went to an entertainment at the house of Pepita. The cross which had stood at the door was now placed in a large saloon on the ground-floor, in which there is a piano, and Pepita presented us with a simple and poetic spectacle— one that I had seen when a child, but had since forgotten.

From the upper part of the cross hung down seven bands or broad ribbons, two white, two green, and three red, the symbolic colours of the theological virtues. Eight children, of five or six years old, representing the seven sacraments, and holding the seven ribbons that hung from the cross, performed with great skill a species of contra-dance. The sacrament of baptism was represented by a child wearing the white robe of a catechumen; ordination, by another child as a priest; confirmation, by a little bishop; extreme unction, by a pilgrim with staff and scrip, the latter filled with shells; marriage, by a bride and bridegroom; and penance, by a Nazarene with cross and crown of thorns.

The dance was a series of reverences, steps, evolutions, and genuflexions, rather than a dance, performed to the sound of very tolerable music, something like a march, which the organist played, not without skill, on the piano.

The little dancers, children of the servants or retainers of Pepita, after playing their parts, went away to bed loaded with gifts and caresses.

The entertainment, in the course of which we were served with refreshments, continued till twelve; the refreshments were syrup served in little cups, and afterwards chocolate with sponge-cake, and meringues and water.

Since the return of spring Pepita's seclusion and retirement are being gradually abandoned, at which my father is greatly rejoiced. In future Pepita will receive every night, and my father desires that I shall be one of the guests.

Pepita has left off mourning, and now appears, more lovely and attractive than ever, in the lighter fabrics appropriate to the season, which is almost summer. She still dresses, however, with extreme simplicity.

I cherish the hope that my father will not now detain me here beyond the end of this month at farthest. In June we shall both join you in the city, and you shall then see how, far from Pepita, to whom I am indifferent, and who will remember me neither kindly nor unkindly, I shall have the pleasure of embracing you, and attaining at last to the happiness of being ordained.

"*Pepita Jiménez.*" *Juan Valera.*

IF SHE COULD ONLY WRITE.

"PLEASE write me a letter, Holy Sir."
  "To Robin, I suppose?"
" You know because one evening dark
To startle us you chose,—
But on my soul . . . "—" No more, a pen
And paper, daughter, give :
'*Beloved Rob,*' "—" ' Belov'd ' ? "—" Then
You don't love him, I perceive."
" Oh yes ! and now you've put it,

It must stay"—"' *If you but knew
How very sad and lonely, dear,
I am away from you!'*"
"Why, Sir, you know my very thoughts!" . . .
"To an old man like me
A maid's breast is of crystal clear
Through which the heart we see.
' *Without you all is bitterness,
But with you Paradise.*'"
"Pray make those letters quite clear, Sir,
And underline them thrice."
"' *And if you no longer love me,
Suffer so much shall I
That*' . . ."—"'Suffer'? 'tis not the word, Sir;
Put ' I shall surely die.'"
"'Twere sinning against Heaven, my child."
"'Die,' sir, in black and white!"
"Not so."—"Alas, your heart's of ice.
Oh! if I could but write! . . .
Dear Father, Holy Father!
In vain you write for me,
If incarnate in the letters
Is not all that I may be.
For Christ's sake, tell him that my soul
Within me will not stay,
That if anguish does not kill me
'Tis because I weep all day.
That my lips, the roses of his breath,
Know only how to close;
And that all smiles and laughter
Long ago within me froze.
That the eyes he thought so lovely
Are heavy with distress,
Since there's nobody to look at them
They shut for wretchedness.

"IF I COULD ONLY WRITE."

That for the echo of his voice
My ears are all athirst;
That of all the torments suffer'd
His absence is the worst . . .
And that it is *his* fault my heart's
In such sweet-bitter plight! . . .
Good heavens, how many things I'd put
If I could only write! . . ."

Campoamor.

DOCTOR PERTINAX.

ST. PETER was polishing the large knocker of the Gate of Heaven, leaving it as bright as the sun—which is not to be wondered at since the knocker St. Peter was cleaning *is* the sun we see appearing every morning in the east.

The holy porter, merrier than his colleagues at Madrid, was humming some little air not unlike *Ça ira* of the French.

"Hola! You get up very early," said he, bending his head and staring at a person who had stopped before the threshold of the gate.

The unknown did not reply, but bit his lips, which were thin, pale, and dry.

"No doubt," continued St. Peter, "you are the savant who was dying last night? . . . What a night you made me pass, friend! . . . I never closed my eyes once, thinking you might be likely to knock; my last orders were not to let you wait a moment, a piece of respect paid to your sort here in heaven. Well, welcome, and come in: I can't leave the gate. Go through, and then straight on. . . . There is no entresol."

"THE STRANGER DID NOT STIR FROM THE THRESHOLD."

The stranger did not stir from the threshold, but fixed his little blue eyes on the venerable bald head of St. Peter, who had turned his back to go on rubbing up the sun.

The new-comer was thin, short, and sallow, with somewhat feminine movements, neat in his attire, and without a hair on his face. He wore his shroud elegantly and nicely adjusted, and he measured his gestures with academic severity.

After gazing for some time at St. Peter working, he wheeled round and was about to return on the journey he had come he knew not how; but he found he was standing above a gloomy abyss, in which the darkness almost seemed palpable, and a horrisonous tempest was roaring with flashes of livid light at intervals like lightning. There was not a trace of any stairs, and the machine by which he dimly remembered he had mounted was not in sight either.

"Sir," exclaimed he, in a vibrating and acrid voice: "May I know what this means? Where am I? Why was I brought here."

"Ah, you haven't gone yet; I am very glad, for I had forgotten something." And pulling his memorandum-book out of his pocket, the saint moistened the point of the pencil between his lips and asked—

"Your name?"

"I am Doctor Pertinax, author of the book stereotyped in its twentieth edition, called '*Philosophia Ultima.*' . . ."

St. Peter was not a quick writer, and of all this had only put down Pertinax. . . .

"Well, Pertinax of what?"

"Of what? Oh, I see, you mean from where? just as they say: 'Thales of Miletus, Parmenides of Elea. . . .'"

"Exactly, Quixote of la Mancha. . . ."

"Write down, Pertinax of Torrelodones. And now, may I know what this farce means?"

"This farce?"

"Yes, sir. I am the victim of a farce, this is a comedy: my enemies, my colleagues, with the help of subtle artifices and theatrical machinery, exalting my mind with some beverage, have doubtless prepared all this. But the deception is useless. My power of reasoning is above all these appearances, and protests with a mighty voice against this low trickery; neither masks nor limelights are of any avail, for I am not taken in by such palpable effrontery, and I say what I always said, and which is enframed on page 315 of my " *Philosophia Ultima*," note *b*. of the sub-note Alpha, *i.e.*, that after death the deception of appearances will not exist, and there will no longer be any desire for life, *nolite vivere*, which is only a chain of shadows linked with desires, &c., &c. . . . Therefore, one of the two: either I have died, or I have not died; if I have died, it cannot possibly be I as I was when alive half an hour ago, and all that I see around me, as it can only be a representation, is not, for I am not: but if I have not died, and am myself, what I was and am, it is clear that although what I see around me exists in me by representation, it is not what my enemies wish me to believe, but an unworthy farce designed to frighten me; but 'tis in vain, for . . ."

And the philosopher swore like a coal-heaver. And the swearing was not the worst, for he lifted up his voice towards Heaven, the inhabitants of which were beginning to awake at the noise, while some of the blest were already descending by the staircase of clouds, tinged some as with woad, others with a sea-blue.

Meanwhile St. Peter held his sides with both hands to keep from bursting into the laughter with which he was nearly choking. Pertinax became more irritated at the saint's laughter, and the latter had to stop to try and pacify him by the following words—

"My dear sir, farces are of no avail here, nor is it a question of deceiving you, but of bringing you to Heaven, which it appears you have merited for some good works of which I am ignorant; in any case, calm yourself and go up, for the inhabitants above are already astir, and you will find somebody who will conduct you to where all will be explained to your taste, so that not a shadow of doubt will remain, for doubts all disappear in this region, where the dullest thing is the sun which I am polishing."

"I do not say *you* are deceiving me, for you seem an honest man; the tricksters are others, and you only an instrument, unconscious of what you are doing."

"I am St. Peter . . ."

They have persuaded you that you are; but there's no proof that you are."

"Dear sir, I have been porter here for more than eighteen hundred years . . ."

"Apprehension, preconception. . . ."

"Preconception fiddlesticks!" cried the saint, now somewhat angry; "I am St. Peter, and you a savant, and like all that come to us, an ignorant fool, with more than one bee in your bonnet . . ."

The gateway was now crowded with angels and cherubim, saints, male and female, and a number of the blest, who all formed a circle round the stranger and smilingly surveyed him.

From amongst them there stepped forth St. Job:—"I think," said he, "that this gentleman would be convinced that he had lived in error if he could see the Universe as it actually is. Why not appoint a commission from amongst us to accompany Doctor Pertinax and show him the construction of the immense piece of architecture, as Lope de Vega says, whom I am sorry not to see among us."

Great was the respect for St. Job, and they immediately proceeded to a nominal vote, which took up a good deal of time, as more than half the martyrology had repaired to the gate. The following were by the results appointed members of the commission:—St. Job, by acclamation; Diogenes, by a majority; and St. Thomas the Apostle, by a majority. St. Thomas of Aquinas and Duns Scotus had votes.

Dr. Pertinax gave way to the supplications of the commission, and consented to survey all the machinery and magic, with which they might deceive his eyes, said he, but not his mind.

"My dear fellow, don't be downhearted," said St. Thomas, as he sewed some wings on to the Doctor's shoulder-blades: "Look at me, I was an unbeliever, and . . ."

"Sir," replied Pertinax, "you lived in very different times, the world was then in its theological age, as Comte said, and I have passed through all those ages and have lived side by side with the "*Criticisms of Pure Reason*" and the "*Philosophia Ultima*"; so that I believe in nothing, not even in the mother who bore me; I only believe in this, inasmuch as I know that I am, I am conscious, but without falling into the preconception of confounding representation with essence, which is unattainable, that is to say, excepting the being conscious, putting aside all that is not myself (and all being in myself) I *know*, by knowing that everything is represented (and I as everything else) by simply appearing to be what it is, and the reality of which is only investigated by another volitive and effective representation, a harmful representation, being irrational and the original sin of the Fall; therefore, this apparent desire undone, nothing remains to explore, since not even the will for knowledge remains."

Only St. Job heard the last word of this discourse, and, scratching his bald crown with his potsherd, he replied—

"The truth is, you savants are the very devil for talking nonsense, and don't be offended, but those things, whether in your head or imagination, as you please, will give you warm work to see them in reality as they are."

"Forward! forward!" shouted Diogenes at this moment; "the sophists denied me motion, and you know how I proved it; forward!"

And they began their flight through boundless space. Boundless? Pertinax thought it so, and said—

"Do you expect to show me all the Universe?"

"Certainly," replied St. Thomas.

"But since the Universe—seemingly, of course—is infinite . . . how can you conceive the limit of space?"

"Conceive it, with difficulty; but see it, easily. Aristoteles sees it every day, for he takes the most terrible walks with his disciples, and certainly he complained that the space for walking ended before the disputes of his peripatetics."

"But how can space have an end? If there is a limit, it will have to be nothing; but as nothing does not exist, it cannot form a boundary; for a boundary is something, and something apart from what is bounded."

St. Job, who was already growing impatient, cut him short—

"Enough, enough of conversation! but you had better bend your head so as not to knock it, for we have arrived at that limit of space which cannot be conceived, and if you take a step more, you will break your head against that nothing you are denying."

And effectually; Pertinax saw there was nothing more beyond; wished to feel it, and bumped his head.

"But this can't be!" he exclaimed, while St. Thomas applied to the bump one of those pieces of money which pagans take with them on their journey to the other world.

There was no help for it, they had to turn back, the Universe had come to an end. But ended or not, how beautiful shone the firmament with its millions and millions of stars!

"What is that dazzling light shining above there, higher

than all the constellations? Is it some nebula unknown to the astronomers of the earth?"

"A pretty nebula!" replied St. Thomas; "that is the celestial Jerusalem, from which we have just descended, and what is shining so are the diamond walls round the city of God."

"So that those marvels related by Chateaubriand, and which I thought unworthy of a serious man . . . ?"

"Are perfectly true, my friend. And now let us go and rest on that star passing below there, for i' faith, I am tired of so much going backwards and forwards."

"Gentlemen, I am not presentable," said Pertinax; "I have not yet doffed my shroud, and the inhabitants of this star will laugh at such indecorous garb . . ."

The three Ciceroni of Heaven all burst out laughing together. Diogenes was the first to exclaim—

"'Though I should lend you my lantern, you would not meet a living soul in that star, nor in any other star."

"Of course," added Job, very seriously, "there are no inhabitants except on the Earth; don't talk such nonsense."

"'This I cannot believe!"

"Well, let us go and show him," said St. Thomas, who was already growing angry. And they journeyed from star to star, and in a few minutes had traversed all the Milky Way and the most distant starry systems. Nothing, not a sign of life. They did not even encounter a flea, for all the numerous globes they surveyed. Pertinax was horrified.

"This is the Creation!" he exclaimed; "what solitude! Come, show me the Earth; I want to see that privileged region; by what I conjecture, all modern cosmography is a lie, the Earth is still, and the centre of all the celestial vault; and round her revolve the suns and planets, and she is the largest of all the spheres . . ."

"Not at all," replied St. Thomas; "astronomy is not

mistaken; the earth revolves round the sun, and you will soon see how insignificant she appears. Let us see if we can find her amongst all that crowd of stars. *You* look for her, St. Job; *you* have plenty of patience."

"I will!" exclaimed the Saint of the potsherd, as he hooked his spectacles round his ears.

"It is like looking for a needle in a bottle of hay! . . . I see her! there she goes! look! look how small! she looks like a microbe!"

Pertinax looked at the Earth and sighed.

"And are there no inhabitants except on that mote?"

"Nowhere else."

"And the rest of the Universe is empty?"

"Empty."

"Then of what use are such millions and millions of stars?"

"As lamps. They are the public illumination of the Earth. And they are also useful for singing praises to the Almighty. And they serve as eke-outs in poetry, and you can't deny they are very pretty."

"But all empty?"

"Every one!"

Pertinax remained in the air for a good time sad and thoughtful. He felt ill. The edifice of his "*Philosophia Ultima*" was threatening ruin. Upon seeing that the Universe was so different from what reason demanded, he began to believe in the Universe. That brusque lesson of reality was the rude and cold contact with material which his spirit needed in order to believe. "It is all so badly arranged, but perhaps it is true!" thus thought the philosopher. Suddenly he turned to his companions, and asked them—"Does Hell exist?"

The three sighed, made gestures of compassion, and replied

"Yes; it exists."

" And condemnation is eternal ? "

" Eternal."

" A solemn injustice ! "

" A terrible reality ! " replied the three in chorus.

Pertinax wiped his brow with his shroud. He was perspiring philosophy. He began to believe that he was in the other world. The injustice of everything convinced him. " Then the cosmogony and the theogony of my infancy was the truth ? "

" Yes; the first and only philosophy."

" Then I am not dreaming ? "

" No."

" Confession ! confession ! " groaned the philosopher ; and he swooned into the arms of Diogenes.

* * * * * *

When he awoke, he found himself in his bed. His old servant and the priest were by his side.

" Here is the confessor, sir, for whom you asked . . ."

Pertinax sat up, stretched out both hands, and looking at the confessor with frightened eyes, cried—

" I say and repeat, that all is pure representation, and that I am the victim of an unworthy farce."——And he expired really.

" *Solos de Clarin.*"   *Leopoldo Alas.*

A FEW THOUGHTS ON LIGHT.

MAN has invented artificial light, he inferred it from natural light ; he has in the same way invented artificial truths, inferring them from supreme truths.

The sun appears every day illuminating space to show us the heavens.

In Madrid the gas is lighted every night that we may see the earth.

Man is to God what a box of matches is to the sun.

Human pride can also write its Genesis.

It can begin like this—

"One day man said—'Fiat lux,' and there were matches."

Henceforward a blaze of light which illumines us perfectly.

The light invented by men is worth more than the light created by God: let us see how.

A thousand sunbeams cost nothing; one box of matches costs a halfpenny.

"*Hojas Sueltas.*" *José Selgas.*

EPIGRAMS.

TO A CRITIC.

THY foolish criticism
   On the plays composed by me
Wounds not my egotism;
But a sore, indeed, 't would be,
Should they be praised by thee.
    Leandro Fernandez de Moratin, 1760–1828.

TO A TRANSLATOR OF THE ÆNEID.

IN bad Spanish great Vergil
You dare to asperse,
And tell us most closely
You follow his verse:
If to imitate Maro
Is your real intent,
Pray will it's to burn
By *your* last testament.

— —

THE mother of young Cupid,
Once her baby sleepless lay,
Fearful lest the child should perish,
Weeping loud in her dismay,

Quickly to the gods repair'd.
Grave Morpheus took it in his care,
Laid it in the bed of Hymen,—
In a trice it slumber'd there.

Love, Morpheus, and I
Shared a maiden fair;
Love took her heart
As his due share,
And Morpheus liked
Her sweet eyes best
So I for myself
Claimed all the rest.

The Devil tried hard
Job's faith to impair,
Loss of property, children,
And health he'd to bear,
But failing to tempt him
To curse his own life,
To make him despair
He left him his wife.

A Mathematician,
Garcia by name,
Was thus sadly address'd
By the wife of the same:

How is't you acquir'd
Such a great reputation
And are so behindhand
In Multiplication?

Pablo de Jérica.

The Sun-dial.

A sun-dial was made by some natives near Quito,
Who thought it so fine (in Spanish " bonito "),
They put up a roof to protect it from rain,
Saying, " We never shall have such a sun-dial again."
But of use it was none, since the roof hid the sun.
And I said in my heart, 'tis a nice counterpart
      Of good laws for our weal
      Spoil'd by fools' silly zeal!

J. E. Hartzenbusch, 1806–1880.

FOLK-TALES.

The Girl who Wanted Three Husbands.

A CERTAIN Pacha had a daughter who had three suitors. When her father asked her which of the three she would marry, she replied she wanted all three. To this he replied it was impossible, no woman ever had three husbands; but the girl, who was wilful and spoilt, persisted, and at last the good Pacha in despair called the three suitors before him and told them he would give his daughter to whichever returned with the most wonderful thing within a year's time. The three suitors set out in quest, and after vainly wandering about the world for many months, one of them met a witch who showed him a looking-glass in which you saw whatever you wished to see. This he bought from her. The second suitor also met this witch, who sold him a strip of carpet, which, when you sat upon it, carried you to wherever you wished to go; while the third suitor bought from her a salve, the which, when applied to the lips of a newly laid out corpse returned the body to life. Now the three suitors met, and showed each other their respective finds.

"Let us wish to see our fair mistress," said one; and they wished and looked into the mirror, when, lo and behold! they saw her dead, laid out in her coffin ready for burial. They were overwhelmed with grief.

"My salve will restore her to life," said the third suitor, "but by the time we get to her she will have been long buried and devoured by worms."

"But my carpet will take us to her at once," cried the second suitor, and so they all sat down on it and wished.

In a trice they found themselves in the Pacha's palace, and the salve was applied to the dead girl's lips. She immediately came to life again, sat up, and looking at the Pacha said—

"I was right, you see, father, when I wanted all three."

(*Abridged from*) *Fernan Caballero.*

Péru's Solution of the Difficulty.

There was in the village of Abadiano a certain farmer called Chomin, who had made a prodigious fortune by his devotion to a number of saints of both sexes.

When first married he possessed nothing beyond his wife and a dog; but it occurred to him to make perpetual family saints of St. Isidro, patron of farmers; St. Antonio, advocate of animals; St. Roque, enemy of the plague; Santa Lucia, protector of the sight; St. Barbara, enemy of thunderbolts and lightning, and other innumerable saints, to each of whom he offered up every night their respective Pater Noster and Ave Maria, and certes, he struck a mine of wealth by so doing, for from that moment he began to prosper, and in such a way that after a few years he had the best house and farm in the district of Gaztelua.

In Chomin's house even a headache was unknown; the wheat, which in Biscay generally produces sixteen bushels for one sown, produced twenty-four for Chomin; the maize, which nearly always produces thirty for one, produced forty for Chomin; not a single head of his cattle had come to grief, although he had many, and when a storm burst upon the heights of Gorbea and Amboto, and the lightning flashed towards Abadiano, it always took good care to make a little round so as to avoid passing over Chomin's buildings and property.

Chomin had a servant by name Péru, to whom he had promised his daughter, Mari-Pepa, with whom Péru was in love, and verily not without motive, for she was the prettiest girl that came to dance on Sundays in the market-place of Abadiano.

Péru was a hard worker, and as honest as the day; but he had a very short memory, and was not over-intelligent; it was related of him among other things, how one day that Péru had to go to San Antonio de Urquiola, his master having commissioned him to kiss the Saint for him, Péru, instead of giving the kiss to the Saint, gave it to the Saint's pig, which always accompanies him. But in spite of this, if he was in love with Mari-Pepa, she was still more in love with him, for we know what women are like; they may dislike a man for being poor, ugly, or wicked, but they don't mind how stupid he is.

One night, the eve of St. James, after the whole family, under the direction of Chomin, had told their rosary, with an extra rosary of Pater Nosters and Ave Marias to the patron saints of the house, Chomin said to Péru—

"Listen, Péru. To-morrow begins the fair of Basurto, and I am thinking of going there to see if I can buy a pair of bullocks to rear and train, so that when you and Mari-Pepa marry you may have a good yoke of oxen, for it is already time to think of settling you."

Péru and Mari-Pepa, upon hearing this, blushed as red as cherries, and looked at each other with eyes dancing with joy.

Chomin continued, "I shall be away for at least a couple of days, for until I come across a pair which will be the pride of the country I won't come back. Meanwhile, Péru, you will have to take my place at prayers, and be careful not to forget the Pater Noster and Ave Maria for each of the Saints who protect us."

"Don't you worry about it," replied Péru, "not a single one shall be forgotten."

"I hope not, Péru, for, you see, we owe them a great deal. My wife and I had only one rag in front and another behind when we made them our Saints, and to-day. . . . Well, you shall see a good few ounces of gold from the sweepings of our stables on your and Mari-Pepa's wedding-day! But suppose you omit, for example, St. Barbara and her corresponding Pater Noster and Ave Maria, and a tempest bursts over us. . . . Lord Jesus, at the very thought my legs tremble! Now let us see, Péru, if you know by heart all the saints to whom you must pray."

Péru recited the names of all the patrons of the family to Chomin's satisfaction, but the latter burdened his fealty in the accomplishment of his task, by threatening that he should not become his son-in-law if he did a single saint out of their respective Pater Noster and Ave Maria, which omission would be sure to be found out by the ill-luck which would certainly happen to the family, house, property, or cattle.

The next morning, after he had attended early mass, Chomin took his way to the fair, now certain that Péru would not pass over a single saint. Poor Péru took the charge so much to heart, and above all the threat, that he passed the whole night and next morning in trying to find a sure way of not forgetting a single saint, but with no avail, however much he racked his brains. And it was a serious case, for Péru said to himself, "I know all their names off like a parrot, but as there are twenty-five besides the Virgin, how can I help it if I give an Ave Maria or so short, and there is an end to my marriage with Mari-Pepa? It would be a pretty to-do if that happened, for I shall not find another companion like her easily, and then Chomin won't let us leave the house without some household furniture, a good yoke of oxen, and fifty ducats for the dowry."

At the fall of evening all the village was dancing to the sound of the tambourine in the market-place of Abadiano, all except Péru and Mari-Pepa. Péru was sitting amidst brambles and furze on a desolate slope overlooking the village. Mari-Pepa was in the market-place close to the village fountain, refusing to dance with anybody, and full of grief at Péru's state of mind.

Suddenly Péru uttered a shout of joy and flew down the hill, seized Mari-Pepa, and began the maddest dance ever seen in Abadiano. He had thought out an infallible way how not to forget a single saint in the celestial city.

That evening, after praying to each of the particular saints appointed by Chomin special patron saints of the family, lest any should have been forgotten he prayed to *all the saints in the celestial city,—and seven leagues without,* in case any should be taking a walk.

A. Trueba.

MIRACLES OF ST. ISIDRO, PATRON-SAINT OF MADRID.

OLD CHRISTOVAL'S ADVICE, AND THE REASON WHY HE GAVE IT.

IF thy debtor be poor, old Christoval cried,
    Exact not too hardly thy due;
For he who preserves a poor man from want,
    May preserve him from wickedness too.

If thy neighbour should sin, old Christoval cried,
    Never, never unmerciful be!
For remember it is by the mercy of God
    That thou art not as wicked as he.

At sixty-and-seven the hope of heaven
    Is my comfort, old Christoval cried;
But if God had cut me off in my youth,
    I might not have gone there when I died.

You shall have the farm, young Christoval,
    My good master Henrique said;
But a surety provide, in whom I can confide,
    That duly the rent shall be paid.

I was poor, and I had not a friend upon earth,
    And I knew not what to say;
We stood by the porch of St. Andrew's Church,
    And it was St. Isidro's day.

Take St. Isidro for my pledge,
    I ventured to make reply;
The Saint in Heaven may perhaps be my friend,
    But friendless on earth am I.

We entered the church and came to his grave,
    And I fell on my bended knee;
I am friendless, holy Isidro,
    And I venture to call upon thee.

I call upon thee my surety to be,
    Thou knowest my honest intent;
And if ever I break my plighted word,
    Let thy vengeance make me repent

I was idle, the day of payment came on,
    And I had not the money in store;
I feared the wrath of Isidro,
    But I feared Henrique more.

On a dark, dark night I took my flight
  And hastily fled away :
It chanced that by St. Andrew's Church
  The road I had chosen lay.

As I passed the door I thought what I had swore
  Upon St. Isidro's day ;
And I seemed to fear because he was near,
  And faster I hastened away.

So all night long I hurried on,
  Pacing full many a mile ;
I knew not his avenging hand
  Was on me all the while.

Weary I was, and safe I thought,
  But when it was daylight,
I had, I found, been running round
  And round the church all night.

I shook like a palsy and fell on my knees,
  And for pardon devoutly I prayed :
When my Master came up—What, Christoval,
  You are here betimes, he said.

I have been idle, good master ! I cried,
  Good master, and I have been wrong !
And I have been running round the church
  In penance all night long.

If thou hast been idle, Henrique said,
  Go home and thy fault amend ;
I will not oppress thee, Christoval,
  May the Saint thy labour befriend.

"I HAD, I FOUND, BEEN RUNNING ROUND AND ROUND THE CHURCH ALL NIGHT."

Homeward I went a penitent,
 And I never was idle more;
St. Isidro blest my industry,
 As he punished my fault before.

When my debtor was poor, old Christoval said,
 I have never exacted my due;
I remembered Henrique was good to me,
 And copied his goodness too.

When my neighbour has sinned, old Christoval said,
 I have ever forgiven his sin,
For I thought of the night by St. Andrew's Church,
 And remembered what I might have been.

  Southey's " Letters from Spain and Portugal."

THE WEDDING NIGHT.

BEFORE Isidro's holy shrine
Hernando knelt and pray'd,
"Now, blessed Saint, afford thine aid,
 And make Aldonza mine;
And fifty pieces I will lay,
The offering of my Wedding Day,
 Upon thy holy shrine."

Hernando rose and went his way;
Isidro heard his vow;
And, when he sued, Aldonza now
 No longer said him nay;
For he was young and *débonair*,
And sped so well that soon the fair
 Had fix'd the Wedding Day.

The Wedding Day at length is here,
The day that came so slow;

Together to the church they go
　The youth and maid so dear ;
And kneeling at the altar now
Pronounced the mutual marriage vow,
　With lips and heart sincere.

And joy is on Hernando's brow,
And joy is in his breast ;
To him by happiness possest,
　The past exists not now ;
And gazing on the wedded maid,
The youth forgot Isidro's aid,
　And thought not of his vow.

The sun descended from the height
Of heaven his western way ;
Amid Hernando's hall so gay,
　The tapers pour their light ;
The Wedding Guests, a festive throng,
With music and with dance and song,
　Await the approach of night.

The hours pass by, the night comes on,
And from the hall so gay,
One by one they drop away,
　The Wedding Guests ; anon
The festive hall is emptied quite :
But whither on his Wedding Night
　Is young Hernando gone?

Hernando he had gone away
The Wedding Guests before ;
For he was summon'd to his door
By an old man cloth'd in grey,

Who bade the Bridegroom follow him ;
His voice was felt in every limb,
   And forced them to obey.

The old man he went fast before,
And not a word said he,
Hernando followed silently,
   Against his will full sore ;
For he was dumb, nor power of limb
Possess'd, except to follow him,
   Who still went mute before.

Towards a church they hasten now,
And now the door they reach ;
The Bridegroom had no power of speech,
   Cold drops were on his brow ;
The church where St. Isidro lay,
Hernando knew, and in dismay,
   He thought upon his vow.

The old man touch'd the door, the door
Flew open at his will,
And young Hernando followed still
   The silent man before ;
The clasping doors behind him swung,
And thro' the aisles and arches rung
   The echo of their roar.

Dim tapers, struggling with the gloom,
Sepulchral twilight gave :
And now to St. Isidro's grave
   The old man in grey is come.
The youth that sacred shrine survey'd,
And shook to see no corpse was laid
   Within that open tomb.

> "Learn thou to pay thy debts aright!"
> Severe the old man said,
> As in the tomb himself he laid;
> "Nor more of vows make light."
> The yearning marble clos'd its womb,
> And left Hernando by the tomb,
> To pass his Wedding Night.

Southey's " Letters from Spain and Portugal."

FATHER COBOS' HINT.

(LAS INDIRECTAS DE PADRE COBOS.)

A CERTAIN Father Superior of, I don't know where, used to take such delicious cups of chocolate as only holy friars do. An intimate friend of the friar, who was extremely fond of chocolate, began visiting him very frequently, and always at the hour in which his reverence drank his chocolate, the friar being so courteous as to always order another cup for his visitor. But as this friend abused the father's hospitality by coming day after day, the latter complained of this sponging tendency, whereupon a lay-friar, whose name was Father Cobos, declared that it fell to him to give him a hint to drop this habit. To this the Father Superior agreed. Noticing soon after that his friend no longer came to the convent, and desirous to know the lay-friar's hint, he asked him after a fortnight what he had said to make his friend leave off coming even to see him.

"I gave him a hint," replied Father Cobos. "I said, 'Look you, Don Fulano, don't be so disobliging as to take your chocolate at home; for the Father Superior says you are such a tremendous glutton that it warms the cockles of his heart every time he sees you.'"

The Father Superior was so amused at this that he divulged the story, and since then the hints of Padre Cobos have become proverbial throughout Spain.

Juan Martinez Villergas.

POPULAR SONGS.

THE PARSLEY VENDOR.

THIS morning as the golden sun
    Was rising, pretty maid,
I saw you in the garden
Bending o'er the parsley bed.
To see you somewhat nearer
Through the garden gate I strayed,
And found when I went out again
I'd lost my heart, sweet maid.
You must have come across it,
For I lost it there, I say.
"Oh, pretty parsley maiden,
Give back my heart, I pray."

A. Trueba, 1819–1889.

PETENERA.

WHEN He made thee those black lashes
God, no doubt, would give thee warning
That for all the deaths thou causest,
Thou must put thyself in mourning.

(*Trans. A. Strettel.*)

ALCALDÉ máyòr, Alcaldé máyòr,
You sentence poor prisoners for theft,
While your daughter walks out with her black eyes,
And robs all our hearts right and left.

La Granadina.

Some tears, my pretty maiden,
If only two or three,
And the goldsmiths of Granáda
Shall set them as jewels for me.

They tell me that you love me,
But 'tis a falsehood bold:
So circumscribed a bosom
Could never two hearts hold.

As I carelessly opened
Your letter, my dear,
Your heart dropp'd out,
Into my bosom, I fear,
So I took it in; but
As there's no room for two,
I have taken out mine,
Which I now send to you.

Bolero.

I saw two stones
Fight in your street
For the joy of being trodden
Under your feet;
  And I ponder'd then,
  If the stones do this,
  Oh, what will men?

BOLERO.

A FAVOUR, Blacksmith,
I ask of you;
Pray make me a lover
Of steel so true.
      And this is what he replies to me:
      It can't be very true
      If a man it's to be.

As we know, God made man first,
And afterwards the womenstock;
First of all the tower is built,
But last of all the weather-cock.

May the Lord God preserve us from evil birds three,
From all friars, and curates, and sparrows that be:
For the sparrows eat up all the corn that we sow,
The friars drink down all the wine that we grow,
Whilst the curates have all the fair dames at their nod:
From these three evil curses preserve us, good God.
              (*Trans. G. Borrow.*)

PROVERBS.

THE Man is Fire, the Woman tow, the Devil comes the flame to blow.

Choose your Wife on a Saturday, not on a Sunday.

While the tall Maid is stooping the little one hath swept the House.

He who hath a handsome Wife, or a Castle on the Frontier, or a Vineyard near the Highway, never lacks a quarrel.

He who marries a Widow, will have a dead Man's Head often thrown in his Dish.

There's not a pin's point between the yes and no of a woman.

Mother, what kind of thing is this Marrying? Daughter, 'tis to spin, to bear Children, and to cry your eyes out.

The honest woman and the broken leg within doors.

Women and hens soon lost with gadding about.

He who stirs honey must have some stick to him.

In the house of the tambourinist, all dance.

No olla without bacon, no wedding without a tambourine.

A partridge frightened is half cooked.

There's many a good drinker under a ragged cloak.

God doth the Cure, and the Doctor takes the Money.

When the Devil hies to his Prayers he means to cheat you.

Change of Weather finds Discourse for Fools.

When all Men say you are an Ass, 'tis time to bray.

A Handful of Mother-wit is worth a bushel of Learning.

A Pound of Care will not pay an ounce of Debt.

A broken head never lacked a rag.

As good bread is baked here as in France.

When loaves are lacking, cake will do.

He who sings, scares away sorrow.

The hen lives on even with the pip.

However early you get up, the day won't break any sooner.

Short cuts, deep ruts.

Patience, and shuffle the cards.

The hare jumps out when you least expect her.

Where you hope to find rashers there are not even spits.

Opportunity is painted bald.

When the heifer's given you, run quick with the halter.

He who is not Handsome at Twenty, nor Strong at Thirty, nor Rich at Forty, nor Wise at Fifty, will never be Handsome, Strong, Rich, nor Wise.

I wept when I was born, and every day shows why.

Buy at a Fair, and sell at home.

Let us be Friends, and put out the Devil's eye.

Women, Wind, and Fortune are ever changing.

> When going up hill
> For a mule I sigh,
> But I like my own legs
> When I downwards hie.

He who will have a Mule without any Fault must keep none.

You should not blame the pannier for the donkey's fault.

The mule said to the donkey, Gee up, long ears.

There's a difference between Peter and Peter.

God keep me from him whom I trust, from him whom I trust not I shall keep myself.

The foot of the Owner is the best manure for his Land.

If your dove-cote never lacks corn, you will never lack pigeons.

Lock your Door, that you may keep your Neighbour honest.

Never mention the rope in the house of a hanged man.

Finger nails come in when wedges are useless.

When the abbot sings out, the acolyte's not far behind.

At night all cats are grey.

One devil's like another.

He who sheared me still handles his scissors.

Once bitten by a scorpion, and frightened at its shadow.

Flies don't enter a closed mouth.

Some have the glory, and others card the wool.

Don't stretch your leg further than the street is long.

What you have to give to the mouse give to the cat.

Smugglers make better custom-house officers than do carbineers.

Money paid, arms soon tired.

Italy to be born in, France to live in, and Spain to die in.

ANECDOTES.

AN astute Gallegan one day presented himself with the most candid air at the shop of a tailor, telling him he had come to draw the fifty reals he had deposited with him two years ago.

The tailor was thunderstruck, and replied that he had no money of his, whereupon the Gallegan began to cry out and complain loudly and bitterly, which soon drew a crowd round the shop door.

The tailor was sure of his fact, since there was no document to attest the imaginary deposit, but fearing the scandal might damage his business, yet unable to confess to the debt after denying it, had recourse to a neighbouring tradesman, who promised to settle the affair.

"Look you here, yokel, why are you making such a fuss about a mistake? Don't you remember that it was to my shop you brought the fifty reals?"

"Oh, yes," slyly replied the Gallegan; "but that was another fifty."

WHILE ascending a steep hill the mayoral opens the door of the diligence every now and then, to shut it with a loud bang, without a word to the passengers.

"Oh, mayoral!" cries one, "why do you open and shut the door like that, we are freezing."

"Hush! it's for the mules: every time the door slams they think somebody has got out, and pull better."

A COUNTRYMAN wrote the following letter to his son, a student in the capital :—

"MY DEAR SON,—This is to tell you that I am very displeased with the bad conduct which I have been told you observe in Madrid. If a good thrashing could be sent by post, you would have had several from me. As for your mother, the good woman spoils you as usual. Enclosed you will find an order for seventy reals, which she sends you without my knowledge,

"Your father,
"JOHN."

HORSE-DEALER, exhibiting a superb animal to probable customer :—

"Take this one, sir. He's a splendid trotter. Mount him at four in the morning at Madrid, and you'll be at Alcalá at five."

"He won't suit me."

"Why not?"

"What should I do at five o'clock in the morning at Alcalá where I know nobody?"

"THE deuce! I do feel bad."

"What's the matter."

"I ate a steak of horse-flesh and it's going round and round in my inside."

"My dear fellow! It must have been a circus-horse!"

A YOUNG girl was taken to see a bull-fight for the first time; and one of the matadors was furiously attacked by a bull.

"Don't be afraid, dear, don't be afraid!" exclaimed her father, while the matador was flying through the air with the impetus of the beast's horns.

"Oh, no, papa, it's the bull-fighter who'll be afraid."

At a Station.

"A peseta for a cup of chocolate! It's very dear. It would be better to lower the price, though it should be of an inferior quality."

"To please you, señor, I will make it three reals, but I can't make it of inferior quality."

In School.

"Now, Pepito, is *huevo* [egg] masculine or feminine?"

(Pepito, thoughtfully) "It's very difficult to tell."

"Difficult? What do you mean?"

"Well, sir, how can one know until the chicken's hatched?"

An Aragonese carman was unmercifully beating a mule who had fallen down in one of the chief streets of the capital. The passers-by stopped to censure the carman's conduct, exclaiming—

"How cruel!"

"Poor mule!"

"What a beast the man is!"

The carman stopped his blows and going to the mule's head, said—

"Caramba! Jocky; what a lot of friends you've made in Madrid!"

In the porch of a church a beggar's stool, on the stool a hat, in the hat a cardboard with the inscription—

"Ladies and gentlemen, do not forget a poor blind man, who has gone to his breakfast."

A dying courtier said to the priest that the only favour he asked of God was to let him live till he had paid his debts.

"That is a good motive, my son, and it is to be hoped that your prayer will be heard."

"Alas, father! If it were, I should be sure never to die."

An Arab of Tetuan asked a Jew, which of the three religions was the best: the Jewish, the Christian, or the Mahometan?

The Jew replied—"If Messiah really came, the Christian is the best; if He did not, mine is the best; but whether or no, yours, Mahomet, is always bad."

ECCENTRICITIES OF ENGLISHMEN.

IT is not to be wondered at that a country so fecund in heroes and men of genius as the home of Nelson, Newton, and Byron, should also produce some very eccentric men. Of no other sons of Adam are such whimsicalities and oddities related as of those born in England. At every step on the other side of the Channel one meets with mad philosophers, who, if they unexpectedly inherit a large fortune, instead of leading a sybaritic life, order a schooner or brig to be built, embark straight away without troubling about their destination, let the wind take them whither it lists, swallow half-a-dozen bottles of rum, double themselves into a berth, and mingle their snores with the roaring of the waves until their craft strands on a shoal, when the dampness of the ocean reminds them it's time to wake up.

I knew an Englishman poorer than a retired Spanish ensign, and more miserly than an old clo'man, who, with the help of a clever Newfoundland, which he loved like a brother, saved the life of a lord's daughter who had fallen into the Thames. Ten years later, when he did not even remember his generous deed, he received from the father of the lord's daughter a gift of £200,000 sterling. This stroke of good luck produced no impression on his mind, to judge by any outward expression of joy; and the following day when his creditors came to congratulate him, they found him, to their surprise, bathed in his own blood. Not far from the corpse lay a letter with the following contents: "Let nobody be accused of my death, ascribe it still less to bad fortune. I was happy in the act of suicide; I had good health and money. And yet I felt inclined to kill myself first, because I felt inclined, secondly, because from a boy I had always wished for a capital of £100,000, and I find myself with one hundred thousand more than I wanted. I leave half my fortune to my Newfoundland dog, to be invested in cat's-meat, of which he is very fond, and the other half to whoever undertakes to buy the cat's-meat for the dog. Witness my signature. . . ."

Needless to say, that all who knew the last will and testament of the deceased, wanted to discharge it, with no further philanthrophy than receiving the recompense. As for the dog, which was present at the reading of his master's will, that so greatly concerned him, he did not show the slightest sign of joy. However, the will was declared invalid, and to avoid all disputes the £200,000 were returned to the chest of the noble lord.

The latter, finding himself again possessor of funds of which he had taken leave for ever, desired to use them to satisfy a caprice, which should give him the fame, throughout the whole country, of a wit. He laid a wager with a rich tradesman that he would not sell a hundred thousand sovereigns at a halfpenny each, though he should take his stand for six hours in one of the most crowded spots of the capital. This proposition deceived the tradesman as it would have deceived anybody, and he agreed to take the bet, the stakes being nothing less than £200,000, convinced that it was impossible he could lose. There was a Court-*levée* that day, and a tremendous crowd of people were crossing the Thames over Westminster Bridge towards St. James's Palace. The tradesman and the lord took up their post one side of the bridge, behind a huge open chest, full of sovereigns. "A ha'penny each, sovereigns a ha'penny each!" cried the tradesman, and the lord at his side did nothing but laugh; the stipulations being that the lord should only be allowed to laugh, and the tradesman to say "A ha'penny each, sovereigns a ha'penny each!" The people passed on, saying: "What a take in! Good heavens! Sovereigns for a ha'penny. What will they be like?" The tradesman began to despair. More than one passer-by took up one of the coins, turned it round and round, and then noticing the laughter which the lord pretended he could not stifle, put the money back, saying, "They are well imitated, but nobody can do me."

"A ha'penny each, sovereigns a ha'penny each!" shouted the tradesman unceasingly, and the more he exerted himself to cry his ware, the more clearly did the public think they saw through the trick by which he hoped to empty their pockets. They stayed thus from nine in the morning till three in the afternoon, the lord laughing and the tradesman shouting. The result was that the latter lost the bet. Only two sovereigns were sold, and these were bought by a medical student, believing them to be false, but hoping to pass them in a gambling den or other low place. When he found they were accepted, he returned post-haste to Westminster Bridge to lay in a new provision, but arrived too late; the lord and the tradesman had already vanished.

A. Ribot y Fontserré.

In the Street.

EXCUSE me, I can't stop. The sermon begins at five, and Padre Macario preaches to-day. His words are worth their weight in gold, I don't want to lose *one*. I thought of going to call on the Zaragatonas to give them a piece of my mind; deceitful things, they wrote an anonymous letter to the head of my husband's department, saying he had the influenza, and that all the office would catch it, which is a vile story; he is quite well, and if he had anything the matter with him I should say so at once. . . . They may be thankful this is Holy Week or I should teach them a thing or two, but I don't want to offend Heaven to-day. The wicked scandalmongers ! . . . They shall hear from me sooner or later. . . . But . . . I can't stop. What's the time? Five o'clock. I must run the whole way. Oh! do you think you could manage to send me some stalls for La Tubau ! [1]

In the Church.

"Hail, Mary," . . . Madam, you are crushing my mantilla. . . . "full of grace," . . . yes, *you*, Madam! "Blessed are thou amongst." . . . Good evening, doña Agustina. . . .

[1] The Spanish Ellen Terry.

No, the sermon has not commenced yet, but it must very soon for I saw Padre Macario go into the sacristy.... Yes, isn't there a crowd, and quite natural too, there are not many orators *like* him.... " Our Father which "... You look rather pale? What's the matter?... Oh, don't speak to me of husbands, there are some wretches amongst them?... What, he wouldn't let you come to the sermon? Heavens, what a man! Mine, thank God, is not like that; on the contrary, so that I might feel quite easy, he has promised to give baby his food. He's a very good husband; fancy, this morning I had to go out to see the dynamiters in court, and he stayed at home to wash out some baby-clothes.... " Thy kingdom come," ... but he has his enemies. Those horrid Zaragatonas; ... they can't bear me because I'm plump.... They're jealous and I've told them so. It's the will of Heaven, for as for eating, I eat very little, and some days a little stewed veal, an omelette, and half-a-dozen oranges satisfy me as much as if I had eaten an ox. But it's no good, they dislike me, because they themselves are so scraggy, and now they've started a nasty rumour about my husband. Suppose he has a little cold in the head, what's that to do with them? " Pray for our sins now and "... *They* are consumptive, if you like: you need only look at them, especially the eldest, who dresses her salad with cod-liver oil. I, of course, respect the sacredness of this week, or I should go and see them, when they would have to look to themselves. Besides, I don't like talking ill of anybody, but they had a lieutenant-colonel lodging with them, who only slept there, for he ate with his mess, and paid them ten reals for a tiny bedroom, and was always making them presents besides; if he had an old pair of trousers, for instance, he would give them to their mother to make a little jacket for herself. Now that all means something. In fact, I don't like scandal, but that lieutenant-colonel, "the Lord is with thee." . . . What? Padre Macario in the pulpit? So he is, and just going to begin.

"Dear Brethren . . ."

What eloquence!

"May you in truth be brethren, with your conscience free from the sin of hatred. . . ."

He's right. People are so uncharitable, those Zaragatonas, for instance.

"Love one another with the love of brethren. Christ pardoned His tormentors. . . ."

(*Much moved*) Ah! ah! It seems impossible that people won't repent. When I think of those Zaragatonas, I don't know what's the matter with me! No, when Holy Week is over, I shall go and hear what they have to say for themselves. Horrid creatures!

"*De todo un poco.*" *Luis Taboada* (*Madrid Comico*).

A COINER of false money was confessing that he had made and uttered dollars (20 reals) which were only worth four reals.

"You must restore the difference," said the priest.

"But to whom can I restore it, father? asked the compunctious penitent.

The priest hesitated for a moment, then said—

"Make as many other dollars worth thirty-six reals."

"*La Ilustracion Española y Americana.*"

Spanish Ceremony.

A VERY ceremonious Spaniard, when asked why he was not present at the funeral of a certain personage, replied—

"Because he owed me a call."

Children.

A governess out walking with two children:—
"Look, that's the white cow that gives us our milk."
"Does that black one give us the coffee then?"

"Oh, children! what are you doing up that tree?"
"Mama, Pepito wanted to pick some pears."
"And you?"
"I got up to persuade him not to."

Rural Sympathy.

"My boy," said a happy mother, "has won the first prize at school."

"I can understand your feelings. Oh, how well I remember how pleased I was when our pig took a prize at the show."

"*Blanco y Negro.*"

In the Stalls.

"Do you notice how fat all the chorus are?"

"Yes, the manager is very economical, and the fat ones get the same pay as the thin but fill the stage better."

"*Blanco y Negro.*"

"Take care they don't give you mule's flesh," said a mistress to her maid, who was going out marketing."
"And how can I tell, ma'am?"
"I don't know, but mind you don't buy any."
"Good, ma'am; I won't take any meat until the butcher has shown me the cow's horns."

"*La Ilustracion Española y Americana.*"

Furious wife to inflexible husband:—

"My health requires it. The doctor has ordered me a change of air."

"Very well, my dear, use another fan."

"*La Ilustracion Española y Americana.*"

The Anarchist Agitation.

Military police to poor wretch found in a miserable garret suspiciously hiding a paper:—

"Some little preparation for the First of May, eh?"

(*Timidly*) "Only a sonnet dedicated to the victims."

"*Madrid Comico.*"

Sunday Rest.

The Congress is at present warmly debating the question as to Sunday rest. As scarcely any of us Spaniards work even on week-days, *why* should we work on a Sunday?

"*Madrid Comico.*"

Woman and Man,
I've a specialist's word,
Are as different quite
As a fish and a bird.
She, like the latter,
Is graceful and sweet,
White feathers, charms many,
Long wings, and short feet.
He, on the contrary,
Sticky as gum,
Has, patent or hidden,
Sharp fins, a fair sum.
They marry each other,
For love possibly,
And the law of their cage
Turns and takes out the key.

Poor things, unaware
Were they, but now larn,
That the well-being of one
Is the other one's harm.
If she longs for air,
For water he cries;
The bird drowns in water,
In air the fish dies.

But some pairs are happy, to me you reply!
Yes, some few amphibious creatures, I sigh.

"*Los Lunes de el Imparcial.*"   *Manuel del Palacio.*

HUMOROUS ADVERTISEMENTS.

Perfumes recently arrived from Heaven.—
Perfumería Americana, Espoz y Mina, 26.

Two elephants pull at a pair of English trousers (Pesquera, Magdalena, 20) without tearing them.

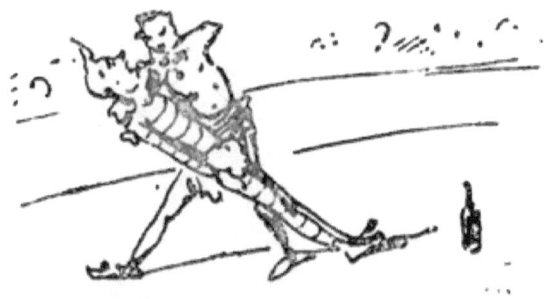

Resuscitation of a dead man, thanks to the fine Brandy of MOGUER, CARMEN, 10.

I had been shaved at No. 40, ALCALA, when an angel flying past told me to follow him, since I was ready.

The athlete, Señor Gomez, has developed his muscles in a most extraordinary way by dining regularly at the restaurant, LAS TULLERIAS, MAYOR 6.

"The earth shook, my sister, the skies were o'ercast, and the clocks stopped."

"Then they could not have been bought at BRANAS, MATUTE 12, father!"

When Love has the toothache,
He is halting and thin,
So get rid of the tooth
If your fair one you'd win.

(TIRSO PEREZ, MAYOR, 73, DENTIST.)

Madrid Comico.

AT THE THEATRE.

The first thing done by every new-comer is to deposit his hat on a chair, to show there are no hooks in the hall.

The startled lover hides himself in a special shelveless cupboard, kept in all houses exclusively for this object.

If anyone becomes a corpse at the end of the drama, the witnesses must all keep the same position until the curtain falls at least.

AT THE THEATRE.

When anything serious happens to the heroine, she must at once take out her hair-pins, which are incompatible with sentiment.

The comic tenor can do nothing less than sing smart couplets to the young ladies, who learn them immediately and repeat them straight away.

Madrid Cómico.

NOTES CRITICAL AND BIOGRAPHICAL.

[*The accent, used in Spanish both for accentuation and pronunciation, has mostly only been given in the names of persons and places in which it is necessary for the pronunciation, as José, otherwise Jose.*]

ALARCON, PEDRO ANTONIO DE, perhaps the most popular Spanish writer of the nineteenth century, was born in Guadix in 1833, and was a member of a noble family of but little means. After studying first jurisprudence, and afterwards theology, he devoted himself to letters, for which he had always shown a strong proclivity. Amongst the best known of his numerous works are "The Three-Cornered Hat," which is based on an old Spanish tale, somewhat Boccaccian in flavour; "The Scandal"; "La Alpujarra," the records of a delightful trip in Andalusia; and several collections of short tales, of which many have been translated into English—notably by Mary J. Serrano (New York).

ALAS, LEOPOLDO, author and critic of the present day.

ALEMAN, MATEO, native of Seville, flourished in the year 1609. He followed in the steps of Mendoza, by the more ample portraiture of the life of a rogue than is the former's Lazarillo, in his "Guzman de Alfarache," which appeared in 1553, forty-six years after its prototype. Little is known of Aleman's life; he seems to have been long employed in the Treasury, and at last to have retired, and devoted the rest of his life to letters. But he claims to be remembered by his work, "Guzmann de Alfarache," the popularity of which was so immediate that, like "Don Quixote," it provoked a spurious "Second Part" before the real continuation appeared, and was soon translated into the chief European tongues, French,

Italian, German, Portuguese, and even Latin, and into excellent English by Mabbe, whose contemporary, Ben Jonson, thus speaks of it:

> "The Spanish Proteus, which, though writ
> But in one tongue, was formed with the world's wit,
> And hath the noblest mark of a good booke,
> That an ill man doth not securely looke
> Upon it; but will loathe or let it passe,
> As a deformed face doth a true glasse."

(Verses prefixed to Mabbe's translation, and signed by Ben Jonson.)

AYGUALS DE IZCO, WENCESLAO, nineteenth century. This author, now often held up as a model to avoid, enjoyed, some fifty years ago, no little popularity as a humorous writer.

"BOOK OF JOKES, THE," is to be found in the collection of "Spanish Salt," edited by A. Paz y Melia, and published in 1890. Señor Paz believes most of the tales in the "Book of Jokes" should be ascribed to Hurtado de Mendoza.

CALDERON DE LA BARCA, PEDRO, the great successor and rival of Lope de Vega, was eminently a poet in the national temper, and had a brilliant success. He was born at Madrid on January 17, 1600. After serving as a soldier he was, on the death of Lope, formally attached to the Court, and was subsequently made a Knight of the Order of Santiago. In 1651 he followed the example of Lope de Vega and other men of letters by entering the Church. He died in 1681, on the Feast of Pentecost, when all Spain was ringing with his autos, and was buried in the splendid church of Atocha. Calderon was remarkable for his personal beauty, and was endowed with a benevolent and kindly character. Of his autos, or religious plays, the "Wonder-working Magician" is the most characteristic of the old Spanish stage (the question has been raised if Goethe had not read it before he wrote "Faust," the plot being very similar). Of the secular dramas, "The Mayor of Zalamea" is in Spain the most popular, and is still frequently represented, while "Life is a Dream" is perhaps pre-eminent for its brilliant flowing verse and philosophic thoughts. "The Mayor of Zalamea," though boisterous and jolly in the act given in the text, winds up a tragedy of the first water.

CAMPOAMOR, RAMON DE, native of Asturias, September 24, 1817, called by Blanco Garcia the Poet "Philosopher" (a title disputed by other critics), is one of the few modern Spanish poets whose fame has crossed the frontier of the Peninsula, his works having been studied in Italy and France. Like his late fellow-poet, Zorrilla, he has reached a ripe old age, and his peculiar style (of which "If She could only Write" is perhaps scarcely typical) has had several imitators.

"CELESTINA; OR, THE TRAGICOMEDY OF CALISTO AND MELIBŒA," is considered one of the chief foundations of the Spanish drama. The first act was probably written by Rodrigo Cota of Toledo, and it may be assumed that it was produced about 1480. The rest was added by Fernando de Rojas de Montalvan. Unhappily, large portions of this vigorous work abound in a shameless libertinism. It was followed by many imitations, and was soon translated into English, German, Dutch, Latin, Italian, and French.

CERVANTES DE SAAVEDRA (MIGUEL) was a member of an old noble family, decayed in fortune, and was born in the month of October in 1547 in Alcalá de Henares. Here he probably received his early education, which it has been conjectured he continued at Madrid, and later on at the University of Salamanca. He discovered a strong predilection for literature, but his necessities seemed to have forced him to seek for a livelihood by some other means. Anyway, in 1570 we find him serving at Rome as chamberlain in the household of Cardinal Aquaviva; and he subsequently entered the navy, and lost his left hand at the famous sea-fight of Lepanto, which fight decisively arrested the intrusion of the Turks into the West of Europe (October 7, 1571). His misfortune did not prevent him joining the troops of the King of Spain at Naples; but when returning to Spain by sea, he was made a prisoner by pirates, who took him to Algiers, where for five years he was kept as a slave. After this period he was ransomed, when he went to Madrid. He married in 1584, and soon after began his first literary efforts, which were for the stage. But after composing some thirty plays with little pecuniary result, his genius was diverted into a different channel, and he produced, in 1605, the First Part of the immortal novel of "Don Quixote." Inimitable in its wit and humour as this work is, it was at first received with comparative indifference. Ultimately, however, it met with the greatest applause, although the author reaped few or none of the emoluments which might have been expected from it. The Second Part was not published till 1615, and was even superior to the first. (Avellaneda's spurious Second Part appeared in 1614.) Needless to say, "Don Quixote" soon became known all over the civilised world, and was translated into a multitude of tongues. The oldest English translation is by Shenton, 1612, which is followed by a vulgar, unfaithful, and coarse one by Milton's nephew, John Philips, 1712; one by Motteux; one by Jervas (Jarvis), 1742, which Smollet used freely in his own, 1755; a few others of lesser importance; and finally, in the eighties of the present century, one by Mr. Ormsby; and Mr. H. E. Watt's learned and faithful work, from which the extracts have been drawn for this volume. The other principal works of Cervantes are "The Journey to Parnassus," his Exemplary Novels, "Galatea," and the unfinished romance, "The Labours of Persiles and Sigismunda," his last work. Cervantes died on the 23rd of April, in the year 1616 (the year of Shakespeare's death), at the age of sixty-eight.

CHRONICLE OF THE CID. Southey's so-called "Chronicle of the Cid" is not a translation of any single work, but is based upon, i. La Cronica del Cid; ii. La cronica general (thirteenth century); iii. El Poema del Cid (twelfth century); and lastly, the ballads of the Cid. The extract given is, however, a word for word translation from the Cronica del Cid. The first and only edition of this chronicle was printed in 1552, but it is impossible to ascertain its age. (The Abbot who published it absurdly supposed it to have been written during the Cid's lifetime.) The incident in the given extract seems to have much amused a mediæval audience, and it was often enlarged and improved upon by the minstrels and story-tellers.

CID, THE (ARABIC, SAID = LORD), DON RODRIGO DIAZ DE BIVAR, also styled *The Campeador*, the national hero of Spain, was born at Burgos about 1040. The facts of his career have been wrapped by his admiring countrymen in such a haze of glorifying myths, that it is scarcely possible to detect them. His life, however, appears to have been entirely spent in fierce warfare with the Moors, then masters of a great part of Spain. His exploits are set forth in the works given in the note to the Chronicle of the Cid; and the story of his love for Ximena is the subject of Corneille's masterpiece,

"Le Cid" (based on a play by the Spanish dramatist Guillen de Castro). The Campeador's last achievement was the capture from the Moors of Valencia, where he died in 1099.

EPIGRAMS. The names of two famous satirists, of Forner (d. 1797) and Pitillas, are, for various reasons, lacking in this compilation.

ESTÉBANEZ DE CALDERÓN, SERAFIN (El Solitario), born in Malaga, 1799, and died in Madrid in 1867, is given the priority of those authors, akin to the Periodical Essayists in English literature, called in Spain writers of "*costumbres*" (manners and customs of the people), who occupy so important a place in the Spanish literature of the nineteenth century, and amongst whom de Larra (Figaro) is pre-eminent. Unfortunately El Solitario employs such subtle style and archaic phrases that the Spaniards themselves complain they have to read his works with a dictionary.

"ESTEBANILLO GONZALEZ, THE LIFE OF," which appeared in 1646, is the autobiography of a buffoon, who was long in the service of Ottavio Piccolomini, the great general of the Thirty Years' War, but it is an autobiography so full of fiction, that Le Sage, sixty years after its appearance, easily changed it into a mere romance (Ticknor).

"FERNAN CABALLERO" (Cecilia Böhl de Faber, daughter of the Spanish scholar), was born in 1796, and married three times. She is sometimes known under her last name, Cecilia Arron (or Arrom) de Azala. Her numerous works, chiefly novelas, were published under the pseudonym of Fernan Caballero, the name of a little village in La Mancha. They give truthful and lively pictures of Spanish (especially Andalusian) life and manners, are eminently national in tone and spirit, and have an excellent moral tendency, which combination soon made her one of the most popular Spanish writers of the nineteenth century. She also shares with Trueba the honour of collecting Spanish Folk-tales and popular songs from the mouths of the people, before the days of Folk-lore societies. Queen Isabella II. made her an offer of a residence in the Alcazar of Seville, of which she availed herself till the revolution of 1868, after which she lived in a modest villa, and devoted herself to charity. She died April 7, 1877.

FOLK-TALES. To a student of Spanish Folk-lore this selection will be unsatisfactory. The tales from Fernan Caballero and Trueba (see *Biographical Notes*) are, however, amusing, while Southey's verses present a sample of the numerous tales current in Spain about the saints, and which are more often than not allied to the ridiculous. *El Padre Cobos* is the title of a famous periodical produced in the years 1854-6 (see *Newspaper Humour*).

"GATOMAQUIA." [Having been unable to find a passage in Lope de Vega's burlesque epic, the "Gatomachia," comprehensive enough in itself to form a good extract, I append some lines descriptive of the hero and heroine, which, though somewhat vulgarised in the English, may give a notion of its humour.]

> On a lofty peak'd ridge of a til'd-roof there sat
> Zapaquilda, the prettiest pussy cat,
> Enjoying a blow and most busy at work
> Cleaning waistcoat and tail with tongue graceful yet perk,
> For as jaunty a cat and important is she
> As if she belonged to a monastery—
> No mirror had she, though a mocking magpie
> Had carried a broken potsherd up on high—
> Who never found student's shirt-collar but he
> Behind a tile hid it as his property.
> When she'd finished her washing, and wetting her paws,
> Had drawn two long stripes down her sides with her claws,
> She sang a sweet sonnet with such style and grace,
> It reminded one of the musician of Thrace,
> And made all the hearts of her list'ners rejoice
> And say, " I am sure that's a pussy cat's voice,"
> While some feline solfas and harmonious chromatics
> Laid a whole nest of rats low with nervous rheumatics.
>
> 'Twas late spring and fair Flora with buskins of gold
> Decked the earth with her roses and flowers manifold,
> When to Sir Marramaquiz, of fame far and wide,
> His squire (of La Mancha, by birth) quickly hied,
> To tell how in the sun Zapaquilda, as fair
> As the roseate dawn, had been combing her hair,
> And now, with a charm and a grace quite her own,
> Was singing a trifle of famed Mendelssohn,
> That enamoured the air. Marramaquiz's heart
> At this news of his squire of dire love felt the smart;

He called for his charger, a monkey acquired
In the war of the Apes and the Cats, and attired
In breeches and boots, worth many a bright dollar,
And a little girl's cuff round his neck for a collar,
In cape, cap and feather, and girt with a sword,
(The feather he'd pluck'd from a parrot whose word
Of defiance had vexed him), used both whip and spur,
And found Zapaquilda still taking the air,—
Who on seeing him, modest as nun 'neath a veil,
Lick'd one paw, droop'd her eyelids and let down her tail,
For of virtuous maidens, 'tis ever the duty
To be more circumspect the greater their beauty.

GUEVARA, LUIS VELEZ DE, born in 1572 or 1574 at Ecija in Andalusia. He wrote a good deal for the stage (four hundred plays), in which he was an early follower of Lope de Vega; but the work which established his fame was the "Diablo Cojuelo," the "Limping Devil," which suggested the idea of Le Sage's famous "Diable Boiteux." Guevara died in the year 1644.

HARTZENBUSCH, JUAN EUGENIO, lived from 1806 to 1880, was born of a German father and Spanish mother. He is one of the first scholars, prose writers, and critics of the century, and like his contemporary, Mesonero Romanos, edited valuable collections of the flower of the old Spanish drama. His masterpiece is the tragedy, "The Lovers of Teruel," which treats upon an old Spanish legend, and is one of the most popular of modern plays. An opera with the same title and subject, by a Spanish composer of the day, is also deservedly popular. "Mariquita la Pelona," which is taken from a collection of short tales by this author, is written in old Spanish, and has a sequel in a modern "Mariquita," who repairs to a convent for a year to obtain possession of a sum of money offered her by some unknown person, on condition she undergoes this temporary confinement, to find at the expiration of the twelve months that the mysterious donor is a slighted suitor, who had vowed to humiliate her.

IGLESIAS, born in Salamanca, wrote a number of poems, the lighter of which have alone retained popularity, the serious and duller ones, written after he became a priest, being justly neglected. He died in 1791.

Isla, Father, was born in 1703, and died in 1781 at Bologna, where, being a Jesuit, he had been sent on the general expulsion of his order from Spain. He was an author possessed of a brilliant and delicate satire, most thoroughly exemplified in his celebrated work, "The History of the Famous Preacher, Friar Gerund," a direct attack on the bad style of preaching then in vogue. Padre Isla is also prominent as the translator into Spanish of "Gil Blas," which, without any foundation, he maintained had been stolen by Le Sage from Spanish literature.

Jérica (Xérica), Pablo de (he was a young man during the French revolution), is very severely criticised by Blanco García in his "History of the Literature of the Nineteenth Century."

Larra, Mariano José de (Figaro), was born in Madrid in the year 1809. Receiving his first education in France, where his father served as doctor in Napoleon's army, he returned to complete it at Madrid, and afterwards repaired to the University of Valladolid, where he began to study law. He wrote his first prose essays at the age of twenty, but it was his later articles, signed "El pobrecito Hablador," which first gave him the undisputed reputation of critic and writer of "*costumbres*," among the host of which, his Spanish contemporaries and imitators, he reigns supreme, while what preserve his fame are the brilliant and satirical articles signed "Figaro," amongst which "The Old Castilian," and "Yo quiero ser comico," are the best known. Unfortunately his private life was disturbed by wild love affairs, and he committed suicide on account of an attachment to a married lady, in 1837, at the age of twenty-eight.

"Libro de los Exemplos" (author unknown). This collection of tales is considered by Don Pascual de Gayangos to be posterior to Don Juan Manuel. The greater part of the tales are taken from Rabbi Mosch Sefardi's "Disciplina Clericalis" (early part of the twelfth century), probably the Latin translation of an Arabic original, which is drawn from Oriental sources, and is itself the common well from which drew, amongst others, the authors of the "Gesta Romanorum," the "Decameron," and the "Canterbury Tales." The story entitled "The Biter Bit" figures, for instance, in the "Disciplina Clericalis" and the Gesta Romanorum. "El Libro de los Gatos" belongs to the same century as the "Libro de los Exemplos" (or Enxemplos).

LOPE FELIX DE VEGA CARPIO was born on November 25, 1562, at
Madrid. This extraordinary Spanish genius, second only to
Cervantes, than whom he was more popular during the lifetime
of both, rose to a degree of fame reached by few of any country.
Epics, serious and humorous (see "*Gatomaquia*"); novelas; ballads;
epigrams; plays—religious, heroic, of intrigue, or of domestic life;
nothing, in fact, came amiss to his pen. But it is as dramatist that
he is best known, and in which quality his facility was such that at
his death it was reckoned he had composed eighteen hundred plays
and four hundred autos (religious dramas), while it is stated that
one of his plays was written and acted within five days. Lope de
Vega's last days were the prey to a melancholy fanaticism. He
regretted he had ever been engaged in any occupations but such as
were exclusively religious; and on one occasion he went through
with a private discipline so cruel that the walls of the compartment
where it occurred were found sprinkled with his blood. From this
he never recovered, and he died on August 27, 1635, nearly seventy-
three years old. His funeral, which immense crowds thronged to
see, lasted nine days; and of the eulogies and poems written on
the occasion, those in Spanish were sufficient to form one volume,
those in Italian another.

MANUEL, PRINCE DON JUAN, born May 5, 1282, at Escalona, died
1349, was of the blood royal of Castile and Leon, nephew to
Alfonso the Wise, cousin to Sancho IV. He first fought against
the Moors when he was twelve, and the rest of his years were
spent in filling great offices in the State, or in military operations
on the Moorish frontier. In spite of a life full of intrigue and
violence he devoted himself successfully to literature, and is the
first great Spanish prose writer. In "Count Lucanor," his best
and more known work, most of the tales are of Oriental origin.
That Shakespeare knew the tale, here given the title of his play,
is indubitable; while "The Naked King" will appear familiar to
readers of Hans Andersen's fairy tales ("The Emperor's New
Clothes" in its turn has given the plot for Ludwig Fulda's drama,
"The Talisman," considered the best German play of the last
three years, and recently introduced into England by Mr.
Beerbohm Tree under the title of "Once Upon a Time").

MENDOZA, DIEGO HURTADO DE, a distinguished Spanish statesman,
soldier, and historian, was born at Granada in 1503. After study-

ing at the Universities of Granada and Salamanca, he entered the service of the Emperor Charles V., and was employed in Italy both as diplomatist and general with equal success. He at last fell under the displeasure of Philip II. of Spain, and in 1567 was banished. He died at Madrid in the year 1575. His greatest work is " La guerra de Granada contra los Moriscos " ; he also wrote some fine poetry ; and claims the merit of producing in " Lazarillo de Tormes " the first model of the *novela picoresca*, peculiar to the literature of Spain. " Lazarillo " was translated into English as early as 1586 by David Rowland, of which rendering as many as twenty editions are known, and which was re-edited in the seventeenth century by James Blakeston, with but slight alterations. Like other books enjoying a wide reputation, it produced many imitations, among them a " Second Part " of little merit. See *Book of Jokes*.

MESONERO ROMANOS, RAMON DE (El Curioso Parlante), born in Madrid, 1803, died in 1882, who appeared in the literary world, almost simultaneously, with de Larra, and together with him and Estébanez de Calderón belongs to the writers of " *costumbres*," seems to an English reader inferior to these two in style and conception, though Spaniards consider his " Escenas Matritenses " one of the great works of the nineteenth century, and they are held by Blanco Garcia to be invaluable photographs of life in the writer's days. Mesonero Romanos was also a composer of light and piquant verses, and distinguished himself in the critical world by his collections of Spanish dramatists, published by Rivadeneyra.

MORATIN, LEANDRO FERNANDEZ, died 1828, the more famous son of a famous father (Nic. Fern. Moratin).

NEWSPAPER HUMOUR. The strictly humorous Spanish periodical literature of to-day is of no great merit, and often borders upon impropriety. Of the papers from which cuttings are here given, *La Ilustracion Española y Americana* (the Spanish *Illustrated News*), is first-rate in its class—Fernandez Bremen is a well-known contributor. The daily paper—*El Imparcial*—devotes a sheet every Monday to lighter and more amusing literature under the direction of Señor Ortega Munilla. Manuel Palacio is the comic poet of the day. Taboada, who writes for *El Madrid Comico*, the nearest approach to our *Punch*, is nothing if not vulgar. *Blanco y Negro* is a fairly successful attempt of humour with propriety. The famous periodical, *El Padre Cobos*, is not represented here as (it appeared in the years 1854-56) it cannot be considered to belong to the present day. It is, moreover, purely political.

OSSORIO Y BERNARD, MANUEL (nineteenth century). A humbler member of the *Spectator* school, or "autores de costumbres."

PALACIO VALDÉS, ARMANDO (nineteenth century). One of the Spanish novelists of the day, and of great popularity, especially in America, where nearly all his novels have been translated into English. "Sister Saint Sulpice" is perhaps his masterpiece. Of his later novels, "Froth" should be avoided as a disagreeable work, and no true picture of aristocratic Spanish circles. "El Maestrante," the last work of this author, is to be brought out shortly by Mr. Heinemann.

PARDO BAZAN, EMILIA, native of Corunna, September 16, 1851, married in 1868, is one of the most gifted women of the times, and in fame the Madame de Staël of Spain. She belongs to the Naturalistic school of novelists; does not, however, lack tinges of idealism. Her critical power is manifest in the review, *El Teatro Critico*, for three years the product of her pen alone, and the issuing of which, it is to be regretted, she has—owing to stress of work—suspended for this year (1894). She is, furthermore, editor of a series of works of special reference to women (whether of fiction, or of scientific, historical, and philosophical interest), for which she has already translated John Stuart Mill's "The Subjection of Women," while she promises, among other volumes, a Spanish version of "Adam Bede." The little tale "First Love" is given here as being suitable for this volume, rather than as typical of Doña Emilia's pen. Her works are too numerous to be here recounted.

"PEDIGREE OF FOOLS." This was versified at a later date.

PÉREZ GALDOS, BENITO, born in Las Palmas (the Canary Isles) in 1845, came to Madrid in 1863, where he took his degree in law. His fame rests upon the "Epistodios Nacionales," in which, following in the steps of Erckman-Chatrian, he illustrates his national history in a series of romances. The first series, to which the volume "Gerona" belongs, covers the period from the battle of Trafalgar to the entry of Ferdinand VII. into Spain (1814). Unlike his French prototypes, Pérez Galdos is furnished with no small amount of humour. In "Gerona" the grim horrors of the siege are well contrasted by passages, such as those given, and a third, in which the two boys Manolet and Badolet catch rats in the cellars, in danger themselves of being devoured by the army of famishing rodents, which are led by a huge fat rat, abused by the boys under the name of Napoleon, and which they finally catch and propose to sell in the market for at least ten reals (2s.) Pérez Galdos changes his residence according to the scenes of the subject at which he is working, and is at present at Santander.

PINEDO, LUIS DE. See *Book of Jokes*.

"POEMA DEL CID." This grand old poem, unquestionably the oldest in the Spanish language, is by Sanchez, who first published it in 1779, given as early a date as the middle of the twelfth century, about fifty years after the death of the Cid. Some spirited fragmentary translations by Mr. John Hookham Frere are appended to the early edition of Southey's "Chronicle of the Cid," and the whole laid before the reader in verse and somewhat epitomised prose by Mr. John Ormsby, whose work is invaluable to English students of the poem, not only for its true rendering, but for the fine introduction. An attempt at old ballad language and style may perhaps be excused in the extract selected, by reason that this, the most humorous incident in the poem, had unfortunately not been put into verse by either Mr. Hookham or Mr. Ormsby, and a fresh departure seemed desirable to avoid invidious comparison. The passage, alas! is also considerably abridged to suit the requirements of the present volume. For the rendering of the old Spanish I have to thank the valuable tuition of Señor Don José Balari y Jovany, of the University of Barcelona, to whom, as a philologist of no small merit, attention has already been drawn in England. The following passage is from Ford's "Guide to Spain"—Burgos Cathedral. "In the ante-room of the chapterhouse is preserved *El Cofre del Cid*, a trunk clamped with iron, and now attached to the north wall, which the Cid filled with sand, and then pledged to the Jews as full of gold, for a loan of 600 marks, which he afterwards honestly repaid."

Polo, Jacinto, flourished in 1630, and is known as the composer of some lyrical poetry and author of prose satires in the style of Quevedo's Visions. It has, however, been doubted by Gayangos and other critics if "The University of Love and School of Interest," from which Ticknor gives the extract "Aunts," was written by Polo.

Popular Songs. Long romances or ballads, like those of the olden times, are also sung in the streets of Spain by the blind minstrels. The so-called popular songs are, however, of the kind here given, which bear a strong family likeness to the *stornelli* and *rispetti* of the Italian peasantry, and which, illustrating the origin of the word *ballad*, are danced to. The verses often embody quaint conceits. The stones in the pavement quarrelling over which should be trodden on by a fair maid is not very far-fetched for a Spanish compliment. A Spanish lover will adore anything that has the remotest connection to his lady-love, and a record "flor" (flower = sweet saying) which hails from South America is, "Blessed be even the razor with which your father shaves himself." The accompaniment to the songs is in dancing rhythm thrummed on the ubiquitous guitar, and often marked by the castanets of the dancers, or, in Oriental fashion, by the clapping of hands of the by-standers. The air sung consists of three or four phrases at most, each a combination of nasally intoned, long-sustained notes ending in odd twists and turns.

Portuguese Epitaphs. The Castilians always sharpen their wits on the Portuguese, who, together with the Biscayans, are laughed at for their simplicity. The Portuguee is also accused of a love of brag. This joking is carried so far that, to take off the poor Portuguese, anecdotes and epitaphs (as in those selected) are written in the Portuguese language by Spaniards. The Andalusian also plays the braggart, and is a reputed payer of fantastic and exaggerated compliments (*flores*) to the fair sex. The Gallegan is credited with the shrewdness of the Yorkshireman.

Proverbs. Many of these "wise sayings drawn from long experience," to which the Spanish people are especially addicted, are given in the English rendering of an old book on Spanish proverbs in the library of the British Museum.

Quevedo, Francisco Gomez de, the eminent Spanish satirist, was born of a distinguished family at Madrid, 1580. He was sent early to the University of Alcalá, where he took his degree at the age of fifteen. He mixed much in fashionable society, but in consequence of a duel he was compelled to quit the court and repair to Naples, where he was received by the Spanish envoy, the Duke of Osuna, who not only retained him in his service, but procured his pardon at Madrid. On the fall of his patron Quevedo returned to court; but scarcely had he arrived there when he was arrested, and confined for three years to his country seat, upon the charge of being the author of certain libels against the Government. In 1641 he was again arrested on the charge of libel, and cast into prison, where he remained for nearly two years. He died sometime after his release in September, 1645. Quevedo was undoubtedly one of the best writers of his age, both in prose and verse. His longest prose satire, "The History and Life of the Great Sharper, Paul of Segovia," first printed in 1626, belongs to the style of fiction invented by Mendoza in his "Lazarillo," and has most of the characteristics of its class. His "Sueños," or Visions, are equally famous, and are extremely original. His works were translated into English by Sir Roger L'Estrange, and passed through about ten editions in forty years, and again by Stevens about the close of the last century. This most original of Spanish writers (excepting Cervantes) distinguished himself by his extraordinary versatility of talent. His poems, collected under the title of "El Parnaso Español," consist of lyrical poems, satires, burlesque pieces, and more than a thousand sonnets of remarkable beauty.

RIBOT Y FONTSERRÉ. The tales current abroad of the eccentricities of Englishmen are many. A Spaniard will gravely tell a tale of how an Englishman, after a serious railway accident on the Continent, in which his valet was killed, gathered together the fragments of the latter's body, packed them in the man's trunk, and despatched this to the family of the deceased. The tale of the somewhat Dundrearyesque lord may, however, be based on fact, for the story is known in England. It is here given from a Spanish humorous publication of the first half of this century. A veteran in journalism like Mr. Sala would probably know the origin, and name the hero of the story.

ROJAS, FRANCISCO DE (ROJAS Y ZORRILLA), flourished during the greater part of Calderon's life, and may have survived him. He was born in Toledo, and in 1641 was made a Knight of the Order of Santiago ; but when he died is not known. Unless he began his career too early to be a mere follower, he certainly belongs to Calderon's school. He is perhaps most successful in tragedies, of which the best play is " None below the King." This work still maintains a position on the stage, and is worth reading if only as an example of the extraordinary sense of honour and allegiance entertained by Spaniards in those past times.

RUEDA, LOPE DE, is the author of four comedias, two pastoral colloquies ("Timbria" is one), and minor works, all written for representation, and which were unquestionably acted before public audiences by the strolling company Lope de Rueda led about. The period in which he flourished is probably between 1544 and 1567. In spite of belonging to the then despised and rejected profession of the stage, he was interred with honour in the great cathedral of Cordova.

SANTOS, FRANCESCO, a native of Madrid, died not far from the year 1700. Between 1663 and 1697 he gave to the world sixteen volumes of different kinds of works for the popular amusement. The oldest of the series is " Dia y Noche en Madrid," the hero of which, a stranger, falls into the hands of a not over-honest servant, who undertakes to serve as guide to him in Madrid. " Truth on the Rack ; or, the Cid come to Life again," is an allegorical work (from it the tale " La Tarasca " is drawn), and is amusing in that the Cid on his return to earth is much disgusted with the traditions and ballads about himself.

SEGOVIA, ANTONIO MARIA, who signed his articles with the pseudonym " The Student," has the fame of being the most classic in style of the Spanish periodical essayists of the nineteenth century.

SELGAS Y CARRASCO, JOSÉ, was born in Murcia in 1824, and died at Madrid, 1882. He was one of the contributors to the famous periodical *El Padre Cobos*, and exhibits an inimitable serious humour in his volumes of " Loose Leaves " (" Hojas Sueltas ").

TIMONEDA, JUAN DE, a bookseller, one of the founders of the popular theatre in Spain, flourished in the year 1590. He was also an early writer of Spanish tales, his first attempt being " Patrañuelo," a small work which drew its material from widely different sources

—some being found in the Gesta Romanorum, others, like the story of Griselda, from Boccaccio, another, familiar to English readers by the ballad of "King John and the Abbot of Canterbury," probably from Sacchetti. Timoneda was a friend of Lope de Rueda, whose works he edited.

TRUEBA, ANTONIO DE, born Christmas, 1819 (?), of poor and respectable parents, within the jurisdiction of the province of Biscay, was sent, at the age of fifteen, to work in a hardware store in Madrid, where he spent all his spare time and hours, stolen from sleep, in reading and writing, until he began to publish, and finally dedicated himself wholly to literature. He is the exponent of humble Spanish life, especially of the country people, and if he is somewhat too rose-coloured in his views, it is, perhaps, not an unpardonable fault. His collection of popular songs was received with enthusiasm, and though he is now out of vogue as an author, the songs and his prose works, of which most are based upon folk-tales, will always be of value for the researches of Folk-lore.

VALERA, JUAN, was born in the province of Cordova on October 18, 1824. He had aristocratic connections, and was early in life enrolled in the diplomatic service, to which he owes his great familiarity with European literature. He subsequently entered politics, and until the age of forty-two had been able to give up to authorship but his hours of leisure, to which we owe his critical studies and translations. "Pepita Jiménez," his first novel, was produced in 1874, and was a "success unparalleled in the history of modern Spanish literature." To continue in the words of Mr. Edmund Gosse:—"This book still remains, after the large development of fiction in Spain, the principal, the typical Spanish novel of our days. . . . It has become a classic in the lifetime of its author, and is studied, imitated, analysed as a book which has passed beyond all danger of the vicissitudes of fashion, and which will unquestionably survive as one of the glories of the national literature. . . . 'Pepita Jiménez' is Spain itself in a microcosm— Spain with its fervour, its sensual piety, its rhetoric and hyperbole, its superficial passion, its mysticism, its graceful extravagance." Later novels are "El Comendador Mendoza," "Doña Luz," and "Doctor Faustino." Valera occupies a pre-eminent position as politician, journalist, author, and critic, and is at present at Vienna as Spanish ambassador to the Austrian Court.

VICENTE, GIL, a Portuguese, but who ranks among Spanish dramatists, as he wrote ten plays in Castilian. (It was a not uncommon practice for Portuguese authors to employ Castilian. Saa de Miranda, the pastoral poet and contemporary of Gil Vicente, wrote six of his eight eclogues in the more sonorous Castilian.) Gil Vicente flourished as a writer for the stage from 1506 to 1536; died in 1557.

YRIARTE (IRIARTE), TOMAS DE, born on the island of Teneriffe in 1750, but educated mostly at Madrid, owes his reputation chiefly to his literary fables, the influence of which was much needed in the age of bad writing in which they appeared, and in which he showed originality by adapting the attributes of animals to only one class of men, namely, authors, and not mankind at large, as had always been done before. Yriarte died in 1791.

ZAYAS Y SOTOMAYOR, MARIA DE. The only information we can gather respecting this lady is founded on the authority of the industrious bibliographer, Nicolas Antonio, who assures us that she was a native of Madrid, and that she composed two series of novels, under the titles of "Novelas Amorosas i exemplares," and "Novelas i Seraos." She is also mentioned by Lope de Vega in his "Laurel de Apolo" in very flattering terms. The style and character of this writer's novels exhibit much of the ease and elegance, with no little of the freedom, of Boccaccio; they abound with incident, both humorous and tragic, and with chivalric or amorous adventure. With little artifice, however, in the plot, and less study of character, there are some striking and effective scenes; while the situations are often well conceived, and the suspense is maintained throughout so as to please or surprise us. "The Miser Chastised" is perhaps the only one of her novels in which the writer wholly adopts a comic tone and spirit, without any touches of a more sentimental kind. With some humour, this story combines considerable ease and originality. Under the same title as the foregoing appeared a drama from the pen of Don Juan de la Hoz Mota, a Spanish dramatic writer of some celebrity, who succeeded in exposing the vice of avarice on the stage in strong and natural colours, and with such bold and happy strokes of ridicule, as almost to merit its being placed in the same rank with the famous "Avare" of Molière (Thomas Roscoe). Doña Maria de Zayas, flourished in the year 1637.

ZORRILLA, JOSÉ, born at Valladolid, February 21, 1817, poet *par excellence* of traditionary and legendary subjects, has for years been prime favourite of the Spanish people, and his inexhaustible vein of poetry showed but scanty signs of diminishing even in the last years of a hoary old age. His most popular work, "Don Juan Tenorio" (1844), a drama in verse treating of the notorious Don Juan, hero of Tirso de Molina's "Seville Deceiver," of Byron's poem, and Mozart's opera, is a masterpiece of harmonious and flowing verse, and of fine dramatic effect. It is played annually in every town where there is a theatre throughout all Spain on the eve of All Saints' Day, when the scene in which the bodies rise from their graves and come to the banquet of Don Juan and his boon companions upon the former's blasphemous invitation is awaited with breathless horror by crowded houses. Other long poems are the "Legend of the Cid," and "The Cobbler and the King." Zorrilla died the 23rd of January, 1893.

www.ingramcontent.com/pod-product-compliance
Lightning Source LLC
Chambersburg PA
CBHW030406230426
43664CB00007BB/772